THE

FRENCH JOURNALS

OF

Mrs. THRALE AND Dr. JOHNSON

Engraved by T. Holloway from the Original Painting

HESTER LYNCH THRALE

From the Engraving by T. Holloway, after the Painting by Sir Joshua Reynolds

THE FRENCH JOURNALS OF MRS. THRALE AND DOCTOR JOHNSON

EDITED

FROM THE ORIGINAL MANUSCRIPTS

IN THE JOHN RYLANDS LIBRARY AND IN THE BRITISH MUSEUM

WITH

INTRODUCTION AND NOTES

BY

MOSES TYSON, M.A., Ph.D.

KEEPER OF THE WESTERN MANUSCRIPTS IN THE JOHN RYLANDS LIBRARY

AND

HENRY GUPPY, M.A., Litt.D.

LIBRARIAN OF THE JOHN RYLANDS LIBRARY

HASKELL HOUSE PUBLISHERS Ltd.
Publishers of Scarce Scholarly Books
NEW YORK. N. Y. 10012
1973

HASKELL HOUSE PUBLISHERS Ltd.

Publishers of Scarce Scholarly Books

280 LAFAYETTE STREET

NEW YORK, N. Y. 10012

Library of Congress Cataloging in Publication Data

Piozzi, Hester Lynch (Salusbury) Thrale, 1741-1821.
  The French journals of Mrs. Thrale and Doctor
Johnson.

  1. France--Description and travel. I. Johnson,
Samuel, 1709-1784. II. Title.
DC25.P5 1973   914.4   72-1263
ISBN 0-8383-1430-9

Published for the Governors of the John Rylands Library at
THE MANCHESTER UNIVERSITY PRESS
23 Lime Grove, Oxford Road, Manchester

Printed in the United States of America

PREFATORY NOTE

In the following pages we print for the first time Mrs. Thrale's journal of the journey to France, which she undertook, in 1775, in company with Mr. Thrale, her eldest daughter, and Dr. Johnson.

Until about a year ago the very existence of the small leather-covered note-book, in which Mrs. Thrale, from day to day, recorded the incidents of the tour, was not only unknown but unsuspected.

It was found amidst a large collection of letters, papers, and other note-books, which at the death of Mrs. Piozzi had passed into the possession of her adopted son, Sir John Salusbury Piozzi Salusbury, and later were inherited by Sir John's great-granddaughter, Mrs. R. V. Colman, from whom they were acquired for the John Rylands Library.

The journal has been reproduced *verbatim et literatim* as Mrs. Thrale left it, except that in the matter of punctuation certain adjustments were found to be necessary. Where passages have been obliterated, or interpolations have been made by Mrs. Thrale, they have been carefully indicated in the foot-notes.

Two accounts of the journey have survived. One is Dr. Johnson's own journal, containing brief notes upon the events of twenty-six days of the tour, which was printed by Boswell in his *Life of Johnson*. The other is Mrs. Thrale's journal, referred to above, which covers the whole fifty-eight days of the tour, and differs from that of Dr. Johnson in that it is much fuller.

For purposes of comparison both accounts of the journey have been printed. That of Dr. Johnson is printed from his original manuscript, now preserved in the British Museum.

In July, 1784, Mrs. Thrale married Gabriele Piozzi, as her second husband, and in the following September they set out together upon a tour through France, Italy and Germany. An account of this tour was kept in two large note-books, which was later written up by Mrs. Piozzi in seven folio note-books, and then rewritten for publication, in which form it was printed in 1789, in two volumes.

Mrs. Piozzi's original manuscript journal of her journey through France on the way to Italy, in 1784, contains so many references to her former visit, and so much information of a personal character which is not found in the printed version, that it has been decided to print this account to accompany the hitherto unpublished journal of 1775.

The collection also contains a large number of unpublished letters, some of which have been drawn upon in the preparation of the present volume. Of special interest are several letters which furnish new evidence concerning Mrs. Piozzi's attitude to her children.

We are indebted to Mr. J. D. Wright of Manchester University, who was responsible for editing the group of unpublished letters of Dr. Johnson, which were printed in the January issue of the " Bulletin of the John Rylands Library," for generously undertaking to read the proofs, and for making valuable suggestions.

The lion's share of the work of preparing the present volume for the press has devolved upon my colleague, Dr. Tyson, to whom I offer my most grateful thanks.

HENRY GUPPY.

THE JOHN RYLANDS LIBRARY,
 September, 1932.

CONTENTS

	PAGE
PREFATORY NOTE - - - - - - - - -	v
INTRODUCTION - - - - - - - -	1
MRS. THRALE'S FRENCH JOURNAL, 1775 - - - -	67
DR. JOHNSON'S FRENCH JOURNAL, 1775 - - - -	167
MRS. PIOZZI'S FRENCH JOURNEY, 1784 - - - -	189

APPENDIX:

	PAGE
I. LETTERS RELATING TO DR. JOHNSON'S FRENCH TOUR -	217
II. DR. JOHNSON AND MISS FRANCES REYNOLDS - -	229
III. GIUSEPPE BARETTI AND MRS. THRALE (PIOZZI) - -	234
INDEX - - - - - - - - -	259

ILLUSTRATIONS

HESTER LYNCH THRALE. From the engraving by T. Holloway,
after the painting of Sir Joshua Reynolds - - *Frontispiece*

TO FACE PAGE

FACSIMILE OF A PAGE OF MRS. THRALE'S FRENCH JOURNAL, 1775 - 68

DR. SAMUEL JOHNSON. From the engraving by T. Cook, after
the painting of Sir Joshua Reynolds - - - 168

FACSIMILE OF PART OF A LETTER FROM DR. JOHNSON TO MRS.
THRALE, IN FRENCH - - - - - - 218

INTRODUCTION

"With *your* wings, Madam, you *must* fly : but have a care, there
are *clippers* abroad."
— *Dr. Johnson to Mrs. Thrale.*[1]

WHEN Dr. Johnson was an undergraduate at Oxford
he was overheard by Dr. Panting, then Master of Pembroke College, to utter the following soliloquy :

"Well, I have a mind to see what is done in
other places of learning. I'll go and visit the
Universities abroad. I'll go to France and Italy.
I'll go to Padua.—And I'll mind my business.
For an *Athenian* blockhead is the worst of all
blockheads." [2]

In later days he showed an increasing eagerness to
travel, both in his own country and abroad, but until
1773 he was never out of England, probably being
restrained from wandering further afield more by lack
of means than through want of enterprise. Journeys
abroad were, indeed, discussed from time to time: [3]
in 1752 there was talk of a visit to Iceland ; in 1763 he
flattered Boswell with hopes of going over to Holland
and of accompanying him in a tour of the Netherlands ;
in 1772 he played with the idea of an expedition round

---

[1] Boswell's *Life of Johnson* (ed. G. Birkbeck Hill, Oxford, 1887),
vol. iii., p. 49.

[2] *Ibid.*, vol. i., p. 73.

[3] *Ibid.*, vol. iii., Appendix B (pp. 449-459). Dr. Hill here collected evidence relating to "Johnson's travels and love of travelling."

I

the world with Mr. Banks and Dr. Solander; and in
1773, while visiting the Hebrides together, he and
Boswell talked of going to Sweden.

Dr. Johnson's tour to the Hebrides was followed in
the next year by a journey into North Wales with his
friends, Mr. and Mrs. Thrale and their daughter
" Queeney " ; and in 1775 by a visit to France with the
same friends and Queeney's Italian tutor, Giuseppe
Baretti. In 1776 the Thrales had completed all their
arrangements for a longer journey to Italy, when the
sudden death of their only surviving son caused them
to put off the visit.

There is no doubt that the abandonment of the
Italian journey was a tremendous disappointment to
Johnson. While the Thrales were still undecided,
Johnson was speaking of the visit to his friends with
considerable animation. " We must, to be sure," he
said, " see Rome, Naples, Florence and Venice, and as
much more as we can." Later when the Thrales had
definitely decided not to go that year, Johnson still
looked forward to a future visit. To Boswell he said : [1]

> " A man who has not been in Italy, is always
> conscious of an inferiority, from his not having
> seen what it is expected a man should see. The
> grand object of travelling is to see the shores of
> the Mediterranean."

In the years which followed Johnson spoke more or
less seriously of visiting the Baltic, the West Indies,
or " some part of Europe, Asia, or Africa," but
Italy was always in the forefront of his thoughts.
Thrale had again planned to go to Italy, when once more
death intervened, Thrale himself dying of a stroke of

---

[1] Boswell's *Life*, vol. iii., p. 36.

apoplexy on the morning of April 5, 1781. In 1784, a few months before Johnson's death, Boswell made an application to the Lord Chancellor, Lord Thurlow, for an addition to Johnson's pension, to enable him to winter in the milder climate of Italy.[1] Early in September it was known that the application had not succeeded.[2] On September 5, Mrs. Thrale, Johnson's old fellow-traveller, was at Dover, ready to set out for Italy with her second husband, Gabriele Piozzi.

Although so many journeys overseas were considered by Dr. Johnson, the visit to France was the only one which materialised, and the evidence of his activities on that occasion has an added interest. We will give the verdicts of two of his companions upon Dr. Johnson as a traveller.

Baretti, in a marginal note, writes : [3]

" Johnson was not fit to travel, as every place was equal to him. He mused as much on the road to Paris as he did in his garret in London, as much at a French Opera as in his room at Streatham. During our Journey to and from Paris he visited five or six libraries, which is the most idle thing a Traveller can do, as they are but to be seen cursorily. With men, women and children he never cared to exchange a word, and if he ever took any delight in any thing, it was to converse with some old acquaintance. New people he never loved to be in company with, except Ladies when disposed to caress and flatter him."

[1] *Letters of James Boswell* (ed. C. B. Tinker, Oxford, 1924), vol. ii., pp. 323-324.

[2] Boswell's *Life*, vol. iv., pp. 348-350.

[3] In his copy of Mrs. Piozzi's *Letters to and from the late Samuel Johnson, LL.D.*, vol. i., p. 315 ; see below, p. 234.

In another note, commenting on a passage in a letter to Johnson from Mrs. Thrale after her son's death in which she says :

> " Baretti said, you would be very angry because this dreadful event made us put off the Italian journey."

Baretti angrily writes : [1]

> " Baretti never said any such thing. He knew Johnson better, and had seen enough of Johnson on the preceding Journey to Paris."

We are not disposed, however, to take all Baretti's statements too seriously, as he seems to have been in no way reliable, and the evidence of his own letters [2] shows how much he looked forward to going to Italy with Johnson and the Thrales both in 1776 and 1781.

A different impression of Dr. Johnson as a traveller is given by Mrs. Piozzi, in her *Anecdotes*. She writes : [3]

> " His desire to go abroad, particularly to see Italy, was very great ; and he had a longing wish too to leave some Latin verses at the Grand Chartreux. He loved indeed the very act of travelling, and I cannot tell how far one might have taken him in a carriage before he would have wished for refreshment. He was therefore in some respects an admirable companion on the road, as he piqued himself upon feeling no inconvenience, and on despising no accommodations. On the other hand

---

[1] Mrs. Piozzi's *Letters*, vol. i., p. 317.

[2] See below, pp. 16, 248 ff.

[3] Mrs. Piozzi's *Anecdotes of the late Samuel Johnson, LL.D., during the last twenty years of his life* (ed. S. C. Roberts, Cambridge), 1925, pp. 110-111.

however, he expected no one else to feel any, and felt exceedingly inflamed with anger if any one complained of the rain, the sun, or the dust. ' How (said he) do other people bear them ? ' "

Elsewhere, in the same work, Mrs. Piozzi adds : [1]

" He delighted no more in music than painting ; he was almost as deaf as he was blind : travelling with Dr. Johnson was for these reasons tiresome enough. Mr. Thrale loved prospects, and was mortified that his friend could not enjoy the sight of those different dispositions of wood and water, hill and valley, that travelling through England and France affords a man. But when he wished to point them out to his companion : ' Never heed such nonsense,' would be the reply : ' a blade of grass is always a blade of grass, whether in one country or another : let us if we *do* talk, talk about something ; men and women are my subjects of enquiry ; let us see how these differ from those we have left behind.' "

Two accounts of the French journey, written up from day to day, survive, however, which enable us to test the reliability of these criticisms. One of these is Johnson's own journal, containing notes upon the events of twenty-six days of the tour : this was printed by Boswell [2] in his *Life of Johnson*, but is reprinted below from the original manuscript. The other account is Mrs. Thrale's journal, which covers the whole journey, and is now printed for the first time.

Johnson's notes are very short, but show, as Boswell

---

[1] Mrs. Piozzi's *Anecdotes*, p. 66.
[2] Boswell's *Life*, vol. ii., pp. 389-401.

remarks, " an extraordinary attention to various minute particulars." Boswell is insistent that : [1]

> " They completely refute the idle notion which has been propagated, *that he could not see ;* and, if he had taken the trouble to revise and digest them, he undoubtedly could have expanded them into a very entertaining narrative."

Johnson could not, however, be persuaded to write up his travels. To Boswell he said : [2]

> " The world is now not contented to be merely entertained by a traveller's narrative ; they want to learn something. Now some of my friends asked me, why I did not give some account of my travels in France. The reason is plain ; intelligent readers had seen more of France than I had. *You* might have liked my travels in France, and THE CLUB might have liked them ; but, upon the whole, there would have been more ridicule than good produced by them."

The impressions left by Johnson's notes and such other records of his remarks and activities as we possess are clear. He does not appear to have paid much attention to the countryside, for as he wrote in the *Rambler*, " the great object of remark is human life," but he did show considerable interest in the foreign birds and animals in the menagerie at Versailles. He did not like the Theatre, and was no ardent lover of art, though he could appreciate Raphael. He spent much of his time in libraries. Most of the people with whom he talked were English : he did not admire the French ; they had no happy middle state as in England ; " they had not the tavern life which is so agreeable in this country, where people meet all upon a footing, without any care or anxiety "; their shops were mean; the meat in their markets " such as would be sent to a gaol in England "; their manners were indelicate. He was, none the less, greatly interested in the French way of life ; he praised some of their buildings, sought to learn something of their institutions, observed the methods of several of their manufactories, and visited, far from unobservantly, a number of their houses.   One very considerable drawback, however, in his investigations, must have been Johnson's disinclination to speak French. He wrote French fairly well, and understood it very well, but could not speak it readily, and his habit of falling back on Latin must sometimes have restricted the conversation.

Mrs. Thrale's journal is very different from Johnson's. It is much more full, and she writes with all her accustomed vivacity.   It is at once evident that she was no Boswell. Her object was first and foremost to record her own impressions, not those of Johnson, but naturally his activities do not go without mention. Mrs. Thrale was also visiting the Continent for the first time. She was eager to make the most of her visit, and was fully prepared to be impressed, and her frequently extravagant praise of the French churches becomes somewhat monotonous. Johnson, himself, did not escape being infected with her enthusiasm. Years later, on her return with Piozzi after a lengthy stay on the Continent, she viewed the same things more calmly. In her journal of 1787 she writes : [1]

[1] Mrs. Piozzi's *Observations and reflections made in the course of a journey through France, Italy, and Germany* (London, 1789), vol. ii., p. 385.

" How fine I thought these churches thirteen
years ago, comes now thirteen times a-day into my
head ; they are not fine at all ; but it was the first
time I had ever crossed the channel, and I thought
every thing a wonder, and fancied we were arrived
at the world's end almost ; so differently do the
self-same places appear to the self-same people
surrounded by different circumstances ! "

Mrs. Thrale also is very severe in her criticisms of
the French, but she tried to correct this tendency.   On
October 1 she writes : [1]

" This Morning however I have been reading
Bocage's Letters on the English Nation, which
have somewhat tended to restrain my Spirit of
Criticism : She had more Opportunities of Observation & I fear more force of Mind besides
than I may have, yet her Information has been
miserably confined I see, & many of her Facts are
false—how should mine be better ! I will relate
only what I see—which can hardly fail of being
true."

Much of Mrs. Thrale's time also was spent with her
own countrymen and countrywomen, and while Dr.
Johnson was pleased to visit the English Benedictine
monks, Mrs. Thrale not infrequently delighted to extend
her acquaintance among the English nuns in France.

When Mrs. Thrale passed through France in 1784,
she still had very vivid memories of her first visit, and
these memories did not fail to influence her account of
her travels with Piozzi.   We have, accordingly, given

[1] See below, p. 94.

below the French portion of her original overseas journal of 1784. This journal is the more interesting in that it contains personal information which is not given in the version printed by her in 1789.

We will now venture to give some account of the persons who went with Johnson to France, and in particular of Mrs. Thrale, concerning whom much new material has recently been brought to light.

The expedition was inaugurated, and all the necessary expenses met, by Henry Thrale.

Thrale was the son of a wealthy Southwark brewer. He had been educated at Eton and Oxford, and had made the grand tour with Mr. Lyttelton, afterwards Lord Westcote. His manners, according to his wife, were those of a gay man of the town, and evidently not incompatible with a close friendship with the light-hearted playwright, Arthur Murphy. He had succeeded to his father's business at the age of thirty, and was elected Member of Parliament for the Borough of Southwark on December 23, 1765, representing the Borough continuously in Parliament until 1780. In 1765 Murphy had introduced Johnson to the Thrale household, and from 1766 onwards, until Thrale's widow let Streatham Park, Johnson often stayed at their house. Thrale had a sincere affection for his learned friend, and tried to serve him in every possible way. Boswell, after visiting Streatham on October 6, 1769, relates : [1]

"Johnson, though quite at home, was yet looked up to with an awe, tempered by affection, and seemed to be equally the care of his host and hostess. I rejoiced at seeing him so happy."

[1] Boswell's *Life*, vol. ii., p. 77.

Thrale also had a powerful influence over the Doctor, and, as Mrs. Thrale tells us, " could make him suppress many rough answers." [1] On the other hand Johnson was no less attached to his friend. Writing to the widow, after Thrale's death in April, 1781, he said : [2]

" I am not without my part of the calamity. No death since that of my wife has ever oppressed me like this."

And again : [3]

" My part of the loss hangs upon me. I have lost a friend of boundless kindness at an age when it is very unlikely that I should find another."

To Sir Robert Chambers, some years later, he wrote : [4]

" One great abatement of all miseries was the attention of Mr. Thrale, which from our first acquaintance was never intermitted. I passed far the greater part of many years in his house where I had all the pleasures of riches without the solicitude. He took me into France one year, and into Wales another, and if he had lived would have shown me Italy and perhaps many other countries, but he died in the spring of eighty one, and left me to write his epitaph."

For nearly ten years before his death Thrale's health was very unsettled, he was liable to become depressed, and it seems that his business ability suffered. This was particularly the case in 1772, a year of many business failures, when Mrs. Thrale records, " a sudden run

[1] Mrs. Piozzi's *Anecdotes*, p. 90.
[2] Birkbeck Hill, *Letters of Samuel Johnson*, vol. ii., p. 209.
[3] *Ibid.*, p. 211.
[4] *The R. B. Adam library relating to Dr. Samuel Johnson and his era* (1929), vol. i., p. 37. A facsimile of the letter is given.

menaced the house, and death hovered over the head of the principal." [1]   In such moments of crisis Mrs. Thrale frequently consulted their family friend, as is shown by many letters between her and Johnson in 1772 and 1773.   We quote a passage from one of her unpublished letters to Johnson, sent on November 7, 1772 : [2]

> " I hope we shall all spend our Christmas comfortably together, & till then I must keep your *roving Wishes* in order, and my own too, which hang upon the Country the more as Mr. Thrale will not stir now he is in Town, nor can all the influence I have over him make him speak a kind word to a Customer when he knows it would save him a house.   You see this is a *private Letter.*   He dined abroad yesterday & I had liked to have had some private Talk with Perkins but I missed the opportunity, & somehow was not sorry for the accident that hindered me, one's whole heart *so* entirely resists a clandestine Conversation and if I ask leave I am *so* sure to be refused : but one Virtue must be violated I suppose to save another, and if I cannot do any good without, I'll try that experiment. Be well My Dear Sir & continue to love us bad as we are ; that thro' all our distresses we may still have the pleasure and Pride of possessing a friend truly matchless."

The following years witnessed an improvement in Thrale's business affairs and a temporary recovery of his health.   Several extracts from an account of her husband by Mrs. Thrale, made at an early date in

---

[1] A. Hayward, *Autobiography, Letters, and Literary Remains of Mrs. Piozzi (Thrale)*, 2nd edition (London, 1861), vol. ii., p. 26.

[2] John Rylands Library, *Thrale-Johnson Letters.*

"Thraliana," the diary which she began to keep on September 15, 1776, will enable us to picture him as he appeared to his wife, about the time of the French tour : [1]

> "Mr. Thrale's person is manly, his countenance agreeable, his eyes steady and of the deepest blue ; his look neither soft nor severe, neither sprightly nor gloomy, but thoughtful and intelligent; his address is neither caressive nor repulsive, but un- affectedly civil and decorous ; and his manner more completely free from every trick or particular- ity than I ever saw any person's. He is a man wholly, as I think, out of the power of mimicry. He loves money and is diligent to obtain it ; but he loves liberality too, and is willing enough both to give generously and to spend fashionably. His passions either are not strong, or else he keeps them under such command that they seldom disturb his tranquillity or his friends ; and it must, I think, be something more than common which can affect him strongly, either with hope, fear, anger, love, or joy. . . . Mr. Thrale's sobriety, and the decency of his conversation, being wholly free from all oaths, ribaldry and profaneness, makes him a man exceed- ingly comfortable to live with ; while the easiness of his temper and slowness to take offence add greatly to his value as a domestic man. Yet I think his servants do not much love him, and I am not sure that his children have much affection for him ; low people almost all indeed agree to abhor him, as he has none of that officious and cordial manner which is universally required by them, nor any skill to dissemble his dislike of their coarse-

[1] Hayward, *Autobiography*, vol. ii., pp. 188-190.

ness. With regard to his wife, though little tender of her person, he is very partial to her understanding ; but he is obliging to nobody, and confers a favour less pleasing than many a man refuses to confer one. This appears to me to be as just a character as can be given of the man with whom I have now lived thirteen years."

It is probable that if Mrs. Thrale had written her Character of Thrale four or five years later, it would have been somewhat modified. The death of his son in 1776 was a tremendous blow, from which he never recovered, and his health rapidly deteriorated. In June, 1779, he had an alarming attack of apoplexy. " From this dreadful situation," wrote his wife,[1] " medical art relieved Mr. Thrale, but the natural disposition to conviviality degenerated into a preternatural desire for food. . . . With a *person*, the very wretched wreck of what it had been, no one could keep him at home. Dinners and company engrossed all his thoughts. . . ." A temporary recovery was followed by another seizure in February, 1780. But this second warning was also unheeded, his habits became still more intemperate, and on April 3, 1781, he was found on the floor in a fit of apoplexy, and died on the following morning.

During the last few years of his life, his bodily disorder seems to have been reflected in his actions ; his business was badly managed ; we doubt if he could now be described as " a man exceedingly comfortable to live with " ; and he is said to have developed a " sentimental affection " for Miss Sophia Streatfield, the handsome, " incomprehensible " young lady, frequently mentioned in Madame D'Arblay's Diary, who im-

[1] Hayward, *Autobiography*, vol. ii., p. 38.

pressed her friends and acquaintances by two remarkable talents, her knowledge of Greek, and her ability to produce tears at will.[1]

There is an overwhelming amount of manuscript material in existence relating to Mrs. Thrale. It includes thousands of letters written by her, thousands more letters written to her, diaries filled with contemporary accounts of events and of her thoughts and actions, brief autobiographies written during the later years of her life, manuscripts of her works, both published and unpublished, note-books, and other miscellaneous records. Much of this material has long been known, more has recently come to light.[2] Much has been written about her and many of her statements have been interpreted in widely different ways, for she seems, both during her lifetime and afterwards, to have had both the gift of inspiring loyal friendships and the misfortune of provoking bitter criticism. We do not aspire to be numbered either with her critics or with those who are sometimes referred to as her " apologists," but merely to relate a few facts, some old, some new, about this remarkable lady.

Hester Lynch Salusbury was born at Bodvel in Carnarvonshire on January 16, 1741. Her father was John Salusbury of Bachygraig, near Denbigh, and was descended in the direct line from Thomas Salusbury, a member of an ancient Welsh family, who was knighted by Henry VII. after the battle of Blackheath. John Salusbury had led a wild life, and is chiefly interesting for his friendship with Lord Halifax, the President of the

[1] Hayward, *Autobiography*, vol. i., pp. 111-124; vol. ii., pp. 34-36.
[2] See Tyson, *Unpublished Manuscripts, Papers, and Letters of Dr. Johnson, Mrs. Thrale and their friends* in the *Bulletin of the John Rylands Library*, vol. xv. (1931), pp. 467-488.

Board of Trade. With Cornwallis he was sent out
to Nova Scotia in 1749 when the town of Halifax was
founded, and a short journal[1] kept by him and several
letters to his wife at home still survive. His wife was
Hester Maria Cotton, daughter of Sir Thomas Cotton,
bart., of Combermere. Hester was their only child.
During her father's absence abroad she and her mother
stayed for a time with Mrs. Salusbury's mother, Lady
Cotton, at East Hyde, near Luton, and afterwards with
John Salusbury's brother, Sir Thomas Salusbury, of
Offley Place, Hertfordshire. She appears to have thoroughly enjoyed her country life, and to have become
a skilful horsewoman. At an early age Miss Salusbury
gave evidence of a quick wit and of an eagerness for
study. Unknown to her people she contributed papers
to the *St. James's Chronicle*; she was interested in natural
history, was instructed in logic and rhetoric, was presented by the great James Harris of Salisbury with an
interleaved copy of his *Hermes, or a Philosophical Inquiry
concerning Universal Grammar*, and gained some knowledge
of Latin, French, Italian and Spanish. There is evidence
enough of her early attainments. A manuscript[2] of
Louis Racine's *Épitre I sur l'homme, à M. le chevalier de
Ramsay*, rendered into English verse, with translations
of letters of Racine, Pope, and Sir James Ramsay, and
several drafts of Prefaces, are noted as " by H. L. S. at
a very early period," and in one preface the young
translator writes :

> " thinking it more impertinently vain to resist
> the sollicitations of Gentlemen so eminent in the
> Literary World [as Dr. Wilson, Dr. Collier, and
> Dr. Parker][3] than to yield to them, I comply'd

[1] J.R.L., *English MS.* 615.   [2] *Ibid.*, 624.   [3] *Crossed through.*

and resolved not only to translate the Essay itself but the Preface and some few Original Letters wch I culled, not w^thout much Trouble from the Author's Collection of Letters."

She also translated from the Spanish the *Vida de Cervantes Saavedra*, by Gregorio Mayans y Siscar,[1] and there are manuscript fragments of translations of the *Don Quixote* of Cervantes, into English and Italian.[2]

Numerous letters to her, written in Latin,[3] from her tutor, Dr. Arthur Collier, survive, and it is clear that she had a good knowledge of that language, though without pretensions to profound classical scholarship. We will, however, give the later verdict of her most bitter critic: writing to his brothers on March 22, 1776, in preparation for the expected Italian visit, Baretti says:[4]

"Mr. Thrale is a very fine man and obviously a thorough gentleman, who likes simple ease and is never out of humour for a moment. He only speaks a very little French, unlike his wife, who talks French and Italian fluently, without troubling about their quality, and likes to talk them, and is bright and lively. She is, however, shocked at the least offence against religion or morality, for she is very fond of her Bible, and you must be sure there is a Latin Bible among the aforesaid books, as she understands Latin perfectly too."

The accomplished Miss Salusbury had several suitors for her hand, before Thrale was introduced by her uncle,

---

[1] J.R.L., *English MSS.* 626, 627.
[2] *Ibid.*, 625.　　　　[3] *Ibid.*, 534.
[4] See Lacy Collison-Morley, *Giuseppe Baretti* (London, 1909), p. 289. Mr. Collison-Morley gives translations of a number of Baretti's letters.

Sir Thomas Salusbury. None of these were approved of by her father, and it was not till October 11, 1763, almost a year after John Salusbury's death, that his daughter became Mrs. Thrale.

The young wife lived a very restricted life, till after Johnson was introduced into the household in 1765, then she quickly gained a reputation as a wit and hostess among a large circle of literary celebrities and bluestockings, attracted by Johnson's presence at Streatham. We can only discuss briefly Johnson's relations with Mrs. Thrale. Boswell writes : [1]

> " He had at Mr. Thrale's all the comforts and even the luxuries of life ; his melancholy was diverted, and his irregular habits lessened by association with an agreeable and well-ordered family. He was treated with the utmost respect, and even affection. The vivacity of Mrs. Thrale's literary talk roused him to cheerfulness and exertion, even when they were alone."

Boswell, who describes Mrs. Thrale as " a lady of lively talents, improved by education," gives immediately afterwards an opinion which he says is that of Johnson himself in his own words : [2]

> " I know no man, (said he,) who is more master of his wife and family than Thrale. If he but holds up a finger, he is obeyed. It is a great mistake to suppose that she is above him in literary attainments. She is more flippant ; but he has ten times her learning : he is a regular scholar ; but her learning is that of a school-boy in one of the lower forms."

---

[1] Boswell's *Life*, vol. i., p. 495.   [2] *Ibid.*, p. 494.

The latter part of this opinion attributed to Johnson is remarkable. Thrale had received a good education, and we know that in 1773 the University of Oxford bestowed on him the honorary degree of D.C.L., but what were his pretensions to regular scholarship? He listened with intense admiration to the conversation and arguments of Dr. Johnson, and delighted in hearing and provoking a war of words; but he contributed very little to general conversation at the Streatham gatherings,[1] and resisted successfully any temptation to appear in print. Dr. Johnson did not write many letters to Thrale, but of his letters to Mrs. Thrale over three hundred were included by Dr. Birkbeck Hill in his *Letters of Samuel Johnson*, printed in 1892, and a good number more have since come to light. Dr. Hill was no favourable critic of Mrs. Thrale, but of Johnson's letters to her he admits : [2]

> " In themselves they required far more annotation than the other letters, for in writing to her Johnson touched on a much greater variety of persons and subjects. He frequently introduced quotations and literary allusions. She was a lady of some learning and many pretensions, who had more wit and more literature, he maintained, than even the great Mrs. Montagu."

We may be sure that Johnson would not have written these numerous letters to anyone for whose literary attainments he had not a high regard, and evidence

[1] His wife wrote, " Johnson has a very great degree of kindness and esteem for him, and says if he would talk more, his manner would be very completely that of a perfect gentleman."—Hayward, *Autobiography*, pp. 189-190.

[2] Birkbeck Hill's *Letters*, vol. i., pp. xi-xii.

that he was justified in this regard is abundantly to be found in the conversations recorded by Boswell, and elsewhere.

Johnson for many years received more than entertainment as a member of the Thrale household, which he delighted to speak of as " home." Thrale was a gracious and attentive host, no doubt, and the " *columen domus*," but a great deal of the credit for the happiness Johnson found there must be given to Mrs. Thrale, upon whom obviously the comforts of the " home " largely depended. It was to Mrs. Thrale that Johnson went, or wrote, for sympathy in his times of mental or bodily suffering.

In addition to her social and literary activities, her care for Thrale and Johnson, her excursions into the realms of business during her husband's illnesses, her occasional electioneering, and her many other diversions, Mrs. Thrale, in the course of fourteen years, bore her husband twelve children. Of these twelve children, one lived a few hours, one lived ten days, one lived seven months, two others lived under two years, another two lived under five years, and their elder son, Harry, died suddenly when nine years old. These losses were suffered, although the mother secured for her children the attendance of some of the best physicians of the day, including Sir Lucas Pepys and Dr. Jebb, both of whom were physicians to the King. Mrs. Thrale's distress is revealed in numerous letters to Johnson, who could only comfort her with assurances that she had done everything possible for her children. The nature of their illnesses would seem to indicate that several of the children were constitutionally delicate, and while we do not stress the fact, we are reminded that both Thrale himself and Mrs. Thrale's father died during sudden seizures, when comparatively young. The four remaining children seem to have inherited their mother's strong constitution : they were Hester Maria, afterwards Lady Keith, Susanna Arabella, who died unmarried, Sophia, afterwards Mrs. Merrik Hoare, and Cæcilia Margaretta, afterwards Mrs. Mostyn. The three elder girls were very different in temperament from their mother, whose efforts to gain their affection were not always very successful. She found them cold, unresponsive, and " superior to any feeling of tenderness which might clog the wheels of ambition," an opinion apparently shared later by both friends and suitors, although the Misses Thrale were " beautiful in person," " cultivated in understanding," not unendowed with worldly goods, and had many admirers. The relations between mother and daughters were not improved by the actions of the tutor, Baretti,[1] whose kindnesses to the children were many, but who did not hesitate to show his contemptuous disapproval of some of Mrs. Thrale's methods in her daughters' presence, and sought to increase his popularity with them by always taking their part against her.

After Thrale's death, Mrs. Thrale and Johnson lived for several years on terms of close friendship : he stayed at Streatham, and after the Streatham house was let, is found going with Mrs. Thrale to Brighton, and visiting her at her house in Argyll Street ; and he wrote many letters to her, sometimes writing daily. On June 19, 1783, in a pathetic letter in which he regrets the diminution of her regard, he nevertheless turns to her with his complaints " as a settled and unalienable friend," and he follows this up with daily letters.[2] Thrale's widow, however, was in a different position from Thrale's wife. Dr. Johnson's mind, also, began to

[1] See *Appendix III.*
[2] Birkbeck Hill's *Letters*, vol. ii., pp. 300-303.

centre more and more upon his bodily infirmities, he now made little effort to conceal his dislikes, and Mrs. Thrale, despite her " veneration for his virtue " and her " reverence for his talents," began to find his increasing demands upon her thought and services irksome. A new factor also entered into the situation in the person of Gabriele Piozzi, the Italian music-master. Piozzi, who by the beginning of 1782 had already shown signs of his regard for the widow, was looked upon by her with growing favour. She saw in him a distinct physical resemblance to her wild but devoted father, John Salusbury, while his gentle manners, his marked admiration both for her person and her talents, his anxiety to do her will, could hardly fail to impress one who freely admitted that she was vain, and who was accustomed to men of more exacting dispositions.

By October, 1782, her prejudices arising from differences in birth and fortune were overcome, and she was favourably considering a marriage which would meet with the strong disapproval of her daughters, of Dr. Johnson and many of her friends, and which would demand great courage in one whose matrimonial intentions had for some time been a subject of unrestrained speculation in the popular Press. We are not competent to discuss the embarrassing " struggles of the understanding and the heart " [1] revealed so fully in the pages of *Thraliana*, the diary of this enamoured middle-aged

---

[1] Many passages are quoted in Hayward's *Autobiography*. In a letter to her adopted son on April 19, 1813, referring to her wishes in event of her death, Mrs. Piozzi, after mentioning several possessions to be given to her youngest daughter, Mrs. Mostyn, adds : " *Thraliana* should be hers—or burned—but you may read it first, if t'will amuse you . . . only let it *never* be printed ! oh never, never, *never*."—J.R.L., *Piozzi-Salusbury Letters*.

lady, which resulted in her parting from Piozzi in January, 1783, and in his recall in the following year. They were married [1] in London by the Spanish Ambassador's chaplain, according to the Romish Church, on July 23, and two days later the Protestant ceremony was performed in St. James's Church, Bath.[2]

Dr. Johnson, as his letters show, had long been aware of Piozzi's admiration for Mrs. Thrale,[3] and, if we accept Miss Burney's evidence, had for months regarded this relationship with more than apprehension. On May 24 Miss Burney wrote to Queeney that Johnson knew the "whole affair," probably referring to Piozzi's recall,[4] but he none the less, received a severe shock when, on June 30 Mrs. Thrale sent him a personal letter,[5] together with a copy of a circular letter sent to all Thrale's executors, announcing that Piozzi was coming back from Italy, and an immediate marriage was intended. Referring to their friendship, she wrote :

> "it requires that I should beg your pardon for
> concealing from you a connexion which you must
> have heard of by many, but I suppose never believed.
> Indeed, my dear Sir, it was concealed only to save
> us both needless pain ; I could not have borne
> to reject that counsel it would have killed me to
> take, and I only tell it you now because all is

---

[1] A copy of the certificate is in the John Rylands Library.

[2] Dr. Birkbeck Hill pointed out that *Jackson's Oxford Journal* for July 31 gives the date of the marriage as "*July* 28, *Sunday*" (Birkbeck Hill, *Letters*, vol. ii., p. 404 *n.*), but he did not note that *July* 25, 1784, was a Sunday.

[3] Birkbeck Hill, *Letters*, vol. ii., pp. 238-239.

[4] The Marquis of Lansdowne, *Johnson and Queeney* (London, 1932), p. 49.

[5] Birkbeck Hill, *Letters*, vol. ii., p. 404 *n.*

irrevocably settled, and out of your power to prevent."

Johnson replied [1] on July 2, with an attempt to persuade her, if not yet married, to see him first, which was coupled with accusations so bitter, as to cause Mrs. Thrale, in her reply on July 4, to conclude a defence of herself and Piozzi with the words : [2]

"Farewell, dear Sir, and accept my best wishes. You have always commanded my esteem, and long enjoyed the fruits of a friendship *never infringed by one harsh expression on my part during twenty years of familiar talk. Never did I oppose your will, or control your wish ; nor can your unmerited severity itself lessen my regard ;* but till you have changed your opinion of Mr. Piozzi let us converse no more. God bless you."

On July 8, Johnson wrote a last letter in a more subdued tone.[3]

"What you have done, however I may lament it, I have no pretence to resent, as it has not been injurious to me : I therefore breathe out one sigh more of tenderness, perhaps useless, but at least sincere.

"I wish that God may grant you every blessing, that you may be happy in this world for its short continuance, and eternally happy in a better state ; and whatever I can contribute to your happiness I am very ready to repay, for that kindness which soothed twenty years of a life radically wretched.

[1] Birkbeck Hill, *Letters*, vol. ii., pp. 405-406.
[2] Hayward, *Autobiography*, vol. i., pp. 240-241.
[3] Birkbeck Hill, *Letters*, vol. ii., pp. 407-409.

Do not think slightly of the advice which I now presume to offer. Prevail upon Mr. Piozzi to settle in England : you may live here with more dignity than in Italy, and with more security : your rank will be higher, and your fortune more under your own eye. I desire not to detail all my reasons, but every argument of prudence and interest is for England, and only some phantoms of imagination seduce you to Italy. I am afraid however that my counsel is vain, yet I have eased my heart by giving it. . . ."

The letter ends :

"I am going into Derbyshire, and hope to be followed by your good wishes, for I am, with great affection,

"Your, &c.,

"SAM : JOHNSON.

"Any letters that come for me hither will be sent me."

Mrs. Thrale's reply, her last letter to Johnson, has only recently been discovered. It was sent from Bath, and is dated July 15, with a post-mark 16 JY. We give it in full : [1]

"Not only my good Wishes but my most fervent Prayers for your Health and Consolation shall for ever attend and follow my dear Mr. Johnson. Your last Letter is sweetly kind, and I thank you for it most sincerely. Have no Fears for me however ; no *real* Fears. My Piozzi will need few Perswasions to settle in a Country where he has succeeded so

---

[1] J.R.L., *Thrale-Johnson Letters.*

well ; but he longs to shew me to his Italian Friends, and he wishes to restore my Health by treating me with a Journey to many Places I have long wish'd to see : his disinterested Conduct towards me in pecuniary Matters, his Delicacy in giving me up all past Promises when we were separated last year by great Violence in Argylle Street, are Pledges of his Affection and Honour. He is a religious Man, a sober Man, and a Thinking Man—he will not injure me, I am sure he will not, let nobody injure him in your good Opinion, which he is most solicitous to obtain and preserve, and the harsh Letter you wrote me at first grieved him to the very heart. Accept his Esteem my dear Sir, do ; and his Promise to treat with long continued Respect & Tenderness the Friend whom you once honoured with your Regard and who will never cease to be my dear Sir

" Your truly affectionate and faithful serv^t."

The signature has been vigorously erased. A post-script adds :

" The Lawyers delay of finishing our Settlements, & the necessity of twenty-six days Residence has kept us from being married till now. I hope your Health is mending."

This letter marked the end of their relationship. Madame D'Arblay in her Diary relates that in November, Johnson said to her of Mrs. Thrale :

" I drive her quite from my mind. If I meet with one of her letters, I burn it instantly. I have burnt all I can find. I never speak of her, and I desire never to hear of her more."

Many letters, however, escaped the fire—well over a hundred are now in the John Rylands Library [1]—and were returned after Johnson's death by Sir Joshua Reynolds. In view also of Johnson's letter of July 8, it is not improbable that some sort of reconciliation would have taken place, if Mrs. Thrale had not uncompromisingly rejected his advice not to go to Italy. He died, however, unreconciled, in the following December.

Mrs. Thrale's behaviour towards Dr. Johnson, and some of her comments and anecdotes relating to him, have justifiably provoked a certain amount of severe criticism, but several of her critics, when reliable evidence is not forthcoming, almost invariably imagine the worst, or, if by any stretch of imagination evidence can be interpreted in more than one way, are inclined to choose the most unfavourable interpretation. Over twenty years' close friendship was ended owing to the unreasonableness, not unnatural, of a very sick man, and the headstrong determination of a so-called [2] infatuated woman. But we find it difficult to reconcile the inherent charity of a Johnson, deeply hurt though he might be, with the attacks on his friend by those who are ostensibly his champions. Boswell was jealous of Mrs. Thrale, and later was annoyed by her *Anecdotes*; he was provoked to biting criticism; but even he would have fallen foul of several of her later critics. We cite a passage from a letter he wrote to Mrs. Thrale as late as July 9, 1782 : [3]

---

[1] J.R.L., *Thrale-Johnson Letters*. *English MSS.* 539-540.

[2] There is much evidence to prove that the marriage was a success, and that Mrs. Thrale's estimate of her future husband was more than realized.

[3] *Letters of James Boswell*, vol. ii., pp. 312-313.

" Last night's post brought me your kind letter
informing me of Dr. Johnson's being so much
better since his jaunt to Oxford. It is needless to
tell you what joy it gave me. I kissed the sub-
scription, ' H. L. Thrale,' with fervency. The
good news elated me ; and I was at the same time
pleasingly interested by the tender wish which you
express to releive my anxiety as much as you can.
My dear Madam, from the day that I first had the
pleasure to meet you, when I jumpt into your coach,
not I hope from impudence, but from that agreable
kind of attraction which makes one forget ceremony,
I have invariably thought of you with admiration
and gratitude. Were I to make out a chrono-
logical account of all the happy hours which I
owe to you, I should appear under great debt, and
debt of a peculiar nature, for a generous mind
cannot be discharged of it by the creditor."

Mrs. Piozzi's *Anecdotes* reveal her pride in Johnson's
friendship, and her sincere veneration for his talents
and his character. A few of her stories, bearing upon
the rougher side of his nature, appear to be disproved
by facts, for when relying on her memory, she was clearly
not always accurate in her association of events and
persons ; but we doubt if her inaccuracies are so injurious to Johnson's reputation as the zealous efforts of
those critics who reflect on his understanding by their
attempts to prove the opinion voiced by Baretti : [1]

" The most unaccountable part of Johnson's
character was his total ignorance of the character
of his most familiar acquaintance."

[1] A marginal note to his copy of Mrs. Piozzi's *Letters*, vol. i.,
p. 309.

If Johnson was deceived as to the character of his "Dearest Lady," the majority of her friends, both men and women, were equally deceived. Even among those who broke with her over the Piozzi marriage, there were some, including the Burneys and William Weller Pepys, who in their letters had shown how highly they regarded her as hostess, friend and mother. The fiercest contemporary criticism came not from those who knew her well, but mainly from journalists and sometimes scurrilous pamphleteers.

Before leaving Mrs. Piozzi, as we shall now call her, three matters of some interest remain to be considered : her behaviour to her daughters ; her later friendships ; and her literary work.

We venture to include here several new pieces of evidence concerning Mrs. Piozzi's attitude to her children, since this has been the basis of several attacks upon her character.[1] When Mrs. Piozzi left England in September, 1784, her daughter, Queeney, was within a few days of her twentieth birthday, Susanna was over fourteen, Sophia over thirteen, and Cecilia about seven and a half. The youngest child was at Ray and Fry's school at Streatham; the other girls were left with a Miss Nicholson, a lady of good family.[2] Miss Nicholson was apparently at first liked by them, for Queeney, mentioning her in a letter to her mother, dated July 27, wrote : [3]

"May I say that I wish you would just write her a Line or two ? it would delight her much, & she is more kind to us than I had the smallest

[1] See also *Appendix III*, pp. 234 ff.
[2] Hayward, *Autobiography*, vol. i., pp. 267-268.
[3] J.R.L., *Letters to Mrs. Piozzi from her daughters. English MS.* 553. The letter is addressed to "Mrs. Thrale, Bath."

Reason to expect. When your last Letter came, I lamented for want of Franks, & she, immediately it seems wrote to her Sister & got me some to you. Only think how polite."

It was not many months before Miss Nicholson and Queeney disagreed; but Queeney, as no doubt her mother was well aware, was by character and capabilities well fitted to take charge in such an emergency, and could always rely upon the support and advice of the guardians nominated in her father's will.

Mrs. Piozzi was kept well-informed about her daughters by means of letters from trusted friends and occasional letters from the girls themselves. During her two and a half years' absence, brought about partly by the need to economize and partly by the sensitiveness arising from the criticism to which she had been subjected, Mrs. Piozzi constantly had her daughters in mind. Among her most prized treasures was a portrait of Queeney, which hung, together with one of Dr. Johnson, in her dressing-room; but stronger evidence of her thought and affection is found in a letter written to Susanna Thrale on August 13, 1786, after about two years' separation. She began : [1]

" Your Request must be my Excuse for meddling with Subjects which it is the peculiar Province of the Clergy to discuss and to explain ; God forbid that I should have an Idea of intruding upon a Profession wch it is our indispensable Duty to revere ; but you used to say my Preachments were the clearest, & that from being accustomed to my Manner of talking on serious Subjects you came

[1] J.R.L., *English MS.* 634.

away better informed than after listening to Discourses more elaborate from Lips more learned than mine. The Distance we have now been so long Time from each other, must serve as another Excuse, since we cannot converse as formerly, when ev'ry Sunday Evening glided away in a sort of grave but useful Talk, for which to say the Truth, I have found few People of your Age express so much Taste as yourself."

A long letter is followed by a dissertation filling thirty-eight folio pages, which Mrs. Piozzi says she has composed

" somewhat upon the Plan of Abbé Fleury's historical Catechism, but shorter; as many of his Chapters were written expressly to justify Opinions & Ceremonies of that Church to which he belonged, & for which he was an avowed Champion. . . . My little Work pretends to nothing further than to recommend with earnestness the Scriptural Precept given by the wise Son of Sirach in the 12th Chapter of Ecclesiastes

' Remember thy Creator in the Days of thy Youth.' "

The attitude of Queeney towards her mother during these years of separation was extremely cold, and this also affected the other two sisters, for though they were described in a letter of October 19, 1784, as " very kind and affectionate," in her Biographical Anecdotes Mrs. Piozzi records that : [1]

" The letters from our daughters had been cold and unfrequent during the whole absence ; a little more so as we approached nearer home."

[1] Hayward, *Autobiography*, vol. ii., p. 68.

This is not surprising when one remembers the proud reserved nature of the Thrale girls, and the malicious attacks on the Piozzis that were made in several of the popular papers. When the Piozzis did return to England, the daughters called and " behaved with cool civility," and in the years that followed, although their affection never appears to have been excessive, there were periods when they were extremely friendly, as letters to their mother, and also to Piozzi, show.

The mother herself, as Johnson had well recognized,[1] had " the quality of being easily reconciled, and not easily offended," and proved this again and again in her relations with her daughters. Lord Lansdowne, whose opinion of Mrs. Piozzi is far from favourable, states in his recent volume on *Johnson and Queeney* [2] that there are extant some 350 letters between the years 1780 and 1821 from Mrs. Piozzi to Queeney. He says that " the correspondence is ostensibly friendly, though amidst expressions of endearment and protestations of affection not a few shrewd hits at her correspondent may be discovered." We find it difficult to follow his suggestion that Mrs. Piozzi wrote these numerous letters, not out of affection, but because, " after her second marriage, Hester was more in the great world than her mother "; for, as will be shown below, Mrs. Piozzi was extraordinarily rich in friends, drawn from all classes of Society, and representative of a great variety of professions and occupations.

Mrs. Piozzi's youngest daughter, Cecilia, differed greatly in character from her sisters. While Mrs. Piozzi was away, she had been moved by her eldest sister from the school at Streatham to Stevenson's in Queen Square.

[1] Birkbeck Hill, *Letters*, vol. i., p. 355.
[2] *Op. cit.*, pp. xxvi-xxvii.

This action annoyed Mrs. Piozzi, and upon her return she took her home and secured for her special masters.[1] Cecilia seems to have shown herself genuinely fond of her mother and of Piozzi, but caused them considerable anxiety. In 1792 an enterprising young man called James Drummond appears to have had "public Banns proclaimed in the Parish of Christ Church, Surrey, between himself & Cecilia Thrale . . . before he could have seen her twelve Times in her Life, without having ever spoken to her alone & so completely without her Consent that she knew not of the Transaction."[2] The "severity of discipline," with which Baretti charges Mrs. Piozzi in bringing up her children, does not appear in the correspondence relating to this affair, which came to an end with the following short note from Cecilia, then fifteen years old : [3]

> "My darling Mother. You will not be a little surprised to find by this that *for the present I give up James Drummond*. At a *future time* however if I find I *really love* him why as we shall neither of us be superanuated I hope all will go on well but *now* I will neither *see, hear,* or *think,* of him and wish you not to mention him or let our Master more to yours ever
>
> "Cecilia.
>
> "I think I will send *no* An[s.] to his letter."

Later Samuel Rogers, the poet, was an unsuccessful suitor for her hand; but in June, 1795, Cecilia, then eighteen, was married at Gretna Green to John Meredith

---

[1] Hayward, *Autobiography*, vol. ii., p. 69.

[2] J.R.L., *Cecilia Thrale (Mostyn) Correspondence. English MS.* 572.

[3] *Ibid.*

Mostyn, a minor. Mrs. Piozzi had not been hostile to the match, as is revealed by her letters, provided that a settlement could be made on Cecilia; but on Saturday, June 6, Mostyn wrote to their friend, Mr. Robert Ray, that he hoped he and Cecilia would determine " no longer to wait for Mrs Piozzi's consent but go to Scotland this night." [1] A short quotation from Cecilia's letter to her mother from Scotland will indicate her feelings towards her mother and Piozzi at this time : [2]

" Pray tell me what has been said & done by the Misses &c. & that you were not frighten'd after you found the *Young Man* was arrived & we had set out safely . . . pray come to us as soon as you possibly can—it seems so odd to be here without you, you can't think, pray do come & stay till Brynbella is ready for you. We shall be very comfortable I dare say—and do you think Mrs Siddons would let the two girls come, surely she could have no objection, do pray write to her & beg for them, they should be no inconvenience to you or Papa. —What does he say to the Affair ? *My godda bless, never I see such a people*—give my love to him—how will he be able to live without *Miss Cecil* to scold and row I wonder—tell him *I'm grieved for his imparable loss.*"

Before Cecilia came of age litigation over her affairs, and high feeling thus aroused, caused a break between the Mostyns and the Piozzis. This feeling died down in time, though both Mrs. Mostyn and her sisters clearly resented the adoption [3] by their mother of a

---

[1] J.R.L., *Cecilia Thrale (Mostyn) Correspondence. English MS.* 572.
[2] *Ibid.* [3] Lansdowne, *Johnson and Queeney*, p. xxv.

young nephew of Piozzi's, John Salusbury Piozzi, who afterwards took the name of Salusbury. When Mrs. Piozzi died in 1821, her three eldest daughters were at her bedside, and in the words of her friend, Mrs Pennington, "their affectionate attention soothed her last moments." At their request Mrs. Pennington wrote a laudatory obituary notice to the Press, which met with their warm approbation. Mrs. Mostyn at the time was in Italy, but she communicated at once with Mrs. Pennington, and the latter wrote to Sir John S. P. Salusbury on July 6:[1]

> " She requests me to say, with her kind Love, how much she shall be obliged if you will reserve for her *something* that *was* her Mother's."

In 1827 Mrs. Mostyn and Sir John were exchanging friendly letters. Of John Salusbury Piozzi Salusbury only brief mention need be made. In 1798, when the Napoleonic wars had brought ruin upon Piozzi's relations in Italy, he and his wife adopted one of his nephews, a small boy then about four years old. In compliment to Mrs. Piozzi, he had been christened John Salusbury after her father, and she was further pleased to find in him some resemblance to her husband. The boy appears quickly to have won the affection of Mrs. Piozzi, who had lost both her own sons, and seems to have liked, and been liked by, boys and young men. He was naturalized, and afterwards, as her daughters were well provided for, Mrs. Piozzi made him her heir. More than 600 letters from her to young Salusbury and his wife between 1807 and 1821 still survive.[2] In 1817 Mrs. Piozzi wrote to Dr. Gray :[3]

[1] J.R.L., *Pennington-Piozzi Letters. English MSS.* 566-568.
[2] J.R.L., *Piozzi-Salusbury Letters. English MSS.* 585-593.
[3] Hayward, *Autobiography,* vol. i., p. 349.

" You remember me hoping and proposing to make dear Salusbury a gentleman, a Christian, and a scholar ; and when one has succeeded in the first two wishes, there is no need to fret if the third does fail *a little*. Such is my situation concerning my *adopted*, as you are accustomed to call him."

Salusbury was appointed high-sheriff of Flintshire in 1816, and in the following year received the honour of knighthood on presenting an address to the Prince Regent.

Mrs. Piozzi had made many friends in Italy and had received many attentions. Her circle of acquaintances was large and interesting. In a letter from Milan, dated January 20, 1785, she wrote : [1]

" The Minister, Count Wilsick, has shown us many distinctions, and we are visited by the first families in Milan."

From Florence, on July 27, 1785, she wrote : [2]

" We celebrated our wedding anniversary two days ago with a magnificent dinner and concert, at which the Prince Corsini and his brother the Cardinal did us the honour of assisting, and wished us joy in the tenderest and politest terms. Lord and Lady Cowper, Lord Pembroke, and *all* the English indeed, doat on my husband, and show us every possible attention."

We have before us a printed tribute paid by the Imperial Chamberlain, the Marquis Araciel, at Varese on July 25,

[1] Hayward, *Autobiography*, vol. i., p. 269. The Prince of Sisterna had presented her with the key of his box at the opera during her stay at Turin (*ibid.*, p. 266).

[2] *Ibid.*, p. 272.

1786, " *Pel fausto giorno delle nozze avvenute in Londra degli ornatissimi Sposi Piozzi. Cantata epitalamica.*"

Mrs. Piozzi returned to England in some trepidation, but found that although her marriage had cost her several old friends of the Streatham days, many others welcomed her with respect and admiration. Boswell, Reynolds, the Burneys, and several others were changed; but Miss Reynolds defended her against Baretti, and later the Burneys were reconciled. In 1807 Dr. Charles Burney wrote : [1]

> " I shall wait on my ingenious & worthy friend Mr. Piozzi with the utmost pleasure. He was the first who let me know what good singing was, & excited in me so strong a desire to hear Pacchierotti, whose style he imitated beyond any other vocal performer."

In March, 1813, Madame D'Arblay made overtures of friendship through her niece, Miss Marianne Francis : [2]

> " My Aunt D'Arblay . . . charges me to say from her, that your early kindness never has been obliterated from her memory, & never can ; that she always preserves amongst her favourite hoards, its eloquent expression ; and that if you were in town, she could with difficulty refrain from seeing if no part of it still remained."

The old friendship does not seem to have been revived till 1818. In the years following her return from Italy, Mrs. Piozzi's friends and correspondents

[1] J.R.L., *Burney-Thrale Letters. English MS.* 545.

[2] J.R.L., *Francis-Piozzi Letters. English MSS.* 582-584. See W. W. Roberts, *Charles and Fanny Burney in the light of the new Thrale correspondence in the John Rylands Library* (1932).

were drawn from all classes. Lord Fife, Lord Hunting-
don, Lord Dudley, Lord Cowper, Lord Pembroke, Lord
Deerhurst, Lord Thurlow and many of the nobility were
on her visiting list; Lady Kirkwall [1] and the Honourable
Mrs. Byron [2] were among her closest friends and corre-
spondents. Among many others we may include Sir
Lucas Pepys,[3] the royal physician; Dr. Michael Lort,
Regius Professor of Greek at Cambridge;[4] Sir Philip
Jennings Clerk, M.P.; Sir James Fellowes, M.D.; Mrs.
Piozzi's executor; James Hutton, the Moravian; the
Rev. G. H. Glasse, the classical scholar; Thomas Pennant,
the naturalist;[5] Samuel Lysons,[6] the antiquary; Daniel
Lysons,[7] the topographer; Samuel Rogers, the poet;
Dr. Samuel Parr; Charles Sheppard, afterwards Attorney-
General of Santa Lucia; George James, A.R.A.; and
John Gillon, a rich West Indian merchant.[8] She had
old friends, also, among her dependants, and there sur-
vives a collection of letters to her old coachman, Jacob
Weston, written " in a familiar gossipy vein." [9]

Her women friends with literary pretensions included
Miss Hannah More; Miss Harriet Lee, the novelist; Lady
Eleanor Butler and Miss Sarah Ponsonby, the recluses
of Llangollen;[10] Miss Helen Maria Williams, authoress

[1] J.R.L., *Kirkwall-Piozzi Letters. English MS.* 580.
[2] J.R.L., *Thrale-Byron Correspondence. English MS.* 546.
[3] J.R.L., *Letters to Mrs. Piozzi. English MSS.* 554-557.
[4] J.R.L., *Lort-Thrale (Piozzi) Letters. English MS.* 544.
[5] J.R.L., *Pennant-Piozzi Letters. English MS.* 575.
[6] J.R.L., *Lysons(S.)-Piozzi Letters. English MS.* 552. See
Hayward, *Autobiography, passim.*
[7] J.R.L., *Lysons(D.)-Piozzi Letters. English MS.* 576.
[8] J.R.L., *Gillon-Piozzi Letters. English MSS.* 577-579.
[9] A. M. Broadley, *Dr. Johnson and Mrs. Thrale*, London, 1910,
p. 59 *n.*
[10] J.R.L., *Ladies of Llangollen-Piozzi Letters. English MS.* 581.

and "Girondist";[1] Miss Anna Seward;[2] Miss Ellis
Cornelia Knight; Miss Marianne Francis,[3] described by
her grandfather, Dr. Burney, as a "monster" of knowledge; and Mrs. Pennington, Anna Seward's "graceful
and elegant Sophia Weston."

Mrs. Piozzi also had many friends among the clergy
and their families; prominent among them were Dr.
Hinchcliffe, Bishop of Peterborough; Dr. Lewis Bagot,
Bishop of St. Asaph; the Rev. Robert Gray, afterwards
Bishop of Bristol;[4] Mrs. Lewis, widow of the Dean of
Ossory; the Rev. Thomas Sedgwick Whalley, poet and
traveller;[5] and the Rev. Leonard Chappelow,[6] of Trinity
College, Cambridge, and of Roydon, near Diss. They,
as well as her lay friends, occasionally discussed with
her their work, sought her judgment, and made use of
her wide general knowledge. Numerous marginal notes
in her Bible [7] and in many theological works show the
deep interest Mrs. Piozzi took in religious matters.

Finally she had an interest of a very different character,
namely, the Theatre. One of the most faithful of all
Mrs. Piozzi's friends, was the actor and author, Arthur
Murphy,[8] who enjoyed a considerable reputation in his
day as a writer of plays, both comedies and tragedies, and

---

[1] J.R.L., *Williams-Piozzi Letters*. *English MS.* 570.

[2] J.R.L., *Seward-Piozzi Letters*. *English MS.* 565.

[3] See above, p. 36, *n.* 2.

[4] J.R.L., *Gray-Piozzi Letters*. *English MS.* 571. Also see
Hayward, *Autobiography, passim.*

[5] J.R.L., *Whalley-Piozzi Letters*. *English MS.* 564.

[6] J.R.L., *Piozzi-Chappelow* and *Chappelow-Piozzi Letters*. *English
MSS.* 559-563.

[7] Her annotated copy of Dodd's edition of the Bible (1770),
left by her to Sir James Fellowes, is now in the John Rylands
Library.

[8] J.R.L., *Murphy-Thrale Letters*. *English MS.* 548.

whose numerous miscellaneous works include an *Essay on the Life and Genius of Samuel Johnson, LL.D.*, and a *Life of David Garrick*. He was a friend of Thrale's before the latter's marriage, and it was he who introduced the Thrales to Dr. Johnson. With the exception of one comparatively short interval of estrangement, Murphy remained for well over forty years a gay companion and trusted adviser of Mrs. Thrale, and when the famous gallery of Streatham portraits was sold in 1816, although the portraits of Johnson, Burke, Goldsmith, Reynolds, Garrick, and other old friends were sold, that of Murphy was reserved for her. Other friends connected with the Theatre included Sarah Siddons,[1] the Kembles, the Holmans, William Augustus Conway,[2] Bertie Greatheed,[3] and Dr. John Delap.[4] Mrs. Piozzi, when eighty years of age, is said to have conceived a sentimental attachment for the handsome twenty-year-old actor, Conway; and in 1842 there was published a volume of so-called " Love Letters of Mrs. Piozzi, written when she was eighty, to William Augustus Conway." [5] Whether these letters have been tampered with or misinterpreted we cannot say; but we are unable to accept unreservedly this tribute to Mrs. Piozzi's romantic disposition. Newly discovered letters, both from Conway and relating to him, indicate that her attitude was rather that implied in a letter she wrote to Mrs. Pennington on June 6, 1820 : [6]

---

[1] J.R.L., *Siddons-Piozzi Letters. English MS.* 574.

[2] J.R.L., *Conway-Piozzi Letters. English MS.* 596.

[3] J.R.L., *Greatheed-Piozzi Letters. English MS.* 558.

[4] J.R.L., *Delap-Thrale Letters. English MS.* 547.

[5] See also Percival Merritt, *The true story of the so-called love letters of Mrs. Piozzi*, Harvard University Press, 1927.

[6] Oswald G. Knapp, *The Intimate Letters of Hester Piozzi and Penelope Pennington*, London, 1914, pp. 322-323.

"Thank God Salusbury and Conway—dear Lads—are young, and likely to last me out. But when they do not write my foolish heart is fluttering for their safety—naughty children as they are in neglecting to send me a Letter."

Bertie Greatheed and Dr. Delap, both minor dramatists, persuaded Mrs. Piozzi to write epilogues to plays, and Henry Hart Milman, afterwards Dean of St. Paul's, invited her, though the invitation was not accepted, to write a prologue for his play " Fazio," first published in 1815, and performed for the first time in London on February 5, 1818.[1] Several manuscripts of Mrs. Piozzi herself show that she also occasionally thought of publishing dramatic works. In her handwriting are a three-act play with the title, " The Two Fountains. A faery tale," [2] and Act I. of " The Humourist. A Comedy " ; [3] in another hand is " The Adventurer. A Comedy in two acts," [4] but there are alterations which have been made by Mrs. Piozzi, and a second copy of the play written throughout in her hand.[5]

Mrs. Piozzi's published and unpublished work, however low or otherwise we may assess its literary merit, is remarkable for the evidence it affords of the wide interests and varied attainments of the writer. During the earlier period of her life, in addition to her writings already mentioned, she contributed a number of short pieces to the St. James's Chronicle and various periodicals, and also a poem entitled " The Three Warnings," to Mrs. Anna Williams's Miscellanies, which appeared in 1766. Of the latter poem Boswell writes : " I cannot

[1] See L. B. Seeley, *Mrs. Thrale*, London, 1891, p. 327.
[2] J.R.L., *English MS.* 649.   [3] *Ibid.*, 650.
[4] *Ibid.*, 651.   [5] *Ibid.*, 652.

withhold from Mrs. Thrale the praise of being the author of that admirable poem, ' The Three Warnings.' " [1]

Her first complete volume was the *Anecdotes of the late Samuel Johnson, during the last twenty years of his Life,* published in 1786; but in 1785 she had contributed the Preface, the Conclusion, and a number of poems to *The Florence Miscellany,* a work which also contains poems by her friends, Robert (" Della Crusca ") Merry, Bertie Greatheed, and William Parsons. The *Miscellany* is a work of little distinction, but Horace Walpole, who did not favour Mrs. Piozzi, wrote to Sir Horace Mann : [2]

> " I should be glad if you could get one for me : not for the merit of the verses, which are moderate enough, faint imitations of our good poets ; but for a short and sensible and genteel preface by la Piozza. . . ."

Manuscripts of other early works survive. They include numerous poems, [3] a few of which, including her witty verses on " The Streatham Portraits," have since been printed by the Rev. Edward Mangin [4] and by Hayward ; [5] a " Dissertation on the God Endovellicus," written long before her marriage to Thrale ; and " Three Dialogues on the Death of Hester Lynch Thrale," [6] written in August, 1779, which were edited in 1932 by Mr. M. Zamick.

Her best known and most discussed work is the volume of *Anecdotes of Dr. Johnson,* of which no fewer

---

[1] Boswell's *Life,* vol. ii., p. 26.

[2] *The Letters of Horace Walpole* (ed. Mrs. Paget Toynbee, Oxford, 1905), vol. xiii., p. 371.

[3] J.R.L., *English MSS.* 646-647.   [4] *Piozziana,* London, 1833.

[5] A manuscript of this poem is in the John Rylands Library.

[6] J.R.L., *English MS.* 642.

than four editions appeared within a year. This entertaining little book was violently assailed by Boswell, and its literary style and haphazard arrangement were strongly and justifiably criticized by Horace Walpole and other writers; but no true Johnsonian can deny its very considerable value. It was written by Mrs. Piozzi in Italy, and she must often have had to rely upon her memory, as many of her papers were in England locked up in the Bank. A number of inaccuracies in her facts have been detected; but her reverence and admiration for Johnson, combined perhaps with a sense of grievance moving her to reveal less attractive sides of his character, which might otherwise have been left unmentioned, probably result in a more or less true impression of Johnson from a woman's point of view. Her comparatively slight work cannot be measured against Boswell's unequalled and monumental *Life of Johnson*, but Mrs. Piozzi was familiar with a Johnson that Boswell could never know, for, while Boswell was the trusted, if subservient, friend and boon companion, Mrs. Piozzi saw more of him in the home. It may not be insignificant that many of Johnson's women friends, of whom we may mention Mrs. Lewis (Charlotte Cotterell), Miss Frances Reynolds, Miss Anna Seward and Mrs. Montagu, disagreed with Boswell. Miss Hannah More's verdict on the *Anecdotes*, given in a letter to her sister in April, 1786, was as follows : [1]

> " Mrs. Piozzi's book is much in fashion. It is indeed entertaining, but there are two or three passages exceedingly unkind to Garrick which filled me with indignation. If Johnson had been envious enough to utter them, she might have been prudent enough to suppress them."

[1] See Hayward, *Autobiography*, vol. i., p. 291.

Mrs. Montagu, the " Queen of the Bluestockings," at the time of the appearance of the *Anecdotes* was, it should be noted, very annoyed with Boswell on account of a passage in his *Tour to the Hebrides*, in which, with reference to her *Essay on Shakespeare*, Johnson is reported to have said :

> " Reynolds is fond of her book, and I wonder at it ; for neither I, nor Beauclerk, nor Mrs. Thrale, could get through it."

Mrs. Piozzi contradicted this statement, and Mrs. Montagu wrote to her, on March 28, 1786, a letter from which we take the following extract : [1]

> " I will no longer delay my acknowledgments for a letter which gave me great pleasure, & of a kind superior to that which can arise merely from the vanity of an Author, as it express'd personal kindness to me, as well as approbation of my work. Tho they have a right to *censure freely who have written well*, as you have done, yet the kind partiality you had always shewn for me gave me some right to flatter myself, it would have influenced your judgment & taste, so far as to have prevented any severe censure of my essay, & the mortification I should have felt on the sentence you were said to have passd upon it, was mitigated by the very moderate degree of credit I give to all Mr Boswell has ascribed to, or repeated of Dr Johnson, for tho it cannot be supposed he would utter any wilful falsehood, yet poor man ! he is so often in that condition in which men are said to see double, the hearing in the same circumstances may probably be no less disorder'd.

[1] J.R.L., *Montagu-Thrale Letters. English MS.* 551.

"Your Anecdotes of Dr Johnson my dear Madam are very different from Mr Boswells. Yours do honour to the subject, the Writer, & harm to no one. He indeed tells the World that *Mr. Boswell* thought highly of Dr Johnson, but all he relates of him tends to diminish the Worlds esteem of his Friend, & raise up many particular enemies to his memory, but they must be malicious enemies indeed, who are not more vexd & angry at the disgrace he has thrown upon his deceased Friend than at any reflections or censures he has made him the instrument to throw upon others."

Mrs. Lewis, on May 8, 1786, wrote to Mrs. Piozzi thanking her for her "charming, entertaining, witty, *candid* anecdotes." On August 23, 1791, after the appearance of Boswell's *Life of Johnson*, she again refers to Mrs. Piozzi's book, while she challenges Boswell's accuracy : [1]

"I am & have been very unwell lately however I have at last attain'd to Boswell's curious book, & have pretty nearly got thro' the first Vol : but Miss Sarah has stop'd me in my progress in order to read it herself before she sets out for Devonshire, wch will be next monday at the farthest. It is impossible to read a collection of Johnson's conversations & opinions without receiving both information and amusement, but what I have yet met with don't strike me as exhibiting the Character more perfectly than your Book or even S^r: J : H : [2] & if the other anecdotes are as inacurate as those relating to the Miss Cotterells the trouble he took

[1] J.R.L., *Letters to H. L. Piozzi.* *English MS.* 556.
[2] Sir John Hawkins.

in fixing dates was very Ill bestow'd,[1] for there are
many mistakes both as to time and circumstance
but as the whole of the matter reflects neither credit
or discredit I do not care about it. He chuses to
make Mr Reynolds one of Johnsons comforters
for the loss of his wife, & then says the acquaintance
began at our Lodgings opposite Johnson, in Castle
S^t, the fact was that we never saw Johnson till
some years after his wife died, & it was above (a)
year after that, when Mr Reynolds met him at
Fanny's (for I was not there) in poor Shewards
house, & as to the *agreable conversation*, he puts into
the mouth of Mr Reynolds it is wholly imaginary
we not having loss (*sic*) any friend s^d not give
Sr Joshua room to display a *sentiment* wch raised

---

[1] Boswell had thus described the meeting of Reynolds and
Johnson: "When Johnson lived in Castle-street, Cavendish-
square, he used frequently to visit two ladies, who lived opposite
to him, Miss Cotterells, daughters of Admiral Cotterell. Reynolds
used also to visit there, and thus they met."—Boswell's *Life*, vol. i.,
pp. 244-245.

Boswell wrote: "The ladies were regretting the death of a
friend, to whom they owed great obligations; upon which Reynolds
observed, 'You have, however, the comfort of being relieved from
a burtl..en of gratitude' . . . Sir Joshua told me a pleasant char-
acteristical anecdote of Johnson about the time of their first acquaintance. When they were one evening together at the Miss
Cotterells', the then Duchess of Argyle and another lady of high
rank came in. Johnson, thinking that the Miss Cotterells were
too much engrossed by them, and that he and his friend were
neglected, as low company of whom they were somewhat ashamed,
grew angry; and resolving to shock their supposed pride, by making
their great visitors imagine that his friend and he were low indeed,
he addressed himself in a low tone to Mr. Reynolds, saying, 'How
much do you think you and I could get in a week, if we were
to *work as hard* as we could?'—as if they had been common
mechanicks."—*Ibid.*, p. 246.

Johnson's admiration so much. As to the history
of the Dutchess it was in some degree true, that is,
the Dutchess of Hamilton & Lady Donegal came
to make a visit while S^r J: & Johnson were sitting
with Fanny, she cannot recollect that there was
any offence, nor that any party seem'd offended,
the conversation she does not recollect, except that
when the Ladies were gone, Johnson said to her,
thank you Madam *I was never in company with a
Duchess before*. After all tho' we (have) but little
reason to quarrel with Boswell, it is a most im-
pertinent Book, the figure you are to make in it I
have hardly yet reach'd, but still can't help thinking
& I am sure most ardently hoping that he can not
say any thing that will be of the least Ill consequence
to you. I am all impatience to get thro' it. I
shall certainly get Bozz & Pozz. I am afraid it
will gratify my spleen more than it ought to see the
Book brought to disgrace."

Small inaccuracies such as the above are, we admit,
of little consequence in a work of such magnitude and
outstanding merit as Boswell's *Life of Johnson;* but we
quote the above letter as showing that even the long-
headed Scot, with his numerous note-books and with
informants within easy reach, could err, and that some
of the inaccuracies of the vivacious Welshwoman, writing
far away in Italy, were not inexcusable. Boswell himself eagerly exposed some of Mrs. Piozzi's errors; but
he did not find very many of them, and several of
those he attributed to her were comparatively insignificant or on equally good evidence could be defended.
Other inaccuracies have come to light, and it is perhaps
typical of Mrs. Piozzi that she herself should provide

the evidence for the worst of them, which occurs in her account of their relations with the Abbé Roffette at Rouen.[1]

From the *Anecdotes* it appears that on one and the same day Dr. Johnson and the Abbé Roffette discussed the Jesuits; Johnson pronounced an eulogium on Milton which delighted the Abbé; and Mr. Thrale, seeing them so charmed with each other, invited the Abbé to England, only to be roughly rebuked in his presence by Johnson, who "thus put a sudden finish to all his own and Mr. Thrale's entertainment from the company of the Abbé Roffette."

Her French Journal, written up at the time, shows that they met the Abbé, who is not named, on September 23; that the argument about the Jesuits took place on September 24; that the eulogium on Milton was delivered on the following day; and that after Thrale's invitation, Johnson offered to show the Abbé Oxford. The Abbé excused himself and they parted, to quote Mrs. Thrale, "with great Good Will on every Side." There is no justification for these two very different accounts. It would seem that in the *Anecdotes* either Mrs. Piozzi was being deliberately malicious or that relying on her memory she was deplorably confusing different events. The first view is completely at variance with the character of Mrs. Thrale as revealed by her friends, and by several of her critics; the alternative would probably have been scouted by Boswell and many other critics.

Mrs. Piozzi's next work was her *Letters to and from the late Samuel Johnson, LL.D.*, published in two volumes in 1788. We need only mention several criticisms of

[1] See below, pp. 84-86.

this work, which illustrate how the passage of time may affect judgments. Hannah More wrote : [1]

" They are such as ought to have been written but ought not to have been printed : a few of them are very good : sometimes he is moral, and sometimes he is kind. The imprudence of editors and executors is an additional reason men of parts should be afraid to die."

Fanny Burney also strongly disapproved : [2]

" These letters have not been more improperly published in the whole, than they are injudiciously displayed in their several parts. She has given all —every word—and thinks that, perhaps, a justice to Dr. Johnson, which, in fact, is the greatest injury to his memory."

Miss Burney also records the following speech of the Queen : [3]

" I have always spoke as little as possible upon this affair. I remember but twice that I have named it : once I said to the Bishop of Carlisle that I thought most of these letters had better have been spared the printing ; and once to Mr. Langton, at the Drawing-room, I said, ' Your friend, Dr. Johnson, sir, has had many friends busy to publish his books, and his memoirs, and his meditations, and his thoughts ; but I think he wanted one friend more.' ' What for, ma'am ? ' cried he ; ' A friend to suppress them,' I answered."

[1] See Hayward, *Autobiography*, vol. i., p. 313.
[2] *Diary and Letters of Madame D'Arblay* (ed. C. Barrett, London, n.d.), vol. ii., p. 444.
[3] *Ibid.*, vol. ii., p. 449.

Over a century later the interest in Johnson and a change of view-point resulted in an edition of the available letters under the imprimatur of a great University Press, and now another edition, with numerous newly discovered letters, is in course of preparation. The new editor, Dr. R. W. Chapman, referring to the imperfections of the printed editions upon which the preceding editor, Dr. Birkbeck Hill, had to rely, wrote in a letter to *The Times Literary Supplement* of October 30, 1924:

> " Mrs. Piozzi is the worst offender; she mutilated Johnson's letters both deliberately, by cutting out names, shortening the ' studied conclusions,' and discarding paragraphs which she thought unimportant; and carelessly, by failing to correct serious misreadings made by the printer."

To-day letters from Johnson, which Mrs. Piozzi had either mislaid or had deliberately refrained from using, because of their small apparent interest or valetudinary nature, are welcomed on their appearance in print by many of Johnson's admirers. We hesitate, however, to condemn Mrs. Piozzi for not printing letters of small literary value and for not carrying further a practice which was not regarded as in the best taste by many of her contemporaries, while we feel that motives of delicacy were not entirely wanting in her suppression of many names in the letters she did print. We doubt, also, if she should be judged too harshly, and by the standard of meticulous accuracy aimed at by the best editors to-day, for a certain licence in editorship which it is not unusual to find in similar works by her contemporaries. In so far as Johnson's own letters were concerned she sent the originals to the printer, and as she carefully

preserved them afterwards and many of them still survive she evidently felt perfectly justified in the methods
she had adopted. One serious liberty she took, all the
more lamentable in its reminder how subject to temptation
is humanity, for our sense of shock is not unmingled
with understanding. In a letter of Johnson's, dated
June 19, 1775, one paragraph has been struck out and
an extract from another Johnson letter pasted over it.[1]
Certainly the new paragraph does not affect any argument
or statement in the remainder of the letter; but the paragraph cut out described Boswell as " a very fine fellow,"
and asked her if she had read " Boswell's Journals,"
which he speaks of with some approval. Boswell had
said many bitter things about Mrs. Piozzi, but her suppression of this tribute of Johnson's is both regrettable
and unexpected. Fortunately she preserved the evidence
of her lapse, and in partial extenuation, at least, it may be
noted that she printed Johnson's earlier commendatory
letter of May 22, 1775, in which he said :

> " I am not sorry that you read Boswel's journal.
> Is it not a merry piece ? There is much in it about
> poor me." [2]

Mrs. Piozzi's next work was her *Observations and
Reflections made in the course of a journey through France,
Italy, and Germany* which appeared in two large volumes
in 1789. The work was lashed by Horace Walpole and
other critics partly on account of her occasional use
of what Miss Anna Seward called " the vulgarisms of
unpolished conversation," and certain errors of spelling,

[1] R. W. Chapman, *Johnson, Boswell and Mrs. Piozzi. A suppressed passage restored*, Oxford, 1929. A facsimile of the letter
is given.
[2] Birkbeck Hill, *Letters*, vol. i., p. 320.

especially in respect of foreign words. The book was evidently quite popular; an Irish edition appeared in the same year, in 1790 there was a German translation of selections by G. Forster; while over a century later in 1892 was published *Glimpses of Italian Society in the Eighteenth Century. From the Journey of Mrs. Piozzi. With an Introduction by the Countess Evelyn Martinengo Cesaresco.*

Less successful was her next two-volume work, *British Synonymy ; or, an attempt at regulating the choice of words in familiar conversation.*[1] This was inscribed " with Sentiments of Gratitude and Respect, to such of her Foreign Friends as have made English Literature their peculiar Study." William Gifford, editor of the *Quarterly Review*, and other critics attacked the work; others were more favourable. Whatever Mrs. Piozzi's claims were as a philologist the book is far from uninteresting. Johnson is occasionally quoted, and there are some entertaining stories. Walpole wrote to Miss Mary Berry :[2]

> " Here and there she does not want parts, has some good translations, and stories, that are new ; particularly an admirable *bon mot* of Lord Chesterfield, which I never heard before, but dashed with her cruel vulgarisms. . . ."

In his recent book Lord Lansdowne records that Horne Tooke's copy of *British Synonymy*, now at Bowood, contains his hostile annotations, but that his criticism is specially directed to her allusions to sex. Tooke's final note, at least, seems less valuable than gross.[3]

[1] A manuscript of this work is in the John Rylands Library, *English MSS.* 637-638. There is also part of an early draft.

[2] *Letters of Horace Walpole*, vol. xv., pp. 284-285.

[3] *Johnson and Queeney*, p. xxvi.

In 1798 Mrs. Piozzi published a slender volume with the title, *Three Warnings to John Bull before he dies. By an old Acquaintance of the Public.* The author of this political pamphlet, of which the manuscript is in the John Rylands Library,[1] does not appear previously to have been identified. The concluding passage will serve to indicate her general political sentiments :

> " But tho' Danger does approach I will yet have hopes, tho' Ruin is at the Door we may yet keep it out. . . . I remember the old Speeches of King George the second resounded always with the same Words *Unanimity* & *Dispatch* . . . he obtained his Purpose certainly, and in the great, the Immortal William Pitt enjoyed the conscious Triumph of possessing a Minister who was surrounded by Unanimity—preceded only by Dispatch—& followed by Victory with Eagle's Wings. Let us with Gratitude remember the Name, and rally round the Man who has the Honour to bear it . . . and let me a little descend from my Elevation to recommend a long Pull, & a strong Pull, & a Pull altogether."

Finally in 1801 she completed an astonishing performance in two large volumes, consisting of over a thousand pages, with the title, *Retrospection : or a review of the most striking and important events, characters, situations, and their consequences, which the last eighteen hundred years have presented to the view of mankind.*[2] Her arrangements with the printer, John Stockdale, were not completed until almost mid-November, 1800, but the book was

---

[1] J.R.L., *English MS.* 642 ; other short prose pieces of a political nature are in J.R.L., *English MS.* 629.

[2] The MS. of the final version of this work and also a preliminary draft are in the John Rylands Library. *English MSS.* 643-645.

ready for publication by the following January. Many Press errors were made, as she was " obliged to print on New Year's Day, during an insurrection of the printers." Mrs. Piozzi's aims are indicated in her Preface :

> " To an age of profound peace and literary quiet I should have considered such an abridgment as insulting : to our disturbed and busy days abridgments only can be useful. No one has leisure to read better books. Young people are called out to act before they *know*, before they could have *learned* how those have acted who have lived before them."

Elsewhere she writes : [1]

> " History herself is often ill prepared enough when sudden questions interrupt her eloquence ; and my poor summary is willing to confess as controvertible the truth of many a fact recorded here : but with the facts, except as a compiler, myself have nought to do."

We may question the utility of such an enterprise and deprecate Mrs. Piozzi's actual performance, but the work is no slight token of her courage.

Retrospection was her last large work. The Rev. Edward Mangin in 1815 saw the manuscript [2] of a work by her with the title "Lyford Redivivus," the idea being taken from a volume, published in 1655, by Edward Lyford, giving an alphabetical account of the names of men and women, and their derivations. We have seen the manuscripts of other works of hers, which

---

[1] Vol. ii., p. 185. Mr. S. C. Roberts cites this passage in discussing Mrs. Piozzi's works (Piozzi's *Anecdotes*).

[2] *Piozziana*, pp. 13-18. The MS. was sold at " Sotheby's," June 4, 1908, No. 772.

were, as far as we know, never published. The MS. of one work, "begun in April and ended in July, 1791," is headed, *Una and Duessa, or a set of Dialogues upon the most popular subjects* ; [1] an MS. with the title *Sketch of Europe in* 1797, *unrolled by Dumouriez, colour'd &c. by H. L. Piozzi,*[2] and another MS., giving a later version of the same work, and having a Preface, with the title *Miniature Picture of Europe by Dumouriez in* 1797,[3] were based on the "Tableau Speculatif de l'Europe" of C.-F. Dumouriez, which appeared early in 1798 and of which an English translation was published in London the same year ; and there are also the MSS. of numerous short pieces both in prose and verse.[4]

The above formidable series of writings is, at least, ample proof that Mrs. Piozzi thoroughly agreed with the dictum which she has attributed to Dr. Johnson, "any thing is better than Vacuity."

Mrs. Piozzi died on May 2, 1821. To the end she had retained her courageous outlook on life, and age had failed to weaken her intellect or to repress her liveliness. In his Diary on April 28, 1819, Thomas Moore, the poet, had written : [5]

> "Breakfasted with the Fitzgeralds. Took me to call on Mrs. Piozzi; a wonderful old lady; faces of other times seemed to crowd over her as she sat,—the Johnsons, Reynoldses, &c., &c. : though turned eighty she has all the quickness & intelligence of a gay young woman."

In September and October, 1819, she was frequently bathing in the sea, and part of the entry in her journal for October 14, 1819, runs :

---

[1] J.R.L., *English MS.* 635.   [2] *Ibid.,* 640.   [3] *Ibid.,* 629, 647.
[4] *Ibid.,* 641.   See also P. Merritt, *Piozzi Marginalia,* 1925.
[5] Hayward, *Autobiography,* vol. i., p. 361.

> " Bathed in rougher weather than I liked;
> Walked a good Deal."

On January 27, 1820, she had given a concert, ball, and
supper at Bath to celebrate her eightieth birthday. Her
health was proposed by Admiral Sir James Sausmarez,
and afterwards, when the dancing began, she led off
with Sir John Salusbury. The following day she showed
no signs of fatigue, and to the enquiries of her friends
she replied : [1]

> " This sort of thing is greatly in the mind, and
> I am almost tempted to say the same of growing
> old at all, and especially as regards those usual
> concomitants of age : laziness, defective sight, and
> ill-temper."

In March, 1821, while going from Penzance to Clifton,
Mrs. Piozzi met with an accident causing an injury to
a leg. The injury was severe, but she only joked about
it. To her friend, Miss Willoughby, she wrote : [2]

> " Dr. Forbes will be very sorry, for poor
> H. L. P., always a blue, now a black and blue, lady,
> bruised say you, from top to toe ? ' My Lord,
> from head to foot.' "

There are a number of other letters later than this
all in the beautiful and vigorous handwriting which
revealed so clearly the strength and individuality of her
character; and her last letter to Sir John Salusbury,
dated April 10, 1821, shows that she retained her interest
in events and persons, and still looked after her own
business affairs.[3]

Her death took place after a short illness of only ten

---

[1] Hayward, *Autobiography*, vol. i., p. 362.
[2] *Ibid.*, vol. ii., p. 462.
[3] J.R.L., *Salusbury-Piozzi Letters*.

days. She is said to have greeted the news that her daughters had arrived with the remark, " Now I shall die in state." [1] Her friend, Sir George Smith Gibbes, the Bath physician, told the Rev. Edward Mangin of his last visit : [2]

> " When the dying lady saw him at her bedside, she signified by her looks that she knew him well, and that neither his benevolence nor talents could be of any use ; and, unable to speak, conveyed her mournful conviction of her situation, by tracing in the air with her extended hands, the exact outline of a coffin, and then lay calmly down."

Her last words, told to Mangin by Mrs. Pennington, were :

> " I die in the trust, and fear of God."

Before bringing these prefatory remarks to an end, it remains to mention briefly the two other members of the party which visited France, namely Queeney Thrale and Baretti, and also two friends whom they met there.

Hester Maria Thrale, the eldest of the Thrale girls, celebrated her eleventh birthday in France. She is best known as " Queeney," the name Dr. Johnson himself originated, though her mother occasionally refers to her as " Niggey." Miss Burney later described " Queeney " as " a very fine girl, about fourteen years of age, but cold and reserved, though full of knowledge and intelligence." [3] Her disposition does not seem to have been demonstratively affectionate ; but Dr. Johnson was genuinely fond of her and wrote her a number of

[1] Hayward, *Autobiography*, vol. i., p. 363 *n*.
[2] *Piozziana*, p. 8.
[3] *Diary and Letters of Madame D'Arblay*, vol. i., p. 21.

charming letters,[1] which, with a few of his surviving letters to several other children, throw light on a pleasant side of his character. Queeney married in her forty-fourth year Admiral George Keith Elphinstone, Baron Keith of Stonehaven Marischal, a widower of sixty years of age, and an officer of very considerable distinction—he was appointed commander-in-chief of the Channel fleet in February, 1812, and was made a viscount in 1814. This marriage is an instance of that difference in temperament between Lady Keith and her mother, which made it often difficult for Mrs. Piozzi to understand her daughter. In the face of great opposition and ridicule, Thrale's widow, in her forty-fourth year, heedlessly obeyed the dictates of her heart and married an Italian music-master ; at the same age, and with general approval, Queeney accepted the hand of her elderly Scottish sailor after a long and gentle courtship, during which her health was apparently a frequent object of anxiety to the Admiral. Queeney in return, Lord Lansdowne tells us,[2] sent him presents of ginger and " a special brand of lime water of her own making, which seems to have greatly assisted his digestive processes."

Giuseppe Baretti, the Italian tutor, was responsible for many of the arrangements on the French tour, which, he informed his brothers, cost Mr. Thrale eight hundred and twenty-two louis d'or.[3] His activities there are described in *Thraliana* : [4]

[1] Printed by the Marquis of Lansdowne in *Johnson and Queeney*.

[2] *Ibid.*, pp. xx-xxi.

[3] Lacy Collison-Morley, *Giuseppe Baretti*, p. 284. This work gives a full account of Baretti's life and activities. For Baretti see also the publications of the Italian scholar, Luigi Piccioni, in particular, *Giuseppe Baretti prima della " Frusta Letteraria "* (*Giornale storico della Letteratura Italiana, Supplemento*, Nos. 13-14); also Carlo Segre, *Relazioni letterarie fra Italia e Inghilterra*.

[4] Hayward, *Autobiography*, vol. i., p. 94.

"France displayed all Mr. Baretti's useful powers—he bustled for us, he catered for us, he took care of the child, he secured an apartment for the maid, he provided for our safety, our amusement, our repose ; without him the pleasure of that journey would never have balanced the pain. And great was his disgust, to be sure, when he caught us, as he often did, ridiculing French manners, French sentiments, &c. I think he half cryed to Mrs. Payne, the landlady at Dover, on our return, because we laughed at French cookery, and French accommodations. Oh, how he would court the maids at the inns abroad, abuse the men perhaps ! and that with a facility not to be exceeded, as they all confessed, by any of the natives. But so he could in Spain, I find, and so 'tis plain he could here."

Later, in 1776, when an Italian tour was being planned, Baretti explained to his brothers, who evidently had been protesting, that it was not degrading for a man of letters to go as travelling companion with a man of wealth, and instanced Johnson, who was honoured to accompany Mr. Thrale. Baretti had, indeed, sound pretensions to be a man of letters. In his own country he had a high reputation, in particular as the editor of the periodical *La frusta letteraria ;* in England he was well known for his many writings, which included *An account of the manners and customs of Italy ; A journey from London to Genoa, through England, Portugal, Spain, and France ; A Dictionary of the English and Italian languages,* and other grammatical works.

Johnson thought well of him : [1]

"I know no man who carries his head higher in conversation than Baretti. There are strong

[1] Boswell's *Life,* vol. ii., p. 57.

powers in his mind. He has not, indeed, many hooks; but with what hooks he has, he grapples very forcibly."

Mrs. Piozzi, also, did not allow his enmity to her to blind her to his many qualities : [1]

" he was—*Dieu me pardonne*, as the French say— my inmate for very near three years ; and though I really liked the man once for his talents, and at last was weary of him for the use he made of them, I never altered my sentiments concerning him ; for his character is easily seen, and his soul above disguise, haughty and insolent, and breathing defiance against all mankind ; while his powers of mind exceed most people's, and his powers of purse are so slight that they leave him dependent on all. Baretti is for ever in the state of a stream dammed up : if he could once get loose, he would bear down all before him."

Baretti was capable of unselfish acts of friendship, and was very tender with young children, but he was a merciless critic and an unscrupulous enemy. Evidence we have had to give elsewhere [2] confirms the generally accepted view that he was by no means reliable in his facts or opinions when his anger was aroused; and certainly he did not in his fury hesitate to injure either man or woman with totally unsupported aspersions and innuendoes.

The two friends whom they met in France were Mrs. Strickland and the Count Manucci.

Mrs. Strickland,[3] elsewhere described by Mrs. Thrale

[1] Hayward, *Autobiography*, vol. i., p. 103.

[2] See below, pp. 234-257.

[3] Cecilia, only daughter of William Townley, Esq., of Townley, Lancashire, and of his wife, Cecilia, daughter of Ralph Standish,

as her " oldest friend," met the party at Rouen, evidently by arrangement, on September 22. She remained with them until the evening of October 29, when she had to leave the party, to Mrs. Thrale's great regret. Dr. Johnson also seems to have been favourably impressed by Mrs. Strickland, for Boswell in a note upon a letter from himself to Johnson, dated July 9, 1777, in which he refers to a proposal for a meeting at Carlisle, writes : [1]

> " Dr. Johnson had himself talked of our seeing Carlisle together. *High* was a favourite word of his to denote a person of rank. He said to me, ' Sir, I believe we may meet at the house of a Roman Catholick lady in Cumberland, a high lady, Sir.' I afterwards discovered that he meant Mrs. Strickland, sister of Charles Townley, Esq., whose very noble collection of statues and pictures is not more to be admired, than his extraordinary and polite readiness in shewing it, which I and several of my friends have agreeably experienced."

Many years later Mrs. Thrale, then Piozzi, stayed with Mrs. Strickland at Sizergh Castle in Westmorland. The Piozzis were then on a journey through North England, Scotland, and Wales, and on August 19, 1789, Mrs. Piozzi wrote from Liverpool to her friend, Mrs. Byron : [2]

Esq., of Standish, and of Lady Philippa Howard. Her eldest son, Thomas Strickland, succeeded to the Standish estates on the death of his uncle, Edward Townley-Standish, on March 28, 1807, and later assumed the surname and arms of Standish.

[1] Boswell's *Life*, vol. iii., p. 118, *n.* 3.

[2] J.R.L., *Byron-Thrale MSS.* : Mrs. Byron was the wife of Admiral the Hon. John Byron (Foulweather Jack), and grandmother of the poet.

" We have been detain'd from this Place longer
than was our Intention by the renewed Kindnesses
of an old Friend you must have heard me speak
of many Years ago : Mrs. Strickland of Sizergh
in Westmorland, who was one of my *earliest* In-
timates ; her Maiden Name *Townley :* her Grandmother Lady Phillippa Standish, Daughter to the
old Duke of Norfolk. She was in France with
Mr Thrale & me in the Year 1773 (*sic*) I think—
but various Accidents have kept us long asunder.
The first thing I heard at Kendal, however, was
that She had taken Pains to waylay, and carry us
to her House instead of the Inn, so with her, &
her Son, who is married to Sir John Lawson's
Daughter, a pretty pleasing Girl whom Mr Piozzi
& I had met with at Brussells in our Way to England,
we have been living this last Week, & are now half
killed with the Heat, tho' travelling as slowly as
possible."

Mrs. Strickland had also married again since 1775.
Her first husband, by whom she had had three sons and
a daughter, was Charles Strickland of Sizergh ; her
second husband, to whom she was married on April 15,
1779, was her cousin, Gerard Edward Strickland, Esq.,
of Willitoft, Yorkshire. There were two sons of the
second marriage, George and Gerard.

In another letter to Mrs. Byron, dated September 1,
Mrs. Piozzi wrote : [1]

" Had we known that young Mrs Strickland's
Family & yours were intimate we should have had
still more Chat. The amiable Woman you remember
tall, active & elegant, tho' never handsome—is

[1] J.R.L., *Byron-Thrale MSS.*

now chained to her Chair by Infirmity : She has to comfort her however the attentions of her *second* Husband, and the Dutyful Fondness of her Son by the *first ;* besides two little Babies whose Birth has been followed by their Mother's *Loss of Limbs.*"

On June 9, 1795, immediately after her marriage with Mr. Mostyn, Mrs. Piozzi's daughter, Cecilia, visited Mrs. Strickland at Sizergh. In a letter from Preston on June 11 to her mother Cecilia wrote : [1]

" My dearest Mother. We slept at Kendal last night & before we set off for this place the young Man & I went to see Mrs Strickland—wasn't that very pretty, & proper ?—I sent word *Miss Cecilia Thrale* for of course she would not have remember'd me and she was delighted to (see) us, only a little amazed till we told her we were come off *a long journey.* She directly said—Oh ! you have been to Scotland !—You have no idea how much better she is and how extremely well she looks—so much less —her Physicians give her hopes of walking about & doing as she did before. I am sure you will be very glad to hear this. She means to write soon & she has invited the young Man and me to come & see the Lakes next Summer & spend the time at Syzergh instead of at Inns—in short civiller & kinder than any body ever was. We have promised to go & most likely shall I think."

Mrs. Strickland immediately fulfilled her promise to write to Mrs. Piozzi. We will quote a relevant passage from her letter written on June 11, 1795. It reveals

[1] J.R.L., *Cecilia Thrale (Mostyn) Correspondence.*

that she, like many other charming and gifted ladies of her day, was not strong in spelling or punctuation.[1]

" What a perturbation the sight of Old friends puts one into. The world goes on & remaining friends are good and kind, & willing to make one forget the loss of those who are gon from us— here have I just parted with your Dear Daughter My Cecilia—she looks Charmingly—all life & pleasing Manners. I do assure you she quiet delighted me, & her fine Husband, looks all that one can wish for her, & affords a happy prospect, I think, for you, give me leave to present my harty Congratulations on her Marryiage both to you & M[r] Piozzi, tis an event must give you both pleasere now, & be a lasting comfort. It was very kind & pritty of her to call at my Solitary house, & she did it so prittyly, by sending up to say, that Miss Cecilia Threal and M[r] (I can't yet make out his name) my servant said Moyston, were below and desir'd to know how I did. There needed no more intimation to make me gues that a Marryage had taken place, but the where, & the how, remain'd to be explaind—& this they did to me, with so much Naïvete and Sweetness, & every thing intresting about them, that they won my heart & made me embrace her with the Sincerest Cordiality Not as a Name sake, but realy as a Mother, and I take my pen instantly to congratulate you my Dear Lady, tho no post can go from hence till Satturday, but I can not rest till I have written to you, and while my heart is deverted from its own afflictions is the Sweetest Moment to express my gratitude for your kind remembrance and concern for me."

[1] J.R.L., *Letters to H. L. Piozzi.*

In the following years letters passed from time to time between the two old friends, and Mrs. Piozzi was always anxious that Mrs. Strickland, immediately her infirmities permitted, should visit her Welsh home, Brynbella. Mr. and Mrs. Mostyn in the summer of 1796 planned to go into Westmorland on a shooting party and to visit Sizergh.[1] In the following year on July 2, Mrs. Strickland, in her last surviving letter to Mrs. Piozzi, referred with much pleasure to a visit paid by her daughter Mary, then Mrs. Stephenson, to her friend at Streatham Park, and was so improved in health that she was looking forward with confidence to an early meeting at Brynbella.

The other friend, Count Manucci, was unknown to any of the party in France, except Baretti, before a dinner given by the French authoress, Madame du Boccage, on October 5, 1775. He was a Florentine nobleman of high birth and engaging manners, described by Baretti as " a good and most pleasing man, who had read very little in his language and next to nothing in any other." Shortly after his meeting with Johnson and the Thrales, he came over to England, and in the spring of the following year was often with them and made the acquaintance of Boswell. It was his servant who carried the news of the death of the Thrales' young son, Harry, on March 23, 1776, to Baretti.[2] In May he was in London with Johnson, with whom he intended to join the Thrales at Bath. On May 6, Johnson wrote:[3]

> " Count Manucci is in such haste to come, that
> I believe he will not stay for me; if he would, I
> should like to hear his remarks on the road."

[1] Oswald G. Knapp, *The Intimate Letters of Hester Piozzi and Penelope Pennington*, p. 137.

[2] *European Magazine*, vol. xiii., p. 314.

[3] Birkbeck Hill, *Letters*, vol. i., p. 392.

Mrs. Thrale replied on May 8 : [1]

> " Count Manucci is a Goose Cap *not* to wait
> for you ; one good only will attend his coming
> sooner, I shall make Seward,[2] who speaks Italian,
> shew him what is to be seen by pretty Men in the
> Cards and Dancing way, & Seward leaves Bath
> this Day sevenight."

Manucci, however, postponed his departure from day
to day in the hope that Johnson could travel with him,
until on May 14, Johnson, who did not get to Bath on
this occasion, wrote : [3]

> " Manucci must, I believe, come down without
> me.   I am ashamed of having delayed him so long,
> without being able to fix a day ; but you know,
> and must make him know, that the fault is not
> mine."

On May 16 he had written to the Count " to
find his own way." [4]   Almost immediately afterwards
Manucci must have set out for a tour in Ireland.   On
July 18 Boswell wrote to Johnson from Edinburgh : [5]

> " Count Manucci came here last week from
> travelling in Ireland.   I have shown him what
> civilities I could on his own account, on your's,
> and on that of Mr. and Mrs. Thrale.   He has had
> a fall from his horse, and been much hurt.   I re-
> gret this unlucky accident, for he seems to be a
> very amiable man."

[1] J.R.L., *Thrale-Johnson Letters*.
[2] William Seward, a friend of Johnson and the Thrales.   His
writings include the five-volume work, *Anecdotes of Some Distinguished Persons*, 1795-1797.
[3] Birkbeck Hill, *Letters*, vol. i., p. 395.
[4] *Ibid*., p. 398.   [5] Boswell's *Life*, vol. iii., p. 89.

This account was modified in a later letter dated August 30 : [1]

> " For the honour of Count Manucci, as well as to observe that exactness of truth which you have taught me, I must correct what I said in a former letter. He did not fall from his horse, which might have been an imputation on his skill as an officer of cavalry ; his horse fell with him."

We do not know how long Manucci stayed in this country. Years later when Mrs. Thrale was in Milan with her second husband, she met the Count again. The story of the meeting is best given by her in a short account of her stay in Italy : [2]

> " *Au reste*, as the French say, few things befell us worth recording, except Count Manucci's visit. He had been intimate with Mr. Thrale in England, as Johnson's letters abundantly testify, and had taken a fancy to Mr. Piozzi at Paris, when he was there with Sacchini.[3] Hearing, therefore, of his marriage, he came one morning, but never had a notion that it was with *me* he had connected himself. ' Ah, Madame ! ' exclaimed the Count, ' quel coûp de Théâtre ! ' when the door opened, and showed him an old acquaintance with a new name. This was the nobleman who, I told you, lamented so tenderly that his sister's children were *counterfeited*."

---

[1] Boswell's *Life*, vol. iii., p. 91.

[2] Hayward, *Autobiography*, vol. ii., p. 68.

[3] Fanny Burney in her Diary, under July 16, 1781, during a stay at Streatham, wrote : " You will believe I was not a little surprized to see Sacchini. He is going to the Continent with Piozzi, and Mrs. Thrale invited them both to spend the last day at Streatham, and from hence proceed to Margate." She then described at some length this famous Italian composer.

MRS. THRALE'S
FRENCH JOURNAL
1775

Mrs. Thrale's French Journal fills 147 pages of a small quarto note-book, the leather cover of which bears the title "French Journal, 1775". The period covered by its contents extends from September 15 to November 11, 1775, inclusive. On Mrs. Piozzi's death in May, 1821, the manuscript passed, with her other papers, into the possession of her adopted son, Sir John Salusbury Piozzi Salusbury. It was acquired in 1931 for the John Rylands Library, Manchester, from Sir John's great grand-daughter, Mrs. R. V. Colman. It is now "J.R.L. English MS. 617".

28: Octr We went nowhere today but to the great Toyshop called
the Petit Dunkerque. I bought a Trinket or two,
& longed for a snuffbox of exquisite beauty. at
Night Strecky took one Coach & paid Visits while
the Men went to the play — I was not well e:
:nough to venture so Mr. Johnson sat at home
by me, & we critizised & talked & were happy in
one another — he in stuffing me, & I in being stuffed

29. Octr This day I took final leave of my amiable Nuns
at the Fossée — Miss Canning promised mes her
Correspondence, & thanked me a thousand Times
for my little present of Books I had sent her the
Rambler & Mrs Fermor the Rasselas: I kissed
them through the Wicket, and wished them most
sincerely well — Miss Fitzherbert has promised
to send me a Pair of Ruffles to take care of for
her Mama I shall be glad to see something
from the House from hence I waited on Mad:
ame de Barlançon who lives on the outside
of their Convent while She is in Paris

Facsimile of a Page of Mrs. Thrale's French Journal, 1775.

MRS. THRALE'S FRENCH JOURNAL, 1775

NOTWITHSTANDING the Disgust my last Journey [1] gave me, I have lately been solicitous to undertake another.

So true is Johnson's Observation [2] that any thing is better than Vacuity.

15 Sept[r]   We are now going to France. Rochester
1775   Cathedral was the first thing new to me, but
           it was below Worcester or Lichfield, and
nothing I saw in it struck me but the Figures of Faith, Hope and Charity round the Pulpit, which surprized me the more, as the Church bore the manifest Marks of having been defaced by the Puritans—and how these little Images escaped amazed me.

Canterbury Cathedral has not had Justice done it in Description—there are more and greater Curiosities in it than ever I saw of the solemn & sacred kind. I was never so struck with the sight of any Cathedral before —it is truly grand & majestick.

Here we lay & had good Beds but Queeney was forced to sleep in the same Room.

16   We loitered in the Morning at Canterbury so
         long that when we got to Dover and met Baretti,
he was grievously fretted to think that we had lost so

---

[1] Johnson and the Thrales had been in Wales in 1774; see *A Diary of a Journey into North Wales in the year 1774 by Samuel Johnson, LL.D.* (ed. R. Duppa, London, 1816). Mrs. Thrale's journal of the tour is printed in A. M. Broadley's *Doctor Johnson and Mrs. Thrale* (1910).

[2] Johnson's views on the vacuity of life are given by Mrs. Piozzi in her *Anecdotes*, pp. 99-101.

fine a Tide as had just launched off a Ship as We came in : however we saw the Castle & the fort, and flung Stones down Julius Cæsar's Well to hear the Reverberation. The Shore at Dover is wonderfully pleasant, the finest Coast I think I ever saw. I am hitherto vastly pleased with my Journey. We thought we were to sail in the Night but it seems nine in the Morn^g will do, so all goes well, & Niggey gives me no Trouble. She is all alive and well & merry.

17   Queeney's Birthday. She is now eleven Years old, God preserve & continue her Life till mine is spent : on this day we weighed Anchor in a very neat Sloop—Captn Baxter,[1] Commander, an old Schoolfellow of Mr Thrale's. The Weather was lovely—the Ship all our own, the Sea smooth & all our Society well but Queeney, whose Sickness oppressed her beyond Conception. Sam and Molly too were cruel sick, but Queeney worst of all or I thought her so.

I was vastly surprized when I landed at Calais to see the Soldiers with Whiskers and the Women mostly so ugly and deform'd. They however seemed desirous to hide their frightfulness, for all wore long Clokes of Camlet that came down to their Heels.[2] The Inn at this Place kept by Dessein[3] is the most magnificent I ever saw—

---

[1] In the Rev. William Cole's *A Journal of My Journey to Paris in the year 1765* (ed. F. G. Stokes, London, 1931), the name of the captain of the packet on which Cole crossed from Calais to Dover is given as Baxter (p. 361).

[2] See below, p. 193, *n*. 1.

[3] Dessein was the innkeeper at the *Hôtel d'Angleterre* at Calais. Cole writes : " I remained at his Inn, which was new built, & was a fine large Quadrangle, with most sumptuous Apartments & elegantly furnished : &, which was preferable to all, the Master of it a very civil & obliging Man."—*Paris Journal*, p. 358.

the Mount at Marlborough is nothing to it.   We had
an excellent Dinner which a Capuchin Fryar [1] enlivened
by his Company.   When it was over we were entertained
with a Sight of his Convent, Cells, Chapel & Refectory ;
the Library was locked, & I was not sorry, for M^r
Johnson would never have come out of it.   The Fryer
was a handsome Man, had been a Soldier & ended his
Pilgrimage a Monk ; he had travelled Europe & seen
Asia, and was as pleasing a Fellow as could be met with.
Johnson said he was as complete a Character as could
be found in Romance.   The book open in his Cell
that he had been reading was the History of England
& he had a Fiddle for his Amusement.   We saw a Ship
such as might serve for a Model of a Man of War hung
up in the Chapel of the Convent.   I asked the meaning
& the Fryer told me it was a Ship some honest Man had
made, & grown more fond of than it is fit to be of any
earthly Thing—so he had piously given it away to the
Capuchin Chapel.   Johnson observed that I ought to
give them Queeney.

18 Sept   We slept here in Ease & even Splendour,
            & on the 18 : Dr. Johnson's Birthday, we
walk'd early to the great Church ; I had forgotten the
Accounts of magnificence of this kind and was much
struck by it—they are not precise I see in placing their
Altars to the East ; I counted nine in various Parts of
the Church.
    From hence Baretti took me to a Convent of
Dominican Nuns [2] where I chatted at the Grate with
a most agreable English Lady who said She had been
immured there 26 Years ; She was of course not young,
but an elegant Figure & had entirely the Manners &

---

[1] Father Felix, see below, p. 192, *n.* 1.   [2] See below, p. 192.

Look of a Woman of high Fashion.   She asked me what
Diversions we had in London now, as She was an
English woman, & we chatted about M[r] Foote & his
Controversy with the Duchess of Kingston.[1]   She was
the Superior of her Convent, & related to Lady Pennyman [2]—her name is Gray : She begged to see me at
my return, & wished me to take a Letter to her Relations
which I promised, bought some Trifles of her & we
parted.   I observed she wore a brilliant Ring & had
a very fine Inlaid Snuff Box on her Table.   So much
for the Nun.   The Capuchin Friar came to see us this
Morning and brought Queeney a little Present of a
Toothpick Case in return for our Civilities : we had
given a Louis D'Or to his Convent over Night.

18   Well then, we set out, and drove rapidly to
continued   S[t] Omer, where we were shewn the Jesuits'
            College & Schools [3]—they were more than
complete, they were pompous—and the Theatre much
finer than that at Brighthelmstone—it is kept in order
purely for the use of the Boys—a stupid Fellow shewed
us the place who could tell us nothing—so we were not
much delighted afterwards with the Thought of having
spent so much Time when we ought to have been at
the Cathedral.   Oh how stupendous is the Pile, & how

---

[1] This refers to the controversy arising from Samuel Foote's
play, *A Trip to Calais*, satirising the Duchess of Kingston, the
Roman clergy and the English in France. This unacted play
appeared later on the stage in a revised form as *The Capuchin*.

[2] Lady Pennyman, wife of Sir James Pennyman, Baronet, was
the daughter of Sir Henry Grey, first Baronet, of Howick.

[3] The Society had been expelled from France in 1762, but at the
invitation of the Government the clergy of the English college at
Douai managed a school there.

curious the Ornamental part of this noble Edifice—let us never more talk of English Churches.

A Silver Shrine placed in the middle, and beautifully chased, exceeded all I have ever seen & there was another to be looked at through Glass like a Show Box more rich & curious than even that. St Bertin, another Church here at St Omer's, was still more filled with Ornaments : a Silver Crook Seven Feet high, a Crucifix with Diamonds for Nails, & adorned with many other precious Stones, took much of my attention ; and with the Sight of these we clos'd the Evening. On the following Day, 19 Sept^r, we drove to Arras, & Mr Baretti charged me not to forget an agreeable Widow who sold us fruit at Lillaire [1] as we came along. Arras has a Cathedral [2] which for the first Coup D'Oeil exceeds them all, so highly vaulted is the Roof, so massy & magnificent the Pillars. These Churches rise upon one, I wonder where their splendours will have an End. The Benedictines' new Edifice gave us likewise a pleasing Hour ; The Hall or Refectory as they call it is little less spacious than Christ Church, & their Library resembles All Souls exceedingly in Size and Disposition ; I was loitering on the Stairs foot half wishing to go up, when one of the old Fryars reproved me somewhat roughly, & told me their Dormitory was no place for Ladies. We had a worse Inn here at Arras than we have yet experienced, but it may be borne easily enough. Baretti's Plan of rising so very early, & coming to one's Inn time enough to admit of our running about the

19

[1] Lillers.

[2] The old cathedral church of St. Vaast, built between 1030 and 1396, was one of the finest Gothic buildings in Northern France. It was destroyed during the Revolution. The present building was begun in 1755.

Town is wonderfully favourable for the purpose of seeing every thing curious, but it is displeasing enough to get up so very betimes when one has been worn out all Day with pacing about the Towns.   Our Dinners seem to me to be all very good—and likewise the Wines.

20   On this day we quitted Arras, the Idea of which with its Ornamented Churches, peevish Benedictines and Women in black Clokes will not be easily erased from my Memory.   I have this Moment got a Quarter of an hour to employ in general Observations. I counted nine Crucifixes erected on the public Road between St Omers & Lillaire.   I have seen but two Maddonas out of Churches from Calais here to Amiens —the Churches indeed are full of them, & mostly well done ; I have seen but one with which a Puritan could have been offended & that was at [. . .]¹ where some poor Devotee had dressed up an Image of the Virgin in a long Laced Hood or Pinners, I know not what. I could count but three Gentlemen's Houses between St Omers & Amiens, but those were neat ones—the Gentlemen do not live in private Houses it seems in France or Flanders, they all flock to the larger Country Towns excepting the Richest & grandest [among 'em] ² who go up to Paris to spend the Rents ³ [which] their [poor] Tenants [pay 'em] in the distant Counties.   The Roads are not only good, but appear like long Avenues to Noblemens Seats, being planted on each Side with Trees & paved up the middle.⁴   The Agriculture is I believe eminently good and the Country so fertile that since I was two Miles on this Side Calais I have not

¹ Name omitted.
² Throughout the text words in square brackets have been inserted later by Mrs. Thrale.
³ Of *crossed through*.   ⁴ See below, p. 195, *n*. 1.

seen a Spot of Common or neglected Land. There are more Pigs than Sheep upon the Hills & the Cattle are miserably poor, but where there is no Grass how should they be fat, they must not eat Wheat I suppose & cannot digest Tobacco. The Post Horses are wretched enough, & the Tackling so bad it could not be ridiculed in a Farce, but the Horses one meets by Chance under people of Fashion are usually very fine ones. I see no Sportsmen about, nor any Dogs for Pleasure, tho' the Country is more inviting to the pursuit of Game by Hunting, Coursing & Setting than any I ever saw in England, & for a far greater Extent of Ground. The Dresses I have been able to observe were not only unbecoming, but almost uncivilized in their Appearance : at Calais long Camblet Clokes of various Colours, Black pieces of Cloth or Serge or some such strange Thing wrapt closely round them is the Ornament of the Females at St Omer's—no Ribbon is worn except by Women of very high Condition, & many of the lower sort have only printed Linnen Caps. Bibs & Aprons of some sort are universally to be seen on the Women, & the Men for the most part are adorned with Mustachoes. Politeness does really seem to be the grand Characteristick of this Nation [however for] if you meet a French Gentleman on the Road he always pulls off his Hat to you, & the very Custom House Officers behave with a respectful Civility.

20 continu'd　　We set out from Arras in good Time & came early to Amiens, where the Cathedral exceeded every thing I have seen yet, for Profusion of Labour & Expence :—here I saw the Paschal Lamb in White Marble, lying on the Altar for the first Time, & a Statue of the Virgin with a Dagger in her

Bosom—they call her Nôtre Dame des Douleurs. I will not try to describe the Glories of this Building—a vain Repetition of the Words Splendor and Magnificence is all I could do towards it, & those Words, or indeed any other I ever heard, would only disgrace the Cathedral of Amiens. Here we supped in Mr Johnson's Bed Chamber, the Meat is good, the Lodging not very excellent—the Weather wonderfully hot.

21 Sept^r   On the 21st I rose from the vilest Bed I yet ever lay down upon; we slept with our Windows open & were still greatly incommoded by the Heat, and narrowness of the Bed. On our Journey forwards we passed a large heavy Stone House which from its Size, & the unfrequency of such Objects, took our Attention; but how was I astonished to hear it was the Seat of the Duke of Penthiever [1]—utterly void of Dignity or Ornament & depending merely on the native Beauties of the surrounding Country. I saw neither Park nor Garden which could raise Admiration in the Beholder or delight in the possessor. How mean is such a place in Comparison of our Gentlemens Houses in the distant Counties of England—no need to speak of Blenheim or of Chatsworth, Lord Besborough's Villa at Roehampton is Paradise in Comparison. Taste however except in Cookery I have not yet found—perhaps it is confined to Paris, we shall see one of these Days. The Splendour of the Churches form(s) a strange Contrast to the meanness of the private Houses, and now we are turned off from the high Road we are in perpetual Danger of Overturning, between the wretchedness of the Cattle & deepness of the Ruts. The Inn at Neufchatel where

---

[1] Penthièvre. The chief seat of the Duke of Penthièvre, however, was at Sceaux.

we sleep tonight is the meanest we have lain at hitherto
but the Supper was incomparable and I believe we should
have Wax Candles in this Country, if we housed in a
Barn : I have seen no Public house without them.

21 con-   This Day I saw a Gentleman shooting upon
tin^d   the Hills, which unite all the Beauties that
            Extent and Cultivation can bestow : the
prospects are wonderfully fine, & the natural Situations
everywhere delightful. The Poultry too are extremely
beautiful both at the Barn Door & the Table. I will
endeavor to get some of them.

22 Sep^r   Our Chamber last Night was spacious, our
            Beds soft & clean, I had an uninterrupted
Sleep in mine for nine Hours. If my other Children
are as well in their Health as Queeney is, what Reason
have I to be content !—She has ail'd nothing since she
came on Shore, and I really believe the Sea Sickness
was of use to her. Today we go to Rouen, where I
shall hear from the Girls at Kensington,[1] & write to
poor Harry.[2]

22 con-   We arrived at Rouen about three O'Clock,
tinued   the Situation of this Town is uncommonly
            delightful, somewhat resembling the Situa-
tion of Bath ; surrounded by Hills of wonderful Beauty,
& adorned with Trees mingled among the Churches, as
if it had originally been contrived merely to excite the
Admiration of Travellers. When we came down the

[1] The Thrale girls were, it appears, educated at the house of
a certain Mrs. Cummings, or Cumyns, in Kensington ; see below,
p. 253.

[2] Harry Thrale. The Thrales had lost one son, Ralph, in the
preceding July ; Harry, their only remaining boy, died suddenly
on March 23, 1776.

Hill however, we found it an old ill built Town enough ; the Inn indeed is a good one, not like those of Calais or St Omer but better than the Inns of Shrewsbury, Lichfield or Birmingham. We dine in a Bedchamber it must be confest, but a high Tester'd Bed of Crimson Silk Damask, with a Coverlid of the same, brings to one's Mind no Image of its being lain in, & rather looks [a] stately Sopha than a Bed. Mrs Strickland found us at Dinner, commending the Repast, which I am always sure to do, the Provision is so excellent. She made an Appointment for me to go at 6 o'Clock to the play with her, less for the Pleasure of the Representation, than for the Sake of getting acquainted with her Friend Mad^{me} Du Perron [1]—a Lady of Rank and Fashion, & Sister to Madame des Bocages, the celebrated Wit of Paris, who translated Johnson's Rasselas [2] into French : I went to the play accordingly, & found Madame Perron all that Mrs Strickland had said ; some civil things passed between us, & she invited all our Society to sup with her on Sunday Night next—now for the Play. Our Theatre was wretched to be sure, not bigger I think nor certainly half so clean as that of Brighthelmstone ; but by the richness of the Dresses & Tumultuous Applause of the Spectators, I gather that the Actors are thought very considerable in France. The Phædra of Racine was the performance exhibited, and after having seen that part so [lately] played by M^{rs}

---

[1] She was the widow of M. du Perron, conseiller au Parlement de Rouen. It was to her that Madame du Boccage addressed her *Lettres sur l'Angleterre, la Hollande et l'Italie.*

[2] In 1760 a translation was published with the title *Histoire de Rasselas, prince d'Abissinie, par M. Jhonnson* [*sic*], . . . *et traduite de l'anglois par Mme B*****. It has been attributed to Madame Belot, afterwards Durey de Meynières.

Barry,[1] I was much disgusted by the Action of this Woman who will however probably make a Figure in Time upon a Stage where great Grossness is permitted, & Grimace dignified by the Name of Expression. A Riot however in favour of this Player pleased me better than the play itself, as it proved the falseness of Baretti's Assertion that such Brutalities are confined to London, where I never heard so much Violence expressed on any Occasion during my twenty Years acquaintance with the Stage. When I returned at Night to my Inn, I found the Gentlemen had picked up Companions, & bought Books. I put my Queeny to Bed in perfect Health & Spirits and laid myself to rest at 11 o'Clock. Mr Johnson has made a little Distich at every Place we have slept at, for example

A Calais	St Omer	Arras	A Amiens
Trop de frais.	Tout est cher.	Helas !	On n'a rien.

Au Mouton.   The Sign of the Mouton D'Or a(t) Neuf Chatel.
Rien de Bon.

23: Sept^r   This Morning my Curiosity was abundantly gratified by visiting two Convents of Religious Women. The first were Gravelines or poor Claires into whose House however I was not permitted to enter further than the Chapel through the Grate of which I conversed quite at my Ease with them—the more as they were all my Countrywomen, & some still retained a strong Provincial Northern Dialect. They were truly wretched indeed, wore only one Petticoat, and that of the very coarsest Stuff, they were bare legged and bare footed, & had no Linnen about them except

[1] Mrs. Ann Spranger Barry evidently played the part of Phædra at Covent Garden on Feb. 21, 23, 1774 (see Geneste, *Some Account of the English Stage*, v., p. 463).

a sort of Band, which was very dirty though I had Reason
to think I was expected. The Sister at the Speak House
look'd more like Lungs in the Alchemist [1] than any
thing else, and smelt very offensive when I saluted her,
which I find is the Custom at all Convents,—they are
43 in Number, I saw four of them only—the Speak-
house Sister, the Superior (who is her Sister by Blood—
their Family Name Vavasor),[2] the Mother Vicaress, and
a Mrs Williams who makes artificial Flowers to shew
at the Grate. Their Fingers all seem knotted at the
Joynts, their Nails broken & miserably disfigured,
they are extremely lean too, excepting the Vicaress, who
is 81 Years old, has her Teeth, Sight & Hearing as good
as ever I suppose, and seems a cheerful comfortable old
Woman, the other three are dismal Objects indeed, &
so cold when one touches them; but no matter I will
have another Touch with 'em to-morrow—so now to
the Benedictines. Mrs Strickland carried me from this
Scene of Misery to a Convent of the highest Order,[3]
where there is a Royal Abbess—so they call those whom
the King chuses. When we told our Names at the
Speak House and had in the civillest Terms requested
Admission to the Interior of the Convent, a very elegant

[1] This play of Ben Jonson's was acted at Drury Lane Theatre
on Oct. 24, 1794 (Geneste, v., p. 441). Face, the housekeeper, is
occasionally addressed as Lungs by the knight, Sir Epicure Mammon.

[2] A description of this convent is given in A(lban) B(utler)'s
*A Short Account of the Life and Virtues of the Venerable and Religious
Mother, Mary of the Holy Cross, Abbess of the English Poor Clares at
Rouen* (London, 1767). A note (p. 65) says: " Sister Margaret
Teresa, alias Vavasour, made her religious Profession, on the 8th
of September, 1727; was chosen Abbess on the 26th of August,
1756, and still governs this Monastery after the Example of her
Predecessors."

[3] The Benedictine priory of Saint-Louis; see below, p. 122.

Lady said she would answer for the Abbess & immediately ran to enquire. The Lady Abbess [1] presently appeared herself, said She would be glad [to] finish her own Dinner during which Time one of the Nuns should wait on us, and satisfy the Curiosity of the *Dame Angloise*, after which She would hope for our Company in her Apartment. Accordingly two or three Sisters, as they call them, were fixed on to attend us & we were shewn the Refectory, Cells, Garden & all Curiosities of the Place. The Lady shewed us her Dress which was a light Black Stuff turned back with fine Cambrick at the Cuffs—the Head Clothes let no Hair be seen, yet was exceedingly becoming—they change their Linnen every day & are most delicately clean. The Refectory was not large, but the Table Cloths were of good Diaper & perfectly neat—each Nun had a Silver Fork I observed and a Silver Cup : there is a Pulpit in the Refectory for one of them to read in, while the rest eat. By this Time the Abbess joyned us, tho' not before I had been shewn the Priests Vestments which are worked chiefly as I understand in this Convent—the good old Woman who shewed them me was ridiculously zealous for my Conversion, but I got rid of such Talk very quickly. The Lady Abbess then shewed me the way to her Apartment which was very elegant indeed, & herself, the Prioress, & four of the principal Nuns sat down to chat agreeably with Mrs Strickland & me. We talked of Literature, of Politicks, of Fashions, of everything, the Abbess was a mighty pleasing Woman indeed, and seemed very desirous of Information. She was particularly curious [2] to have me explain to her the Nature & Cause of the Rebellion in America. Their House is

[1] Madame Barbançon ; see below, p. 144.
[2] Desirous *crossed through*.

6

full of Lap Dogs, Cats & Parrots; but the Abbess's Favrite is a great *English* Mastiff, which She recommended to my Friendship as a Countryman. They were wonderfully civil to Queeney & extremely complaisant to me—said it was strange I could have a Daughter of her Age, and enquired—as if they were in Earnest—whether in so cold a Climate as England Girls were married at 12 Years old. They gave me Cakes of their own making & I promised the Abbess a French Translation of Johnson's Rasselas : but may I read it? says she. Vestals might read it, Madame, replied I.[1] Why you know *we are Vestals*, said the Abbess. Many things more passed in this Conversation, but I cannot get Time to write 'em down; from hence however we drove to our Inn & I gave Stricky a Guinea for our poor Claires desiring another Talk with them tomorrow.

In the Afternoon we went to a Library belonging if I mistake not to the Benedictines;[2] here we picked up an Abbé[3] who conversed in Latin with Mr Johnson, who had hitherto been unlucky in not finding Company he could talk to—nobody resorting to us on that Acct but an old stupid Priest who could talk English *once*, a Father Wilson.[4] However with this Abbé or Chanoine as they called him he seemed wholly at his Ease. I am now desirous to stop at the Description of the Cathedral where this Gentleman shewed us the Tomb of Cœur de Lyon near the Altar, the Decorations of which consist of a magnificent Palm Tree overshadowing the Lamb of the Apocalypse, with the Wounds. In some Chapel of the Cathedral[5] I think it is that we were shewn a

---

[1] *MS.* it.   [2] See below, p. 85.
[3] The Abbé Roffette; see below, p. 85.
[4] See below, p. 170.   [5] *MS.* Cathedrad.

very capital Picture by [. . .] [1] who has represented the Child in swaddling clothes as St. Luke's Gospel informs us he was wrapped.

24   Here I will end this long but entertaining Day, and begin the 24. by telling how I paid a slight Visit of Ceremony to Mad^me du Perron, & then drove forward to my poor miserable Gravelines who thanked me most humbly for my Guinea & said it was only too much, too much. I had today a great deal of Conversation with them, and found 'em miserably involved in Ignorance & Superstition telling wild Stories of St Francis's receiving as a favour the Wounds of our blessed Saviour, of St. Winifred restoring one of the Ladies to her Sight, &c.

I have now acquired pretty good Notions of the Monastick Life, and have found that these Austerities are never chosen by any Women who have the least Experience of any other Mode of Life : but Parents who want to be rid of their poor Girls send them at the Age of ten or eleven to these Convents where they —seeing these Nuns perpetually & seeing nothing else —fall into the Snare, & profess Poverty, Misery & all which the rest of the World unite to avoid—much less from Religion than Stupidity. However some of them must absolutely be taken, as Mrs Williams told me, & forced to warm themselves in Winter, or they would kill themselves by using Severities on their wretched Persons to distinguish themselves by Sanctity from the rest. Can such blind Superstition be pleasing to God ? Surely not, it can only be pardoned I think as involuntary Error. The Nuns gave me Artificial Flowers of their own Work, & we parted with great expressions

----

[1] Name omitted.

of Kindness. The Abbess's Jubilee is to be celebrated
on the 8: of September next, & they are to have fresh
Fish and White Bread, and they speak of it even now
with Rapture.

24 con-   I went to High Mass at one of the most
tin^d   considerable Churches in the Town, & was
    astonished at the want of Devotion in the
Audience; some were counting their Money, some
arguing with the Beggars who interrupt you without
ceasing, some receiving Messages and dispatching Answers, some beating Time to the Musick, but scarce
any one praying except for one Moment when the
Priest elevates the Host. When the Nicene Creed was
repeating, my Friend pressed me to be seated pleading
my Fatigue &c., and adding that as I did not believe the
Contents I had still less Reason to stand & tire myself
for nothing. I was quite shocked.

The Military Mass for Officers & Soldiers is celebrated with still more noise & still less attention. From
that Church I drove to Mrs Strickland's Lodgings where
I found Father Kennedy & another Confessor to the
Claires, with them I would have had chat concerning
what we had seen; but Mrs Strickland would not suffer
any Controversial Conversation to begin: She said
afterwards that She would not trust the Cause of the
Romish Religion in such wretched hands. It is indeed
a fine Religion wholly run to Seed; all Pomp, all External Shew, & no Intelligence as I can find or any true
Devotion. I am more & more delighted with my own
dear Religion & Country.

24 con-   We supt this Night with Madame du Perron
tin^d   & her Circle of Wits, where Johnson once
    more met his Friend the Abbé & entered
into a most ingenious Argument with him concerning

the demolition of the Jesuits.   Mr Thrale was enchanted
with the Conversation & I never knew his Judgment
fail: I had myself no Power to attend to their Talk,
I had so much trouble to make myself understood;
which however I contrived to manage somehow.
Before we went to Supper at this fine Lady's, I took a
Drive down their publick Walk, and found the Situation
of Rouen with its Bridge of Boats, its Hills & its River
perfectly beautiful.   We were served in Plate at Mad^{me}
Du Perron's & had a magnificent Supper but a dirty
Table Cloth.

25 Sept   We walked over the Courts of Judicature,
           bought a Book or two, saw the Benedictine
Library in good earnest—the other was belonging to
the Church: the Gentlemen have seen many Things
today I believe, but I write only for myself, 'tis as much
as I can do to keep my own Account but here I am up
to the hour.

25 Sept^r   We spent a most agreeable Afternoon with
continu'd   our little Abbé who came to take his Leave
             of us.[1]   We read & chatted, & criticized and

---

[1] The following account of their acquaintance with the Abbé
is taken from Mrs. Piozzi's *Anecdotes of the late Dr. Samuel Johnson,*
pp. 66-67.   The inaccuracies now revealed are commented on in
the Introduction (p. 47).

" When we were at Rouen together, he took a great fancy to
the Abbé Roffette, with whom he conversed about the destruction
of the order of Jesuits, and condemned it loudly, as a blow to the
general power of the church, and likely to be followed with many
and dangerous innovations, which might at length become fatal to
religion itself, and shake even the foundation of Christianity.   The
gentleman seemed to wonder and delight in his conversation: the
talk was all in Latin, which both spoke fluently, and Mr. Johnson
pronounced a long eulogium upon Milton with so much ardour,

Johnson's Eulogium upon Milton *in Latin* was truly sublime.   Mr Thrale invited the Abbé to return with us, and Mr Johnson promised to shew him Oxford—it was matter of Amusement to me to see the Man divided so between Curiosity & Cowardice: he longed to see England & thought this, I believe, no bad Opportunity —but to leave his Connections & run to an Heretical Nation with People he had known but Three days, required some Pause, & indeed who could wonder at his Hesitation! in a Word he excused himself & we parted—I think with great Good Will on every Side.

[Mad^{me} du Perron likewise took her Leave of us this Even^g with the utmost Politeness.] [1]

Tomorrow we leave Rouen, where much Civility & some kindness has been reciprocated.   I shall love Rouen for ever !   Adieu encore un fois.

26   In the Morning poor Baretti was sick but I cou'd not persuade [him] to take anything. [2] People unused to Medicine have a dread of every thing that sounds Physical ;   & Mr Baretti could not help thinking an Emetick more dangerous than a Dram. I think him mistaken, to be sure, but that's his Affair. How delightfully well my Queeney continues.

eloquence, and ingenuity, that the Abbé rose from his seat and embraced him.   My husband seeing them apparently so charmed with the company of each other, politely invited the Abbé to England, intending to oblige his friend ; who, instead of thanking, reprimanded him severely before the man, for such a sudden burst of tenderness towards a person he could know nothing at all of ; and thus put a sudden finish to all his own and Mr. Thrale's entertainment from the company of the Abbé Roffette."

[1] In the margin.

[2] Mrs. Thrale appears to have enjoyed playing the physician, and her efforts in this direction later afforded an opening for Baretti in his virulent attacks upon her ; see below, p. 246.

26 con-   We travelled on the Banks of the Seine
tinu'd   which we crossed three Times in this very
          pleasant Day's Journey, we slept at Vernon
—a true French Inn but the cleanest we have met with.
This was the first Day I ever saw a Vineyard, and of
course the first day I was disappointed on that Side.
Nothing but the Value of the Fruit can make one pay
any Respect to the Tree during Growth, it is short &
ragged & not half so pretty to the Eye as a Hop Garden :
it is however wonderfully pleasing to pluck ripe Grapes as
you drive along a high Road.   The Roads are fine again
today & the Gentlemen's Seats on the Road improve
upon one.   Mr Johnson observed that we now reaped
pleasure of following the Sun into a warmer Climate.
In the Afternoon we sat on the Bridge, & enjoyed the
beautiful View of the Seine, which winding among
Islands, and watering the most fertile Plains in the World
perhaps, delight(s) the Eye inexpressibly, & fill(s) the
Heart with Gratitude to the great giver of all things.
The Rocks are just high enough to strike the Fancy,
and distant enough not to disgust the Eye, the Valley
is [in] some Respects superior to that seen from Richmond
Hill and Wood alone is wanting.   The French Taste
in Gardening, I see, exactly resembles the English Taste
[of] Fifty Years ago.   High Walls, straight Lines, &
Trees tortured into ugly and unmeaning Forms com-
pose all the Variety of which these People's Imagination
seems Susceptible—but I should stay my Censures till
I have seen more.

27 Sept.   We rose from our Beds at Vernon all well
            & in good Humour, and admired the
Vineyards which stretched down quite to the Road ;
though the white Sticks up which the Grapes crawl
give them upon the whole something of an unpleasing

Appearance. The Banks of the Seine however are surprizingly beautiful, & the whole Country carries an Air of Fertility that is inexpressibly delightful : to see Cherries, Apples, Grapes, Asparagus, Lentils & French Beans planted in large portions all around one, & inviting the Traveller to partake the Bounties of the Nation is so perfectly agreeable that one frets to see so many People *beg*, where one is morally certain nobody can starve.[1]

These Reflexions are interrupted by the Recollection of a Frightful Accident which befel the Carriage in which were Mr Thrale, Baretti and the Girl : their Postillion fell off his Horse on a strong Descent, the Traces were broken, one of the Horses run over and the Chaise carried forwards with a most dangerous Rapidity, which Mr Thrale not being able to endure till somebody came up—jumped out with intent to stop the Horses for Baretti & Queeney—however he only hurt himself & they went on till Sam came up, who had been miserably embarrassed with a vicious Horse which had retarded him so long, and afterwards flung him. This was therefore a day of Distress, & my Master found himself so ill when we arrived at St Germains that the Surgeon he sent for, advised him to go on to Paris & get himself bled & take a good deal of Rest which he hoped would restore him. He left us therefore at St Germains & Mr Baretti kindly went with him to give him Assistance, & get us some Habitation to receive us at Paris. Dr Johnson's perfect unconcern for the Lives of three People, who would all have felt for his, shocked and amaz'd me,[2]—but that, as Baretti says, is true Philosophy ;

[1] See below, pp. 209-10.

[2] Mrs. Piozzi refers to this incident in her *Anecdotes* (p. 177) in discussing Johnson's love of travelling by coach : " On this account

Mrs Strickland did not give it so kind a Name, I soon saw her Indignation towards him prevailing over her Friendship for me. We slept at St Germains where we had excellent Beds, & on the next day I perceived Queeney had hurt her Side in yesterday's Scuffle, but

28 : Septr how much Reason have I to rejoyce that no more Harm befel her.

The Politeness of these French People is of an odd Sort, the Servants will come & stare at *you* in such a Manner while you are purchasing or talking that it is astonishing, & the very Gentlemen make you such strange Compliments upon your Dress &c. resembling their own that one scarcely knows whether to laugh or be angry. This Evening we arrived safe at Paris, the Approach to wch is very fine indeed and more than answered—exceeded my Expectations : I should have mentioned seeing the Castle of St Germains in the Morning as the French it is plain think highly of it, and praise the Prospect from the Garden Terras as we praise Windsor. The manifest Inferiority charmed me,

28 con- and to see the Man shewing off a Royal tinu'd Pleasure Ground not twice as big as our own Kitchen Garden, with little trimmed Hedges & small Shrubberies which he called a Forest,[1]

he wished to travel all over the world ; for the very act of going forward was delightful to him, and he gave himself no concern about accidents, which he said never happened : nor did the running-away of the horses on the edge of a precipice between Vernon and St. Denys in France convince him to the contrary ; ' for nothing came of it (he said), except that Mr. Thrale leaped out of the carriage into a chalk-pit, and then came up again, looking *as white* ' ! When the truth was, all their lives were saved by the greatest providence ever exerted in favour of three human creatures ; and the part Mr. Thrale took from desperation was the likeliest thing in the world to produce broken limbs and death."

[1] Was this a misunderstanding on Mrs. Thrale's part ?

was comical beyond Expression. The Afternoon brought us to Paris, where I found M[r] Thrale better, and a long Letter from home full of Accounts of our House's Prosperity & our Son's Health. The Surgeon who came at Night to attend my Master gives us great Encouragement & says I ought to thank the *Virgin Mary* for the miraculous Escape we have had.

29   This Morning Mrs Strickland's Friends and Acquaintances came about her, and Milliners & Monsieurs encreased the Bustle. It is on all Accounts delightful to have her Company, who knows so many people of Fashion & none but those of Character and Reputation. We have made it up all with Johnson who protests it was not unconcern for M[r] Thrale but anger at me that [made] him sullenly forbear Enquiry, when he found Me unwilling (as he thought it) to give him a ready or rational Answer.

We are lodg'd not only conveniently but elegantly. Baretti thinks & provides for all : Queeney has already got a Maitre de Langues. The Comfort of our Society is, that we all seem to love one another—except Queeney

29 : con-   who loves not me : I thought likewise that
tinued   She had not cared for her Father, but She certainly did feel [a little] for him when he was hurt, [or he thought so].

Well She has now hurt herself, & in a strange way too ; crushed her great Toe, poor Creature, in a surprizing [manner] & all out of that odd Bashfulness [1] which I have some hopes this Journey will contribute to cure—this is my second Vexation, I cannot call it

[1] Baretti, writing to his brothers on Mar. 22, 1776, comments on Queeney's shyness and " una certa timidissima ritrosia che la rende taciturna con tutti, e familiare e insolentella con nessun altro che con me."—*Lettere famigliari di Giuseppe Baretti*, Torino, 1857.

a Fright : there can come no harm of it, I hope & believe. Today I saw poor old Leviez,[1] he seems broken up, but was glad to see me ; he must get my Niggey a Dancing Master when her Toe is well. At Night I took the Coach while M[rs] Strickland was at the Opera & saw the Guingettes [2] as they call it & the Boulevards which are Places of publick Amusement for the ordinary Sort of People & consist of rooms, Arbours, Walks, &c. filled with Fiddles, Orgeat, *Lasses and other Refreshments* but no Wine, Beer or Spirits are sold, so that there is Gayety without Noise, and a Crowd without a Riot. We are always grudging the low people their Amusements, the French I see wish to promote them—this seems to be a difference—a distinction rather, between the Characters of the two Nations, but we should remember that no Entertainments would please our English folks without Drink, & that drink cannot be permitted on account of the coarseness of its Consequences.

30   We went this Morning to wait on Madame de Bocages, who meant I am sure to be extremely civil to us, and ought to express her meaning more perfectly for She has written & has travelled—& is at home—however I did not like her as much as I expected. Her Niece the Countess of Blanchêtre [3] seems very agreeable. We were however invited for Thursday next to Dinner so then we shall see more. From this Visit we were running to Shops, when by Chance we met the Procession of Carriages attending the Princesse D'Artois [4] from the Church of Notre Dame where she

[1] Charles Leviez, dancing-master. He died about 1778. A portrait of him by J. E. Eccard was engraved by James MacArdell.
[2] Guinguettes.   [3] Blanchetti.
[4] Marie-Thérèse of Savoy, wife of the future Charles X. of France.

had been to return thanks after her Lying In. The
Equipages were superb—& that of the Lady herself
so magnificent that nothing of the Sort I ever saw in
England could at all come in Competition with it.
I was also forced upon an Observation which occurs
too often—the Superiority of Appearance which the
French Soldiery has over ours. At Night we drove
round the Foire St Ovide [1] which exhibited a Show
totally new to me : there stands in the middle of a large
open Place an Equestrian Statue [2] of Lewis 15th : & round
it—but at a considerable distance—are Shops which

30 : con-
tinued

form a Circus of the gayest Appearance I
ever saw and perfectly singular—the Shops
are temporary, & slight enough of course,
but adorned with a sort of Frippery Finery, Ribbons,
Looking-Glasses, Cutlery, Pastry, every thing one can
imagine that is at once brilliant & worthless—but which
when illuminated with numberless Lights gives an Air of
Festivity which not even the Philosophy of an Englishman can despise nor the Stupidity of a Dutchman neglect.
Lamps formed into Pyramids surround the Statue, &
the Circus of Shops at a proper distance, glittering in
the Eyes of a Crowd of Spectators, who walk round this
gay Place every Evening, tempt some to buy & some to
talk, & brought to Johnson's Mind the Image of Cran-
born Alley [3] on a Saturday Night.

[1] This annual fair took place in the *Place Louis XV.*, afterwards
the *Place de la Concorde.* In 1777 shops and booths were destroyed
by a great fire.

[2] The statue was destroyed by order of a decree passed on
Aug. 10, 1792.

[3] A market for cheap goods and clothes, especially straw
bonnets and millinery. The name Cranbourne Alley was often
applied to a paved thoroughfare, begun in 1678, from Castle Street
to the north-east corner of Leicester Square, though the actual

1 : Oc-   We have driven about the Town ever since
tober   11 or 12 o'Clock & I have stolen half an
           hour for my Journal & general Observations.
Nothing can be truer than what Bareuti says, that the
Extremes of Magnificence & Meanness meet at Paris :
Extremes of every sort are likewise perpetually meeting.
Yesterday I was shewn a Femme Publique dress'd out
in a Theatrical Manner for the Purpose of attracting the
Men with a *Crucifix* on her Bosom [1] ; & today I walked
among the beautiful Statues of [the] Tuilleries, a Place
which for Magnificence most resembles the Pictures of
Solomon's Temple, where the Gravel is loose like the
Beach at Brighthelmstone, the Water in the Basin
Royale cover'd with Duck Weed, & some wooden
Netting in the Taste of our low Junketting Houses at
Islington dropping to Pieces with Rottenness & Age.

1 Oct.   The Place de Victoire is formed in a Round
continued   not unlike the Circus at Bath but far less
            elegant & about the Size of Red Lyon
Square ; with an Equestrian Statue of Lewis 14 : so
immensely large that you can hardly drive two Coaches
abreast between [2] it & the Houses. The Place de
Vendôsme with its Ornaments in the middle is somewhat
less disproportionate, but would shock any Eye except
a French one. I fancy these are their only Squares,
& I do not understand that it is any distinction to inhabit
them : their great Houses are [all] shut from the Street
in the manner of Burlington House & are said to be

alley was a short passage leading into Little Newport Street.   Gray,
writing to the Rev. J. Brown on June 6, 1767, says : " I have seen
His Lordship of Cloyne often.   He is very jolly, and we devoured
five raspberry puffs together in Cranbourne Alley, standing at a
pastry-cook's shop in the street."   See also H. B. Wheatley and
P. Cunningham's *London : Past and Present* (London, 1891).

[1] See below, p. 201.   [2] Round *crossed through*.

princely. I have not yet seen any. Their Streets are
more noisy than those of London, being narrower one
hears every carriage on both sides the way, & there being
no Terrace for Footpassengers, they come up close to
one's door. The Houses too are so very high that they
make an Echo, & every Sound is so reiterated that
1 Oct.   it stuns one. I was mentioning how Ex-
continued   tremes meet. Madame de Bocages yesterday
after loading us with superfluous Civilities,
praising our Wit, our Beauty &c. told us if she had any
Pudden to give us, we should dine with her. This
was such a hint as I had no Notion could be given without
Intent to offend, yet I am morally certain She desired
we should be pleased with her. Her Niece had on [in
the morning] a pair of Lappets Value at least 50£, & a
Gown so ordinary & so nasty that if my Dairy Maid
wore such a one [at home] I would not drink the Cream
[she skimmed]—No Ruffles had she—even to her Shift
—but what struck me [still] more was the flat Silver
Ring like that of a London Alewife which she wore on
her finger.

This Morning however I have been reading Bocages'
Letters on the English Nation, which have somewhat
tended to restrain my Spirit of Criticism : She had more
Opportunities of Observation & I fear more force of
Mind besides than I may have, yet her Information has
been miserably confined,[1] I see, & many of her Facts
are false—how should mine be better ! I will relate only
what I see—which can hardly fail of being true.

1 Oct.   Among the Objects perpetually pressing
continu'd   upon one's Eye is uncommon deformity
—such various modifications of Ugliness I
could not have conceived, nor am very fond of observing ;

[1] See below, p. 201.

the Pictures in the Church of Nôtre Dame give one
[some] [1] Relief, I am glad to turn my Looks upward
for all Reasons.   We got to Church too late for high
Mass, so I attended Low Mass at one of the by Altars ;
and as I could not hear nor understand one Word the
Priest said—I collected my Thoughts & read the Office
of Spiritual Communion by Wilson, Lord Bishop of
Sodor & Man.

1 Oct[r]:   The purity of the Air in a Metropolis so
continu'd   crouded is truly surprizing ; no Sea Coal
             being Burned, the Atmosphere of the narrow-
est part of Paris is more transparent & nitid than that
of Hampstead hill, I have seen no Rain since I left
England except one slight Shower at S[t] Omer's & the
Sun is so strong on this 1st of October [This 1st of
October is Sunday] [2] that one is tempted to fret because
of the intense heat & strong Glare.

The good behaviour of the people too deserves to be
commended ; a Crowd here is far less rude & dangerous
than in London, & you are sure to meet no Insults
from the Populace of Paris, where every Man thinks
himself the Protector of every Woman.   This Species
of Gallantry goes through all ranks of People as far as
I have been able to observe.

This Evening I went to their Colisseum,[3] a new
Amusement imitated from our Pantheon,[4] but vastly
small in Comparison,—well adorned however & kept
clean.   The Fireworks were exquisitely pretty, & in the
middle under the Dome were a Set of Children dancing

---

[1] More *crossed through*.   [2] In the margin.

[3] The *Colisée* was opened to the public for the first time in 1771,
it was demolished within ten years.

[4] The Panthéon, opened in Jan., 1771, was first used for mas-
querades and afterwards for opera.   It was burnt down in 1792.

Cottilions &c. for the Diversion of the Company who formed a Ring about them.   Here I met Bob Cotton.[1]

2 Octr This Morning Queeney began French with her new Master; a man I like exceedingly, & who talks English with a fluency of which few Natives are capable.   The rest of the Morning was spent in the Persecution of Mantua makers, Milliners &c. to get Clothes ready for our Journey to Versailles, where at last we were not likely to go because the Court removes to Choisy forsooth, & there we may see 'em instead. The Evening carried us to the Theatre, where I was pleased to find the Cid[2] upon the Stage acted by Players of no mean Powers of Performance, I understood every word they said.   The Play House is a Wretched one, Foote's little Theatre[3] is a Palace to it, for size, magnificence and Elegance of Decoration.   The first [Excellence of a Theatre however are the Actors & those are good].   There has been a Shower of Rain today.— I have picked up but little for my Journal today.   Sunday seems here to be the great Time for all Sorts of Business & Diversion.

3 Oct[r] The Morning of this day was spent in running about from Church to Church to see the Splendour of the Romish Religion; St Sulpice was the first & largest that we looked at: it is well built in the modern Italian Taste—spacious & majestic.   The high Altar is overshadowed by a Canopy of pure & solid Brass very magnificent & kept not only clean but bril-

[1] Probably Robert, eldest son of Sir Lynch Salusbury Cotton. He had been with the Thrales and Johnson in Wales.

[2] Pierre Corneille's famous tragedy.

[3] Samuel Foote's new theatre in the Haymarket had been opened in May, 1767.

liant. The Balustrade round the Communion Table is likewise brass—& here are two natural Shells, the largest I ever saw for the purpose of holding Holy Water. They were given by the Republic of Venice [1] to Lewis 15 : who had them lipped with Brass to preserve them. Here is a very strange Picture too of the Trinity with Eagle's Wings stretched round a Groupe of human Figures supposed to represent the Faithful. So much for S[t] Sulpice. From hence we drove to the Carmelites where we were shewn the famous Magdalen of Le Brun, said to be the Portrait of La Valiere in her State of Penitence : [2] M[rs] Strickland then introduced us to a Convent of English Benedictine Monks,[3] the Prior of which Society was particularly civil & shewed us the Corpse of James the 2[d]: deposited here & the Model of his Face in Plaister of Paris or Wax, I know not which. We were then shewed the Val de Grace,[4] the high Altar of which pleased me infinitely, Joseph & Mary Statues as large as Life standing on each Side [of] the Infant Jesus who lies in the middle & is exquisitely well performed. The whole is of White Marble wonderfully fine.—In

---

[1] Mrs. Thrale here confuses the facts. The Rev. William Cole, in 1765, writes of " two of the most sumptuous & largest Sea Shells, edged with gilt copper, & fixed against the Pillars, for Holy Water Basons, or *Benitiers*, that ever were seen ; they were sent as a Present 2 Centuries ago by the Republic of Venice to the King of France (François I), & were 'till lately, always kept in his Cabinet of Curiosities, when King Lewis the well-beloved bestowed them upon this church for that purpose."—*Paris Journal*, p. 250.

[2] Louise de La Vallière retired to this Carmelite nunnery, in the Rue St. Jacques, in 1675, and died there in 1710. See also Cole's *Paris Journal*, pp. 133-137.

[3] Cole describes a visit to this convent (*op. cit.*, pp. 283-284).

[4] See Cole, *op. cit.*, pp. 131-133.

this Morning's Ramble the late Cardinal de Richelieu's Monument must have a place as it is said to be one of the greatest Works in Europe—and even the Italians permit that to be said.[1]

The Evening once more took us to the Play where I was well entertained by a new Comedy called the Gamester.[2] The Actors are really excellent; *better than our own*, but every thing shews how far the French are behind us. They suffer a Repetition of the same Stage Tricks, & those the lowest, in a manner that would not be borne in London, nor even at a strolling Theatre in [England]. The Queen of France was at the Play tonight sitting in one [of] the Balcony Boxes like any other Lady, only that she curtsied to the Audience at going out & they applauded her in Return. She is wonderfully pretty, & I fancy perfectly amiable; for She clapped the Players when they pleased her,—& chatted with her Maids in a Manner most engaging[ly] free & lovely—I wished her a better Theatre & handsomer Box to sit in.

4 Oct^r   We were called [from Breakfast] by some of our new Friends to see a Horse Race or rather a Match between two Princes of the Blood Royal:[3]

---

[1] In the church of the Sorbonne.   See Cole, *op. cit.*, pp. 128-131.

[2] Cole (*op. cit.*, p. 101) in 1765 went to a play called *Le Joueur*, or *The Gamester*. This was probably Edward Moore's play, *The Gamester*, which was translated into French in 1762 by Bruté de Loirelle as *Le Joueur*, and by B.-J. Saurin as *Beverlei*.

[3] Horace Walpole, writing to the Hon. Henry Seymour Conway from Paris on Oct. 6, 1775, says: "There was two days ago a great horse-race in the Plain de Sablon, between the Comte d'Artois, the Duc de Chartres, Monsieur de Conflans, and the Duc de Lauzun. The latter won by the address of a little English postillion, who is in such fashion that I don't know whether the Academy will not give him for the subject of an éloge."—*The Letters of Horace Walpole*, vol. ix., p. 263.

Such is the ingenuity of French Horsemanship that they gave the greatest Weight to the slightest Horse [1] —but they had the Sense to send for Riders from England : Singleton, the Marquis of Rockingham's Jockey, lost, & no wonder—there was not [any] Proportion at all between the Horses, either in Strength or Speed ; add to this that one of 'em was four Years old who carried the weight, & the other was eight Years old who carried the feather.

The Queen of France came to see the Sport, & was placed in a Booth much worse than Astley [2] provides for the 12 penny Company at Westm^r Bridge ; in which Booth there was no Chair to sit on till one had been fetched from Paris, [&] the Race Ground was 4 Miles from the Town. The Queen is still handsomer by Day than by Night, tho' dress'd with the utmost Simplicity : She praised the Jockey who won, & stroked the Horse : She & her Ladies clapped their Hands, & almost shouted when the Winner came in.

4 Oct^r   We had to dine with us Father Cooling,[3] continued Prior of the English Benedictines that we visited Yesterday, he seems learned & polite, and likes me, I believe, which is always the first good Quality in my Eyes : We had also Queeney's Abbé who is a mighty companionable Creature, & afterwards there came a Mr Le Roy [4] who has been to England, has seen Athens, & even (been) to Constantinople. I

[1] For Johnson's opinion of French horse-racing, see below, p. 230.

[2] Philip Astley, in 1770, had opened " a wooden theatre, with sheltered seats, but with an unroofed circus, in a timber yard at the foot of Westminster Bridge."—*Dictionary of National Biography.*

[3] Father Cowley ; see below, p. 223.

[4] Julien-David Le Roy, French architect, 1728-1803.

fancy upon nearer Acquaintance we shall find him very agreeable.

I have always heard that Basket work was most frequently [found] in England, but here the Stage Coaches, & Lighters which carry Charcoal up the Seine, are chiefly made of Wicker, & when they make a handsome Sedan [for a Lady] that likewise is of Basket Work —[daubed of a dirty] blue.

I saw a painted Dame in one this very day. Such [instances of intolerable Gross][1] ness [however][2] never [had place I hope][3] in any [civilized] Nation but this; The Youngest and prettiest Ladies of the Court will hawk and spit straight before them without the least Attention to Delicacy, & today at the Horse Race we were shewn a Woman of Condition riding astride w^th: her thick Legs [totally][4] uncovered except by her Stockings [ye whiteness of] which attracted all Eyes to look on them. (Nothing could surely be so ridiculous as their Contrivance of dressing all the Jockeys alike & chusing Green out of all the Rainbow as if to prevent one's seeing them at a Distance.)[5] But the most [surprizing thing I ever heard of][6] in this Respect was the Riot raised [at ye Course today] by forty three Fishwomen who surrounded the Queen, & [with the loudest Voices and frantic Gestures] uttered a thousand Gross Obscenities in her Ears till She was forced to give 'em Money to be rid of them. When I expressed my Astonishment at such Things being permitted; Ah, says a French Gentleman [with

4 Oct^r
continued

---

[1] instances of Magnificence & Mean *crossed through.*

[2] Are *crossed through.*   [3] Met *crossed through.*

[4] All *crossed through.*

[5] The passage within brackets is crossed through; *cf.* below.

[6] Curious part of the show *crossed through.*

great Composure], que ces Gens la sçachent bien la Methode d'attraper les Ecus! & another presently informed me that these were the Women who kissed Louis quinze one Day in a fit of riotous Madness, & that they had this very Morning forcibly saluted the King's Brother, Comte D'Artois, who happens to be a pretty Young Man & pleas'd their Fancy. Now let English Liberty be talked on ever so loudly, such Licentiousness as this was never tolerated [with us] even at a contested Election, much less [at] an Amusement intended for the Court & principal Nobility to partake of. I have not yet done with the Horse Race; our Jockeys in England are always dressed in different Colours that they may easily be discerned at a Distance, and Green is supposed the worst for the purpose because of the Trees & the Grass making that Hue difficult to be distinguished—here all the Riders were habited in *one colour*, and that Colour was *Green*.[1]

The Shops here at Paris are particularly mean & the Tradespeople surly & disagreeable; a Mercer will not shew you above half a Dozen Silks & those he will not cut,—they run in Pieces for Gowns & you are obliged to buy all or none. I must however mention the great Civility of one Man who sells Hard Ware, Cutlery, &c. & seeing us distressed for a Place the Day Mad^me D'Artois returned Thanks for her Child at the Church of Nôstre Dame—he called us into his House, & placed us in a Window from whence we could conveniently see the Parade of Equipages go by.

This Man however had been seven Years in England.

I have at last finished my fourth of October, tomorrow we dine at Madame de Bocage's which will [furnish] matter enough no doubt, & then I'll begin a new Page.

[1] *Cf.* Johnson's remarks on this colour; see below, p. 233.

5 Oct[r] The Morning was spent in adjusting our Ornaments in order to dine with Madame de Bocages at 2 o'Clock. There was a showy Dinner with a Frame in the middle, & She gave us an English Pudding made after the Receipt of the Dutchess of Queensbury. We saw nothing particularly pleasing at this Visit but the Beauty of Madame de Bocage's Niece, the Countess of Blanchetie, whose husband was so handsome too—that being a Frenchman—I wonder'd. In the Course of Conversation however he turned out an Italian, & there was another Italian Nobleman there, who hailed Baretti, & made himself agreeable to us all. Nothing would serve him but attend us at Night to the Colissée, which, after leaving our Names with the Sardinian Ambassadress,[1] we were willing enough to permit. In Madame de Bocages' Drawing room stood the Busts of Shakespear, Milton, Pope & Dryden ; the Lady sate on a Sopha with a fine Red Velvet Cushion fringed with Gold under her feet, & just over her Head a Cobweb of uncommon Size, & I am sure great Antiquity. A pot to spit in, either of Pewter, or Silver, quite as black & ill coloured, was on her Table ; and when the Servant carried Coffee about he put in Sugar with his Fingers.[2] The House these People live in is a fine one, but so contrived that we were to pass through a sort of Hall where the Footmen were playing at Cards

---

[1] Henrietta Jane Speed, Comtesse de Viry. In a letter to the Hon. H. S. Conway, dated Sept. 8, 1775, Walpole writes : " The Harry Grenvilles are arrived. I dined with them at Madame de Viry's, who has completed the conquest of France by her behaviour on Madame Clothilde's wedding, and by the *fêtes* she gave."— *Letters of Horace Walpole*, vol. ix., p. 250.

[2] For Johnson and Baretti's accounts of this incident, see below, pp. 231-232.

before we arrived at Madame's Chamber. When our new Italian Friend,[1] & a Hungarian Nobleman [2] he introduced to our Society, came home with us from the Colissée at Night, we set to criticising the Dinner of the Day—one Dish was a Hare not tainted but putrified, another was a Leg of Mutton put on the Spit the moment the Sheep was killed & garnish'd with old Beans, there was one Dish with three Sausages only [upon it] & one with nothing but Sugar plumbs. Here is Abuse enough however—and with this Abuse we finished the Evening's Conversation.

6 Oct^r   Mr Dominick Mead made a pleasing Addi- tion to our Society, he went with us— (Foreigners & all)—to the Duke of Orleans's Palace, where we were shewn a Cabinet of Cameos, Intaglios & other curious Gravings of great Antiquity. There was among them a Seal said to be that wch Augustus Cæsar used commonly, & carried in his Pocket—'Tis an Omphale's Head—the handle has been enriched with Diamonds by some of its late Possessors. The Collec- tion of Pictures at this Palace is by far the finest I ever saw. They are chiefly the School of Titian, but In my Mind the three Maries at the Sepulchre by Annibal Caracci [3] exceeded all the rest. I will not try to remember

---

[1] Count Manucci; see above, pp. 64-66.

[2] Bathyani; see below, p. 108.

[3] The Orleans collection is described in *La Galérie du Duc d'Orléans au Palais Royal* (Paris, 2 vols.), and G. F. Waagen, *Treasures of Art in Great Britain* (London, 1854), vol. i., pp. 18-21; vol. ii., pp. 485-503. The pictures were brought to England in 1792, and sold here. Among the many pictures acquired by the Duke of Carlisle for the Castle Howard Collection was " The Three Maries," for £4000. Mrs. Thrale was an ardent admirer of Caracci.

half the Rareties I saw today but must not forget the Head of a Parthian engraved on some precious Stone with an Inscription in that Language illegible to the most learned Antiquarians. I was likewise struck with the Head of a Hannibal on Onyx, expressing the Anguish of that Eye which he lost in the Marshes of Italy.

This Evening we drank Tea with an old Maid, Sister to Sir John Moore,[1] who has been settled here 30 Years & so far accomodates herself to the Manners of this Country as to receive Company in her Bed Chamber & sit with the Close Stool as near her as possible.

The Weather is now Broken up & the rainy Season begun; but we must bear the Cold if we can. I am told that Firing here would stand us in a Guinea a Day. This has been my happiest Day hitherto; I have spent it with English Men & among Italian Pictures.

7 Oct[r]   We saw the famous Church of the Jesuits and very fine it is still; though stripped of many rich Ornaments at the Time the Order was abolished: it is built in a most elegant Taste, and decorated with well carved Representations of our Saviour's Passion; there are two Angels of the human Stature holding the flaming Heart, on each Side the Church, in solid Silver, besides a large Crucifix surrounded by the Virtues of equal Size—all in Bronze, and some Basso Relievos of eminent Workmanship. From this fine Church we drove to a Convent of English

---

[1] Probably Sir John Moore, of Fawley, Berks. Sir John's brother, James Benedict, died in 1775, when Prior of the English Benedictine College at Douay. Cole met the Prior in 1765 (*Paris Journal*, pp. 18-19).

[2] The Church of St. Louis and St. Paul in the Rue St. Antoine (see *ibid.*, pp. 290-295).

Nuns,[1] where Lady Annastatia Stafford [2] is the Abbess, and several Women of Quality are immured. I saw Lady Lucy Talbot,[3] Mrs Howard,[4] a Miss Parker,[5] & Lady Mary Stafford,[6] and with them—of the same Society —I saw a Woman of very different Rank *in the World* but the same *in a Cloyster*.[7] This Woman had been a Maid Servant to Mrs Strickland's Father, & went over to Paris to be Lay Sister, as it's called, & do the Office of a Servt to these Ladies, who finding her Devout & docile, I suppose, and happy in a fine Voice, admitted her tho' Moneyless to their Sisterhood & She was profess'd a Nun seven Years ago. She kissed Mrs Strickland's hand & expressed the Sense she had of being much honored by her present Situation : I observed however

---

[1] The Blue Nuns. The history of this convent is given in *The Diary of the " Blue Nuns " or Order of the Immaculate Conception of Our Lady at Paris, 1658-1810,* edited by J. Gillow and R. Trappes-Lomax for the Catholic Record Society, London, 1910.

[2] Lady Anastasia Stafford, 2nd daughter of William Stafford-Howard, 2nd Earl of Stafford.

[3] Lady Lucy Talbot, youngest daughter of George Talbot, Earl of Shrewsbury.

[4] The Hon. Anne Howard, daughter of Bernard Howard, of Twyford, Hants. She was elected Abbess in 1751, 1754, 1761, 1764, holding office for four terms of three years.

[5] Dorothy Parker, daughter of Captain Thomas Parker (2nd son of Alexander Parker of Bradkirk Hall, near Kirkham, Lancs.).

[6] Lady Anne Stafford (Sister Mary Winefred), the younger sister of Lady Anastasia.

[7] Sister Simpson (see below, p. 136). The Diary of the Blue Nuns describes her as Elizabeth Simpson, daughter of Richard Simpson of Preston, and of Mary, daughter of Richard Withington of Ribbleton, outlawed in 1715. Sister Simpson went to be a religious on Sept. 12, 1767, took the veil on Nov. 27, 1767, the habit on Oct. 19, 1768, and was professed on Feb. 7, 1770. Two of her brothers and many others of her family joined the Benedictine Order.

that she called the Women of Quality Sister as they did each other, sate down with them at the Grate & seemed perfectly at her Ease. She was however easily distinguishable by her Vulgarity, and begg'd some Converse with Mrs Strickland's Maid.

7 Octr The Ladies were all very civil, & M^{rs} continued   Howard remarkably so ; She was likewise particularly kind to Queeny, & the Abbess promised to obtain leave of the Bishop for our admittance into the Convent some future Day. Some of these Nuns talked to Mrs Strickland about a Mrs Hooker who they said was sick. As we came home She gave me the History of that Woman's Husband : [1] he is the Man it seems who brought over the Manchester Manufacture hither from England in Resentment against (the) Government which would not grant him a pardon for his Treachery in the Year 45 : he made that Pardon a Condition of Peace between him & his Country, & that Condition not being complied with, he established his Manufacture of Cottons & Linnens here at Paris & has furnished the French, I find, with all the Things of that kind I have seen in their Nation.

We staid at home this Evening, Madame de Boccages drank Tea with us & I think has a mind to make an Intimacy. Our two agreeable Foreigners came [in] after the Italian Comedy, and we had a good Deal of Literary Chat, sometimes in English, sometimes in French, sometimes in Latin, sometimes in Italian ; we

---

[1] This would appear to be the well-known Jacobite, John Holker, son of John Holker of Stretford, Manchester. Holker married Elizabeth, daughter of John Hilton, or Hulton, a Manchester tradesman. He accompanied the Young Pretender on his secret visit to London in 1750. (See *The Dictionary of National Biography*.)

all made Mistakes & those Mistakes made us laugh—
Johnson is quite in Love with little Bathyan—the
Hungarian—it is an amiable Boy indeed. Harry will
be like him I hope.

8 Oct^r   We spent very uncomfortably; one
                   Panchaud,[1] a Banker, invited us to his
Country House where we found a Woman who went
by his Name indeed but having all the Mien &
Manners of a Harlot. I thought her such, & did
not treat her with abundance of Respect. Her Behaviour was so grossly indecent that as we came home
I complain'd to Mr Baretti in very rough Terms, to
Mr Thrale in very severe ones, of being introduced to
such Company. Baretti's Excuse was worse than the
Offence—he said She was Company good enough for
Mrs Cholmondeley,[2] and for that insolent Speech I
thought I had good right to rebuke him, which I did not
spare to do. My Anger however as it is vehement is
never durable—we are all good Friends again, at least
I will answer for myself.

In the Evening we saw the Villa of the Duc de
Pentheiver;[3] it is not so fine as Wanstead [4] upon the

---

[1] Horace Walpole occasionally asked for his letters to be directed
to M. Panchaud. On July 19, 1769, also he wrote from Arlington
Street to Sir Horace Mann : " Panchaud, a banker from Paris,
broke yesterday for seventy thousand pounds, by buying and selling
stock."—*Letters of Horace Walpole*, vol. vii., p. 299.

[2] Is this the Hon. Mrs. Robert Cholmondeley, wife of
Horace Walpole's nephew Robert, 2nd son of George, Earl of
Cholmondeley ? She was Mary, sister of Mrs. Margaret Woffington,
the actress.

[3] Probably at Sceaux.

[4] Wanstead House. This splendid mansion was built by Sir
Richard Child in 1715, and demolished in 1822. It was for a time
the residence of the Prince of Condé.

whole but finer than Wimbledon.[1] The floors are eminently curious, & the Gardens handsome in the French Taste.

9 Oc-   Our two Foreigners dined with us, & had
tober   a Mind to retail Voltaire's Criticisms on
         Shakespeare. Voltaire has indeed a most prodigious Power over the Minds upon the Continent: Scripture seems to have but few Champions who dare oppose him; Shakespeare ought to have fewer, and Homer is, I fancy, almost given over except by a few solitary Scholars. These two Young Fellows however are very extraordinary People; I long to entertain Count Marucci[2] at Streatham, poor Bathyan we shall never see again, he is going from hence to Italy, and is then to settle at Vienna, where his Father (a Hungarian Prince) resides in the Service of the Empress's Court. He invited Johnson thither, who said he must apply to me. Bathyani then never ceased beseeching us to see Vienna in the Course of our Travels—it would be odd enough if we should ever go. Manucci is going to England in a few weeks—he is a Florentine Nobleman of high Birth;—the other is just come from England where he fell in Love with a Young Woman of Quality —I think—Lord Northington's Daughter:[3] so much for our Friends—they are both well skill'd in Literature.

10 Oct[r]   We went to see St Roque's Church, which
             I like better than any I have seen upon the Continent, Amiens alone excepted:—so skilful & so

---

[1] The house of John, 1st Earl Spencer.

[2] Manucci. Mrs. Thrale several times in her *Journal* in error writes Minucci. See also above, pp. 64-66.

[3] Robert Henley, 1st Earl of Northington, Lord Chancellor, died in 1772. In 1775 two of his five daughters were as yet unmarried.

pleasing is the Disposition of the Altars. The description is contained in every Book, so I will not repeat it.
From thence we went to the Tavistock Street [1] of Paris,
a sort of Place like Exeter Change [2] but with better Goods
in it & greater Variety,—every thing was cheap too
[so] I bought a few Trifles for Presents. The next
Flight was to their Foundling Hospital,[3] which is
boasted as a boundless Charity ; & indeed the Woman
said they had already taken in five Thousand two hundred
Children since last January : the Place was wonderfully
clean, cleaner than any I have seen in France, and the
poor Infants at least die peaceably cleanly and in Bed—
I saw whole Rows of swathed Babies pining [away]
to perfect Skeletons, & expiring in very neat Cribs
with each a Bottle hung to its Neck filled with some
Milk Mess, which if they can suck they may live, & if
they cannot they must die. The very young ones,
I have a Notion, seldom get through—those who are
not put in till 8 or 9 Months old seem to do well enough.
The Evening of this Day was disposed of at the Italian
Comedy where the famous Carlini [4] exhibited his Theatrical Talents in the Character of a speaking Harlequin.
The Buffoonery was more gross than anything I ever
saw or could at all have conceived, but the People
laughed, clapped & even shouted with Joy—& Baretti
said plausibly enough that the Multitude were to judge
what best entertained them, & that to criticise a Comedy
without knowing the Characteristicks of the Nation is

[1] Many fashionable shops were then in Tavistock Street,
Covent Garden.
[2] Exeter Change, pulled down in 1829, stood in the Strand,
where Burleigh Street is now.
[3] The *Hôpital des Enfans trouvés*, in the Faubourg Saint-Antoine.
[4] Charles-Antoine Bertinazzi, 1713-83.

impossible : I therefore returned home, not entertained
—because my Taste differs from theirs, but not disappointed, because I have gained some Knowledge ;
I know at least what will delight a Continental Audience.
This Day has been a very good one.

11 Oct^r   Is our Wedding Day ; I little thought of
            ever spending it at Paris. Monsr L'Abbé
François was the first to give us Joy, & present us with
a Large Bouquet of the most beautiful Flowers that
any Season could have produced. When we had suited
ourselves with Caps &c. at Mlle Alexandre's we drove
to the Luxemburg & saw the great Gallery filled with
the pictures of Rubens—they perfectly dazzle ones
Eyes. When we returned home we gave a grand
dinner to Mad^{me} de Bocages, her Nephew & Niece,
the Count & Countess de Blanchetie, Minucci, the
Italian Nobleman, a M^r Le Roy who has travelled a
vast deal, two Monks from among the [English] Benedictines & L'Abbé François [besides] our own Family
which now consists of six Persons. In the afternoon
we went to the Boulevards—a sort of Sadlers Wells [1]
where Rope Dancing, Tumbling and Pantomimes preside—it was more entertaining than a Play—and we had
Chat enough with our Gallants who never forsake us—
I mean Minucci & Le Roy.

12 Oct^r   This Day we devoted to the good Abbé
            who promised to provide us with Amuse-
ment—Accordingly a very large Party of us consisting
of ourselves, Count Minucci, Father Prior, a Mr Swaine
who all of us seem to like, a Captain Irwin [2] & his Wife
& Daughter & our Conductor the Abbé set forward

---

[1] The well-known place of public amusement in Islington.
[2] See below, p. 171.

to the Gobelines where we had [all] the Entertainment that glowing Colours and elegant Designs can give: the Work is superior to Moore's in point of Perfection, but not so much as to dispirit an English Woman, when she compares them together in her Mind—the Man who seems to consider himself as the principal Person here is a Scotsman,[1] ran away like Hooker on Account of the Rebellion & settled at Paris to carry on this beautiful Manufacture, of which in all its Branches he seems to have made himself Master. Our next Flight was to the King's Musæum, where the famous Mr D'Aubenton [2] waited to attend us and display the natural Curiosities deposited in this Suite of Rooms & lately arranged by Mr Buffon himself. We saw them therefore, and were extremely pleased with so fine an Exhibition. The Rooms are disposed precisely like those at Leicester House [3] and are, I think, five in Number, but there are in the King's Musæum things of more difficult Attainment than at Lever's—though our Country-man's Birds are far better preserved than these; I was pleased & astonished to see that he could approach them so nearly. Precious Stones however of uncommon Magnitude & Lustre are Rareties fit only for Royal

---

[1] James Neilson, appointed surveyor of the *basse lice* (lower warp) in 1749, eventually had the complete direction of the work-men of the *basse lice* until 1788.

[2] Louis-Jean-Marie Daubenton, the celebrated French naturalist.

[3] Leicester House once stood at the north-eastern corner of Leicester Square. In 1766 it was occupied by the Duke of Gloucester, but shortly afterwards Sir Ashton Lever formed there a famous collection of objects of natural history called the Leverian (or Holophusikon) Museum. Later this collection was offered at a moderate price to the British Museum, but the offer was refused, and the collection fell to the winner of a lottery. It was broken up by auction in 1806.

Collectors, there were some Emeralds here & Topazes too as large as the Egg of any ordinary hen. Among the Birds the Yellow Parrot of Cuba, the Jabiru, a Large Fishing Bird from China,[1] twice the Size of the biggest

12 Oct^r
continued

Stork I know, & the Promerops of Guinea, coal black, about the size of a Magpye, with a Tail two foot long & the Wings bordered with the brightest Green, struck me as new—I think they are not among Edward's[2] or Willoughby's[3] Collection, but am not sure. The Bird Brooke keeps upstairs stuffed, & calls a Pigeon of some foreign Country, is here denominated Faison huppé de Banda. The Bupreste[4] of Chandenagore, & the Green Wasp of China

12 Oct^r
continued

are the most elegant Insects I observed; Lever's Beetles [too] are greatly before those of the French King.[5] The Musæum detained us a long Time, but we did not regret the Pleasure it had produced when we got to Mr de Gagni's,[6] whose house is decorated with a Profusion of Expence scarcely to be credited. Small Pictures of the Dutch Schools—but finished to the utmost degree of Perfection —cover the Walls, which are hung with Silk Damask;

---

[1] The name " Jabiru " is usually used for the large wading-bird of Brazil and South America.

[2] George Edwards, *The History of Birds*, 1743-51.

[3] Probably referring to *The Ornithology of Francis Willughby*, edited, with additions by John Ray in 1678.

[4] The *Buprestidæ* are brightly-coloured tropical beetles.

[5] Mrs. Thrale's interest in natural history is also evident in a passage of a letter (J.R.L., *Thrale-Johnson Letters*) from her to Dr. Johnson in 1772 : " Dr. Goldsmith has sent me his two first Volumes of natural History, the most entertaining Book I have read I know not how long : it will sadly retard the finishing of my work." Goldsmith's *Animated Nature* was published posthumously in 1774.

[6] The intendant des Finances ; see below, p. 171.

Landskips painted by Paul Brill, small Figures by Teniers, Polenburg [1] & old Frank [2] are the nice Ornaments of his Rooms, nine of which are crowded with Curiosities of wonderful Variety & astonishing Value. Terra Cottas, China Vases, Jasper Tables, Porphyry in many Shapes, Lapis Lazuli, rare old Indian Lac, & a Lustre of Rock Chrystal said to have cost 3500£: Sterling took our attention by Turns ; every Corner was filled with some Curiosity, & nothing here was counted curious but in proportion to its being expensive ; what pleased me most was a Picture, about 2 Foot by 1, of David

12 Oct[r]
continued
Teniers representing People Fishing, which was eminently fine indeed; & a Magdalen in the Desart by Bartolomeo, about 8 Inches by four. There were however some Gerard Dows of inestimable Value, & small things of Wovermans & Bergham [3] that as our Conductor expressed it—n'avoit point de Prix. I was sorry to quit this Fairy Palace, & should have been more so, had I known where we were going, [but] M[r] Monville's [4] House waited for our Inspection and gave us no Pleasure when we arrived. It sems to be contrived merely for the purposes of disgusting Lewdness, & is executed as I conceive on the model of some of the Roman Emperors' Retirements —the Ornaments are all obscene—and of no Value than I can perceive unless considered as [perfect] [5] in that Character. The inside of the Harpsichord painted by Rubens is an Exception—that indeed is the only thing I liked in the House, & with seeing this House we finished our long—but upon the whole—agreeable Morning.

[1] Cornelis van Poelenburgh, 1586-1667.
[2] Frans Franken, the elder, 1542-1616.
[3] Nicolaas Pietersz Berghem.   [4] See below, p. 170.
[5] good *crossed through*.

8

Our Friend the Count came home to dine with us, & the Evening was spent in chat, Criticism and good humoured Conversation.

13 Oct[r]   I got the Morning to myself & wrote Letters to England; after which I treated Queeney with a Run in the Gardens of the Luxembourg and a Walk through the Palais Marchand,[1] where we bought Toys to carry home if we can coax the Custom house officers. At Night we went to the Opera, where I had a good deal of Chat with Lord Mount Morris,[2] he seems an exceedingly pretty Young Man, & observed very justly upon the Glitter of the Night's Exhibition that the French had no way of pleasing the Eye except by a Crowd, or the Ear except by a Noise—the Noise of this Evening's Entertainment has indeed almost split my Brains [but it has produced me Information] —I could not have conceived that such [Numbers of] people could contentedly [have sate] & been stunned so with an unmeaning Clamour. This was the first Time I ever saw Heinel,[3] their great Dancer—I see She has not her [high] Reputation for nothing.

I have now stolen another Moment for general Reflexions : there is a Stupidity in this Nation which nothing but Eyesight could convince one of ; they send Fish up to Table—a Carp for example—without taking off the Scales, and adorn the Gardens of greatest Dignity & most publick Resort with Holy Oaks and common Marigolds. These Instances I have seen myself, but Killpatrick, an Irish Gentleman who is settled here for cheap Living & ought to know them better, says they

---

[1] The stalls along some of the galleries of the Palais Royal.

[2] Hervey Redmond Morres, 2nd Viscount Mountmorres.

[3] This famous danseuse had appeared in England, and is several times referred to by Horace Walpole in his *Letters*.

will actually kill a sitting Hen, & serve her up for a
Poularde as they call it.   At the Opera tonight, no degree
of the remotest probability was observed, a Storm was
raised only to shew their Machinery, which was so despicable that it consisted of nothing but Plates of Tin fairly
laid down upon the Stage, and then rolled up—in sight
of the Audience—to imitate Waves forsooth.   The
Opera House at Paris however is larger than that at
London & very like it ; except that there are no Benches
in the pit—every body is contented to stand.   The
Signs in the Streets [1] often afford me amusement.   The

13 Oct^r
continued
Holy Ghost is commonly the Pawnbroker's
choice, the Virgin Mary sits over an Alehouse Door, adorned with real Grapes like
a Bacchante, and Le Nom de Jesus written thus IHS is
at an Old Clothes Shop on the other Side the Bridge—
The Providence—represented by God the Father walking
between a Cornfield & a Vine Yard is a common Sign
—such devices did I never see before.   Self Admiration
seems the Grand Characteristick of the Country—after
We had filled [our] [2] Eyes with delight among the Duke
of Orleans's Pictures where the School of Titian had
for an hour's Time or two glow'd *in* [*our*] [2] *Sight &*
Triumphed in [*our*] [2] *Soul*—they led [us] [3] to a grand
Gallery—for the conclusion—the bonne bouche as they
call'd it—flourished over on the Sides by the gaudy
hand of their dear Country Man—Coypel,[4] whose
Performances charmed their Taste ten Times more than
all the excellence of Italy.   Another day—when the
Tapestry of the Gobelines was shewn us—no Pictures
would they copy from but French ones, & so little is
their Care to preserve imitations of Nature that they make

[1] See below, pp. 130, 201.   [2] my *crossed through.*
[3] me *crossed through.*   [4] Antoine Coypel, 1661-1722.

a Pelican for Example Pink & Green, a Carp Purple & Yellow—merely to shew the Strength of their Colours, & utterly disregarding its contradiction of common Sense—but are perpetually adding with a Sneer—*You have no such fine Things in England I believe*. The Arms of France for ever meet your Eyes; but have the most ridiculous Appearance cut in Turf in the Gardens of the Luxembourg—unless indeed one recollects the Tumblers at the Boulevards who have them worked into their Dresses like a Badge behind their Shoulders —so much for Remarks.

14 Oct[r]   A new Day is now begun and we have large Promises of Amusement from M[r] Le Roy, who seems to be here what Athenian Stewart [1]—as we call him—is in England:

> For much his knowledge to increase
> He lived in France and travelled Greece.

He took us first to the House of M[r] D'Argençon,[2] which I think was all Gold & Glass: his Bed was a Tent of the most costly Tissue, with a ty'd up Bundle of Spears for Posts; & a Helmet with Plumes at the Top —Bows, Arrows, Battle Axes, &c. forming the Back Frame behind his Head. This Bed was repeated eight Times by Mirrors placed accordingly. The rest of the House was Suitable, & the Apartment of the Lady still more gay; her Dressing Room was splendid [even] to magnificence, & her Boudoir or pouting Room was hung with elegant Paper covered with Glass, they

---

[1] James Stuart (1713-83), joint author with Nicholas Revett of *The Antiquities of Athens, Measured and Delineated*, of which the first volume appeared in 1762. In 1758 Le Roy had published his *Ruines des plus beaux monuments de la Grèce*.

[2] See below, p. 172.

shewed us her Shoes which were remarkably pretty & small—Queeney could not have got them on her Foot I am confident. In this Apartment were Books fit for the Place such as Faery Tales, &c. They would not let us see the upper Apartments because they saw us laughing & handling their Books.[1]

The next House we saw was more gilt & more glaz'd & finer of course ; the Rooms were larger too ; one was 50 foot long—walled with alternate Pannels of Green Marble & Looking Glass—this gay Mansion was the Property of a Monsr St Julien [2] who shewed it us himself and was extremely civil. The Covering of his Son's Bed only, the Window Curtains & Chairs of his Apartment were I guess about 500$^£$ Value : they were proportionably meaner than the Father's and I saw nothing that disgraced the finery of the whole except one Shelf filled with wooden Books. A Basket of Flowers in the Garden took much of my Attention—I will have such a one at Streatham. Large Gardens like the Queen's at Buckingham House, in the very Centre of a great Metropolis, strikes an English Spectator with stronger Ideas of Grandeur than all the other Objects put together.

M^r Le Roy took us to his Brother ; a good old Mechanick [3] who has twice received the premium for facilitating the Discovery of the Longitude : he shewed us his Machines, explained their Uses & Properties

14 Octr continued

and flattered me mightily for knowing something of the Matter. His chief & leading Principle seems to be a Spring proof against heat cold & motion & his principal Skill is preserving every one part separate from every other so as to prevent the ill Consequences of Friction. He gave

---

[1] See below, p. 172.   [2] See below, p. 172.
[3] Pierre Le Roy, 1717-85.

me his Treatise [1] on the Subject, and we parted with
great kindness on both Sides.   Minucci dined with us,
and we criticised the French Taste—he laughed at
D'Argençon's disposition of his Mirrors, and said that
to reflect a Bed eight Times over could create no Pleasure
except [what] the Idea of an Hospital [could give].
These people, says he, are rich only in illusion—'Tis
pity but they would likewise count their Louis at a
Glass—but the best Bon Mot I have heard this long Time
is of Vestru their principal Dancer—There are now,
says Vestru, but three great Men in Europe, the King
of Prussia, Voltaire and myself. [2]   Mad^me Boccages &
the Count & Countess Blanchetie spent the Evening
with us—tomorrow we go to Choisy.

15 Oct^r   Choisy is a royal Residence, rather elegant
            than splendid, as it is intended merely for
a Country Retirement or Hunting Seat.   The Prospect
from the Windows is delightful—& the Seine at Choisy
would be very like the Thames at Greenwich, if it had
any Boats or Ships upon it—but sure never were Rivers
so bare of Vessels, or Roads so barren of Carriages, [3] as
in France ; One may travel 20 Miles by Land or Water
and meet absolutely no one.   The Apartments at Choisy
are very handsome but not superbe, and Madame herself
sleeps in a much worse Bed than the Lady will do who
marries St Julien's Son.   There is a sort of old magical

---

[1] *Précis des recherches faites en France depuis* 1730, *pour la déter-
mination des longitudes en mer par la mesure artificielle du temps*, Paris,
1773.

[2] Gaetano-Appollino-Baldassare Vestris (1729-1809).   This
Italian dancer made his home in Paris when quite young.   The
bon mot mentioned by Mrs. Thrale had a wide circulation.

[3] The dearth of carriages was also noticed by Johnson, but his
comments were ridiculed by Baretti.   See below, p. 233.

Table for the King to dine at when he means to be private with a few particular People, whether Counsellors or Mistresses; the Table sinks & rises by Mechanism;[1] & has two or three dumb Waiters at the Sides to Change the Plates &c., by the same Operation—they all fall at last in the Floor—which is inlaid with Brass—and make part of it. We were shewn here a Table of curious Workmanship too in another Way—made of various coloured Woods & finished to a high Degree of Perfection. It is said to have cost 3000£ to the purchaser & 10 Years Labour to the Maker, but I cannot believe it. Choisy is six Miles only from the Capital, of which you have a beautiful View in returning. Paris however does not [look] so well from its Environs as London —when London is clear of Smoke, but this Metropolis is always so, and you may distinguish every Spire in the City as clearly as the Houses at Hampstead. The Stone Quarries all round the Town make Building very cheap, 15 Oct^r & of course invite the enlargement of Paris, continued which from the whiteness of the Ground & Houses resembles Bath more than London —on the whole. The Vineyards & young Plantations however take off the Glare of the Stone very agreeably, & the coming into this City is beautiful on every Side.

What has pleased me most hitherto has been the Duke of Orleans's collection of Pictures, Gagni's Accumulation of costly Rareties, St Julien's Taste & Splendour in his Ornaments—& the serene Situation & simple Elegance of Choisy—I should not have forgotten the inlaid floors at Sçeaux, which in their way excel any thing I ever beheld—the Floor of every Chamber is finish'd like the

---

[1] "It was invented by Louis XV during the favour of Madame du Barri."—*Croker*.

most high prized Cabinet which Mr Cobb [1] can produce
to captivate the Eyes of his Customers.   We spent the
Evening at home with our own Society—Minucci now
always makes a part of it—but he goes tomorrow to
Fontainebleau, I find, whither we shall like arrive
on Wednesday Night, if all our Schemes take Place.
Queeney's Worms now torment her cruelly—& I cannot
steal a Day to give her Physick—this vexes me a little
but we must bear it.

16 Oct[r]   Mr Mead left us last Night, I think him so
            pleasing a Man that if we had known him
longer we should only have regretted him more.   We
are vastly well off for Friends, the Abbé is amiable &
desirous to please, M[r] Le Roy provides us a Variety
of Entertainment, & Minucci makes Verses Improviso
with Mr Baretti.   I must now begin a new Day.

16 Oct.   This Day has been passed—at least from
           10 to ½ after 3—among the Austin Nuns of
the English College [2]—Convent I mean—in the Rue
S[t] Victoire :   the Women are perfectly conversible,
chearful & pleasing—I like them extremely.   The
Prioress [is] of the Fermor Family [3]—Niece to Pope's
Belinda.   We had a great deal of Chat upon the Subject
both of the Poet & the Lady.   Another Nun [4] pleased
me very much.   She has been a Beauty about London
since my Time, & is now eminently handsome :   She
has likewise seen a great deal of the World, has travelled
& has read ;   She has many Books in her Room on

[1] Probably Mr. John Cobb, cabinet-maker, St. Martin's Lane,
Charing Cross.   He died in 1778.   See *Gentleman's Magazine*, vol.
48, p. 392.

[2] Notre Dame de Sion, in the Rue des Fossés St. Victor.

[3] See below, pp. 173, 204.

[4] Miss Canning.   See also pp. 144, 224.

various Subjects, & talks of studying Latin in good earnest. She played on the Church Organ for my Entertainment, & went over Handel's Water Musick with great Dexterity. They [had] gained leave of the Bishop for me to dine in the Refectory; We had Bouilli Beef with Carrots & other Roots, Necks of Mutton with Spinach, & Entremets of which I know not the Names. The Abbess, Prioress & myself sate at the Table which crossed the Top of the Room, the Nuns on each Side. We went to the Chapel after Dinner from whence we soon returned, & I had an Opportunity of seeing all their Cells & hearing the manner of the Monastick Life described to me exactly. There is an excellent Garden, Kitchen Garden & Vineyard, where Queeney ran Races with the Pensioners while I chatted with the Nuns. An hour or two after called us all together to Tea which the Abbess made for us in her Dressing Room & we talked over [it] in Freedom & Chearfulness, abusing the French Customs, wondering at the Hardships suffered by the Claires, telling & hearing in short whatever we had a mind. I was sorry when Dr Johnson came in the Coach to fetch us home: We detained him a while however, & sent the Confessor to him till we had finished our Tea: when that was over, one of the Nuns went with me to the Grate, & Mrs Strickland soon appeared with

16 Octr continued half a Dozen more, they are most of them her Friends, either Schoolfellows or Instructresses. It was in this Convent She was bred.

We parted with great expressions of Kindness—they had given me a mighty delightful Day, & said we had likewise afforded them one. I shall surely lose my heart among these Friars & Nuns: there is something so caressive in their Manner, so Singular in their Profession, which at once inspires Compassion and Respect, that one must love them, and with a Tenderness that would be painful to oneself, but [for] the Consideration that they feel nothing for us. I left these Ladies a Louis D'Or for Wine, and we parted liking each other quite well I believe. The Votaries of St Austin suffer no violent Hardships—Their Beds are soft, their Linnen fine, their Table plentiful & their House convenient : they make Vows indeed of Poverty, Chastity, Obedience to their Superior & perpetual Inclosure ; but as to Poverty—they never feel the pressure of it at all, nor know those Anxieties with which the Fear of it fills half Mankind : a Well endowed Convent is of all others the most perfect Refuge from Poverty. With regard to Celibacy—it is for the [most part] uncomfortable in the World [only] because it is a Disgrace, which

16 Oct^r　Objection is lost in a Convent ; with Regard to Solitude—few Women live in so much Society as four and twenty or thirty [female] Acquaintance—I mean of People in a little way who pass their Time in Prayer, Cards & Prattle just as these do, only going to one anothers Houses instead of all living in one. Obedience is the most objictible (*sic*) of all the Vows, & that too seems to be made very easy : their Abbess is of their own chusing, & they elect a new one or the same over again every three Years : The Lady I saw Yesterday had been 13 Years Superior. I dont know whether I mentioned that the Abbess of St Louis at Rouen—a Benedictine Convent—had [1] told me when I was there that She had obtained Permission to spend the Winter at Paris. I have just heard that She is expected to Night at the Fossée where I have spent my agreeable day. She is a Lady of a noble House in France, Besançon,[2]

---

[1] mentioned *crossed through*.

[2] Barbançon (?) ; see below, p. 144.

I think, and chosen by the King to preside over the amiable Society of french Benedictine Nuns who were so kind to me at Rouen. I will see her again now She is so near me, She is a Woman of elegant Manners & high Rank. Her Convent is more splendid than that of my Countrywomen at the Fossée & the Refectory more ornamented—besides that the Abbess's private Apartment is just as good as any Person of Fashion's I have seen in France, & they have a Library and Billiard Room appointed, while our poor Ladies must be contented with each a Set of Shelves in her Cell, & a Card Table or two, & Backgammon Tables in one of the Apartments destined for Recreation—Some of the Nuns I find are eminently skilful at Chess.

17 Oct^r   I stole an Hour to give Queeney a Run in the Gardens of the Luxembourg as I think She uses too little Exercise for one who is used to so much. Last Night my Head was so filled with the Nuns that I forgot to tell how We spent the Evening at the Boulevards, & saw a Boy dance among Rows of Eggs with surprizing Agility. The Players in France seem to be better than ours, even their lowest performers are not without some degree of Merit, but this new Fashion of Acting, Singing & Dancing without Gloves does not please me much, especially at the Opera, where the Women are dressed with great Magnificence. I was called from these Reflexions to see the Palace of Bourbon which effaced as to Splendour of Architecture and Elegance of Decoration all I had seen before. There was however in one of the very finest Apartments a Basket to hold Wood which was piled up in it accordingly. At Night we had another Touch at the Boulevards— where one of the Representations was Robinson Crusoe, & in another, there was a Mock Engagement of Men

and Women, the Men fighting with Muskets, the Women with Clysterpipes—the Ladies conquered & were much applauded—so much for French Delicacy.

18 Octr We went off for Fontainebleau, & after passing thro' a delightful Country arrived there in good Time, but at a wretched Lodging which Minucci had provided for our Reception. I had laid some Wagers with our fellow Travellers about the Number of hours we were to spend on the Road, & won a Six Livres Piece upon the whole: Every Man & every Maid wished Mr Baretti to win—I believe they made forty Efforts for him to gain his Wager—he did win a Louis of Johnson & fifteen Livers of myself at last with much ado. We passed thro' a lovely Country—the Face of it just about Fontainebleau resembles Tunbridge but more rocky. We supt together merrily & slept sound in our Beds.

19 Octr The Morning was spent in Dressing, the Noon in going to Court, and the Evening was got rid of at the Play. We saw the young Princess Elizabeth dine first—her Attendant was only Madame de Guemené, who took her Plate from her to give it the page &c., but another Gentleman carved for her. Elizabeth is youngest Sister to the King, about twelve Years old or so, not handsome but passable, if She was not so pinched in her Stays as makes her look pale & uneasy to herself. All Children through this Nation I perceive are thus squeezed and tortured during their early Years, and the Deformity they exhibit at maturity repays the stupid Parents for their Pains. The Princess herself suffers in Compliance to her Country's Taste.

The King & Queen dined together in another Room. They had a Damask Table Cloth neither course (*sic*)

nor fine, without anything under, or any Napkin over.
Their Dishes were Silver, not clean and bright like Silver
in England—but they were Silver: their Plates, Knives,
Forks & Spoons were gilt. They had the Pepper &
Salt standing by them as it is the Custom here, & their
Dinner consisted of five Dishes at a Course: The Queen
eat heartily of a Pye which the King helped her to, they
did not speak at all to each other, as I remember, but
both sometimes turned & talked to the Lord in waiting:
The Queen is far the prettiest Woman at her own Court,
& the King is well enough—like another Frenchman.

19 Oct^r   Monsieur & Madame dine together in
continued   another Room; it is a mighty silent cere-
            monious Business—this dining in publick.
They likewise sat like two people stuffed wth straw;
and only spoke to enquire after our Niggey,[1] about whom
the Queen had likewise before been very inquisitive.
She would have our Names written down, & was indeed
very [condescending but] troublesome with her Enquiries. [I got to another Corner of the room & heard
a Gentleman say: That is the pretty English Woman
I am sure by her blushing.] The Count & Countess
D'Artois were the next Couple to be stared at, and at
them also we stared our fill. The Countess is a little
mean figure but has a pretty face enough, & is the only'
one who has brought a Child, so he will probably be
Heir to France.[2] When we had looked at these great
Folks till our Eyes aked, we returned to our Lodging,
changed our Dress, and finished the Evening at the
Theatre, where we had a Comedy incomparably performed: 'tis a new Piece, full of Repartee & Jokes

[1] Queeney. See below, p. 218.
[2] The Comte D'Artois afterwards becames Charles X. of France;
the son, of course, never became King.

new & old;—but the Action!—I am sorry to see the French beat us so in powers of Performance on a Stage. I think however it is the *only* thing they excel us in & that must be my Comfort.

19 Oct^r   Observations.
continued   There were no Diamonds at all at Court
            but the Queen's Earrings, & She had no other Jewels on her Head—a pair of Pearl Bracelets with a picture on each were all that looked like Ornaments of expence—her Gown was Gawse adorned with Flowers—& a sort of Tree in her Head, which is always extravagantly high. The Women attendants are all eminently ugly; not a Face which did not disgust—and the Shape such as might be expected from the management of it during their Infancy—few Ladies here escape some kind of Deformity. The Court Dress is not like ours, but plaited with a particular Fold upon the Hoop, which is large & sloped, they all have their Trains borne, and those who have English Silks are accounted the best dress'd. No more Time to write a Word this Night.

20 Oct^r   This Morning we drove into the Forest as
begins   they call it to see the Queen ride on Horse-
           back. We were early enough to see her mount, which was not done as in England by a Man's hand, but the right foot is fixed in the Stirrup first & then drawn out again when the Lady is on her Saddle. The Horse on which the Queen rode was neither handsome nor gentle, he was however confined with Martingales &c. & richly caparison'd with blue Velvet & Silver Embroidery: the Saddle was ill contrived—sloping off behind—& a Pommel so awkward that no Joyner could have executed it worse,—there was a

Handle by the Side I saw. While we were examining
the Furniture and Formation of the Horse,
20 Octr the Queen came to ride him, attended by
the Duchess de Luignes,[1] who wore Boots & Breeches
like a Man with a single Petticoat over them, her Hair
tyed & her Hat cocked exactly like those of a Man.
Her Majesty's Habit was Puce Colour as they call it,
her Hat filled with Feathers and her Figure perfectly
pleasing. She offered her Arm to the King's Aunts
who follow'd her to the Rendezvous in a Coach, as
they were getting out, but they respectfully refus'd her
Assistance. Our Conductor now told us that this was
the Time to see the Apartments of the Palace as the
Royal Family were gone out a' Hunting. We therefore
drove to the Castle, and saw the Rooms, which exceeded
in Richness and Splendour all we had yet seen, unless
the Hotel de Bourbon because of its newness, & the
cleanliness of its Furniture, might be put in Competition
with it. In the great Gallery however which is adorn'd
by Pictures of Primaticcio, & Sculptures of Cellini,
& through which all the Family & their Attendants
pass to & from Mass &c., there are Shops erected on
each Side for Trinkets, Millinery, Books &
20 Octr all manner of things—particularly Trusses
continued for Deformity—which are indeed sufficiently
wanted.

The Dogs & Horses of the King was our next
Exhibition, the Staghounds are beautiful indeed &
chiefly of English Breeds ; the Horses, (except half a
Dozen kept a L'Anglois, as the Groom called it,) had
no Stalls to stand in, & but 3 foot & a half Space—they
were a wretched Collection indeed—of ugly, blind &

[1] Guyonne-Elisabeth-Josèphe de Montmorency-Laval, duchesse
de Luynes.

lame—add to this that they are all Stone Horses, & vicious of Course. So much for the Kennel & Stable.

20 Octr continued   The Evening was filled up by dressing & going to the Play—not the little Theatre belonging to the Town but the fine Playhouse erected in the Castle for the Entertainment of the King, Queen, &c., who must not go to any other—except incog : None but people of the highest Quality, and those who belong to the Court of course, could be admitted into this honourable Groupe : we therefore had applied some Days ago to the English Ambassador [1] that we might be placed there under his Protection. Johnson and Baretti thinking themselves not brilliant men enough to shine at such a Shew remained at the Lodging—and we were stuck in a Side Box over against Monsieur and Madame, neither of whom—for I watched them—ever uttered a Single Word during the whole Representation which lasted four long hours. The Queen had no mind to dress after her Morning's ride they told us—so sat upstairs incog : just opposite to us & over the heads of the Brother & Sister. Never did I see so glittering a Spectacle ! as no corner of the Theatre was left empty, and no one admitted who was not gayly & splendidly dress'd. Among the women however none tower'd so high in Diamonds & plumage

20 Octr continued   as the Russian Ambassadress,[2] whose Companion was as handsome as her Principal was magnificent. Nine Embassadors were present besides the Pope's Nuncio, & nothing vexed me but the want of Light to see the Pomp I was surrounded with. Sixteen Candles were all we had to shew ourselves

[1] David Murray, 2nd Earl of Mansfield, 6th Viscount Stormont.

[2] The Russian ambassador at Paris was Prince Ivan Sergyeivich Bariatinski.

off to one another with, but the Stage was sufficiently illuminated. The piece was Musical & very tender, well acted of Course, & the principal performer was a Man who had retired on the fortune he had made by Acting, & now only returned to the Stage to amuse the Queen for the few Nights She passes at Fontainebleau. The Crowd was extreme tonight, the heat & Stench excessive, yet Queeney bears it all. We go to Paris again tomorrow.

21 Octr We returned to Paris through a Country beautiful, fruitful & highly cultivated. There are no Hedges in France, where I have travelled at least —nor no Verdure : Corn fields, Towns finely scattered up & down, & built all of Stone as if they were meant to adorn as well as inhabit the Country—with Rivers perpetually winding in your Sight as if intended merely to amuse the Eye—are the Objects which in this Nation engage the Attention of a Traveller, besides what continues to delight me though I am now so much used to it, which is the Game constantly moving on each Side your Carriage as you drive—Hares, Pheasants, Partridges—not now & then a few of them to stare at, but seen as frequently as Magpies among us, and feeding fearlessly by the Roadside. They will not [endeavor to escape] [1] neither as you pass along, unless you make a Noise or throw a Stone for the Diversion of seeing the Hares run, or hearing the Pheasants rise with a rattling Sound of the Wing peculiar to themselves. I have seen no Foxes but am told that there [are] great numbers on the other Side of Paris, & that they lessen the Quantity of other Game very visibly about their Purlieus. It was at first mighty odd

21 Octr continued

---

[1] fly away *crossed through*.

to me to have Partridges for dinner at every wretched
Inn where you had two or three Beds in the room. I
have never yet spoken of their Cookery [1]—no Meat
here has the Taste of Meat in England; Onions &
Cheese prevail in all the Dishes, & overpower the
natural Taste of the Animal excepting only when it
stinks indeed, which is not infrequently the Case:
besides that every sort of Food being dress'd so very
much, & no Flavour of the Food remaining, they are
driven to the Necessity of superadding something else
which is commonly Garlick, Vinegar, Cheese & Salt.

21 Octr continu'd I think I have already mention'd the Signs [2]
—I saw the Virgin today over an Alehouse
door with this Motto,

> Je suis le Mere de mon Dieu
> Et la Gardienne de ce Lieu.

The Grace of God is Likewise a common Sign & wherever
Ribbons, Tapes, &c are to be sold,—there is commonly
God Almighty in the Clouds holding the small end of
a Cornucopia pouring forth the Wares of the Shop
whether Haberdashery, Grocery or any other. Sometimes indeed they make the Vine that grows up their
House their Sign, & write under it: Au pied de la
Vigne &c. We came home very late tonight, it was
quite dark & I vexed for Queeney, but nothing ever
hurts her I think except the Worms.

22 Octr The Abbé was with us betimes in the morning to take us to Versailles & its environs;
the first thing we saw was the Menagerie where nothing
was new to me: it was indeed agreeable enough to see
the Pelican catch fish in a little Bason kept for his own

---

[1] See above, p. 103.   [2] See also p. 115.

use, & to stroke a Siberian Fox who was as tame as a Lapdog. Trianon, a Royal Summer House, was the next thing we were shewn, and a very elegant Summer house it is—contrived for hot weather merely, with open Arches, playing Fountains, thick shady Walks &c. The King however intends to cut down all the Trees in a short Time—it will then be nothing. La Petite Vienne is another Banquetting House about a Mile from the great Palace. Here the Royal Family sleep sometimes, & the Rooms are very happily distributed, for the Reception of the King & his Train. Here the late King sickened of the Smallpox, & from here the present Queen walked to Versailles on her foot—attended by only four Noblemen & four Ladies—that Queen is a Sweet Creature !

22 Octr continued   The Theatre was the fine Thing we were then carried to admire, & so fine it is that Imagination itself can add but little to its Splendour—I had never known what Expence could do when pushed to the utmost had I not seen the King of France's Theatre. We walked on the Stage to look at the House—& now, says I to Dr Johnson, what Play shall we act ?—the Englishman in Paris ? [1] No indeed, says he,—we will act Harry the fifth. [2] Every representation here costs 2500£ Sterling. From the Theatre we proceeded to the Chapel—that was not finer than many I have seen in France—pretty much like our

[1] Samuel Foote's *The Englishman in Paris*, London, 1753.

[2] " When at Versailles, the people shewed us the Theatre. As we stood on the stage looking at some machinery for playhouse purposes ; ' Now we are here, what shall we act, Mr. Johnson—*The Englishman in Paris ?* ' ' No, No,' replied he, ' we will try to act *Harry the Fifth.* ' "—Piozzi's *Anecdotes*, p. 67.

own at Greenwich.[1] The Apartments in the Palace
however effaced every Sight my Eyes have yet seen for [2]
Riches, Pomp, & Beauty.   The Gallery was just 125 of
my Steps—so spacious too! & so adorned! but not
above 70 Foot longer on the whole than All Souls
College Library at Oxford.   The Façade of Versailles
on the great Front is a glorious Pile indeed; the Situation however is not fine, nor is any Prospect to be seen
from the Windows, except some Marble Basons filled
with Water, & oddly disposed on Terraces—one above
another till you come to the highest where the House

22 Oct^r   stands.—With Regard to Furniture nothing
continued   can be more gay & at the same Time more
            rich than the Furniture of Versailles—
Cabinets of Sêve China, such as we are proud to get
a Cup & Saucer of, adorn the Queen's Apartments,
where a rich Coffer of Crimson Velvet embroidered with
Gold serves to keep her Majesty's Diamonds & is called
the Bijouterie.   They are never weary of representing
to themselves their own Magnificence—Pictures of their
Palaces, or of beautiful Spots in their Gardens are the
only Pictures one ever sees except now & then a Cieling
by Mignard with all the Gods & Goddesses paying
homage to the King of France.   The Duke of Orlean's
Collection excepted, & the paintings of Rubens in the
Luxembourg—but I suppose the last are only preserved

22 Oct^r   because they are the History of Henry the
continued   4th's Queen—and not because they are the
            finest Flemish Pictures in the Universe.
    What is very particularly to be observed in seeing

----

[1] The chapel of Greenwich Hospital?   The interior and roof
were destroyed by fire in 1779, and the restoration was based on
a design by " Athenian Stuart."
    [2] in *crossed through*.

the Palaces of Paris is—that however richly the Apartments may be furnished—they never are made convenient. The Queen for Example has only two Rooms in any of her Houses—a Bed Chamber & a Drawing Room—in the first She sleeps, dresses, prays, chats, sees her Sisters or any other Person who is admitted to Intimacy, & lives by what I can understand in a Bustle hardly to be supported all the Morning long. She has no second Room to run to for Solitude, nor even a Closet to put her Close Stool in, which always stands by the Bedside—& was open the day I saw Fontainebleau, while the *Man* was sweeping the Room—I beg my own pardon, it was Madame de Provence's [1] that I saw it in ; but it must have been the same at the Queen's, if we had happened to come in at the same critical Moment before it was shut down.

22 Octr We were shewn today the place where the
continued different Treaties of Peace are kept with
different Nations ; I saw the King of England's Picture hang against that part of the Wall where the English Papers are kept behind Wire & Silk as Books in many Libraries ; the Empress Queen, the King of Spain & the Czarina's Portraits are disposed in the same Manner—& it is a very good one. I have upon the whole been vastly pleas'd with my Day's Diversion, & as we came home I got some Chat with the Abbé concerning French Poetry & Literature in general : he did not acquit himself as *well* as I expec[ted] and I acquitted myself better than I expected so I will go to

[1] Marie Louise Josephine, daughter of Victor Amadeus III. of Savoy. She died in 1810. The Count of Provence became afterwards Louis XVIII. of France.

Sleep in Peace, and think no more of Versailles till tomorrow.

23 Octr begun   On this day I made use of the Bishop's leave to visit the Blue Nuns—so called from having a Cloke of that Colour to wear at Mattins in the Choir when the Cold Weather sets in : I saw the Ceremony of their Dinner & Grace wch they said in the refectory—I expected 'em to go to Choir like the Austins but they did not.   They have a very spacious House & Garden compared to that at the fossée, & their Cells are contrived to contain every possible Convenience—they have warm Beds for Winter, & cool ones (I mean Curtains & Tester) for Summer ;   & there are two small Chapels in the House, besides the Church below which is a Parish one.   There is a Chapter for the Abbess to hold her Court, & consult on any Emergency with the Prioress, Vicaress & next Superior —who together with three more Nuns, that are balloted for, hold a Council to judge of Disputes, punish refractory Novices &c.   They keep 8 Pensioners, who wear a Habit, & never stir without the Walls unless they have the Abbesses Consents—the Abbess is chosen every three Years, but cannot hold her Dignity more than two Elections successively.   They have no more fasting Days than other Romanists—& Mrs Howard told me

23 Octr continued   that at the Epiphany Time they always made a twelfth Cake, and drew King & Queen. Pleasures must be husbanded in Convents, so they think of a Christmas Pye or a Twelfth Cake with ten times the Sensibility that we do.[1]   Tea in the Abbess's

---

[1] This old custom of making a Twelfth Cake and drawing King and Queen on the feast of the Epiphany is well known ; see

Apartment is likewise a vast delight to them ; if Rousseau's Doctrine of Privation encreasing Enjoyment be
true, Nuns are the happiest of human Beings, for they
have the greatest Skill at it.   Silence during
23 Oct[r]   [some][1] Hours in the day gives an Edge to the
continued   Appettite of Talking, & they fast but just
enough to make them pleased with a Flesh day.   After
all this Nuns are *not happy ;* Devotion alone, and an Eye
steadily kept [fix'd] upon Eternity can render Seclusion
tolerable : these Qualities however I have not been
able to discover except in one Nun among the 41 I
have chatted with familiarly—always speaking with exception to the poor Claires, whose auster[it]ies are such
that even 50 Years sufferance cannot dull the Edge of
them, & who are therefore every moment forced by
present Pain to press forward in the great Journey
towards Eternity.   In other Convents where the way of
Life is not strict, as among the Ladies I lived with today,
& my dear Friends at the Fossée ; each seeks as we do
for temporal Felicity, & each—as we do—feels [the
bitterness of] disappointment.   What adds to their
Uneasiness is that if they feel unhappy
23 Oct[r]   they think it is because they are a Nun,
continued   whereas God knows many of those I have
seen today, would have had more Misery by half had

Brand's *Popular Antiquities of Great Britain.*   There is, of course,
the poem, *Twelfe night,* in Herrick's Hesperides, beginning

    " Now, now the mirth comes
    With the cake full of plums,
    Where Beane's the *King* of the sport here ;
    Besides we must know,
    The Pea also
    Must revell, as Queene, in the Court here."
[1] many *crossed through.*

they lived in the World—what Happiness can there be in Store for Women, young, friendless, ugly & poor? of high Quality too for the most part & exquisitely sensible of Offences & Disgrace.   Surely a Convent is their safest Refuge from the Shafts of Poverty & the Corrosions of Care.   It was very pleasing today to see Lady Lucy Talbot, Sister to an Earl, & whose Fortune (for she brought 10000$^£$ with her) has hitherto supported the House; serving the Nuns at Table as her duty demanded because it was her Week of waiting—& running to the Kitchen to heat a little Cabbage for Sister Simson, who had been a Maid Servant in Mrs Strickland's Family.—To see all distinction thus thrown down by Religion is so lovely that I felt myself very much penetrated by the Sight which made a deep Impression—as I told them—Oh, said Lady Abbess, Women of Quality here must learn to wait & Cook too.   Do you remember, said she, turning to Mrs Strickland, the Story of Lady Catherine Howard [1] & the Eggs?—How was it, dear Madam? cry'd I.   Why, said the Abbess, when poor Lady Catherine's Turn came to boyl the Eggs during her Noviciate, She boyled them so hard nobody could eat them; She was reprimanded for this Trick twice, & the 3^d: Time being worst of all, & the Eggs boil'd quite blue as we call it, the Superior used

23 Octr continued

[1] Lady Catherine Howard, eldest daughter of Henry, 6th Duke of Norfolk, was sent to the Convent School in Sept., 1676, but was professed in the English Benedictine Abbey at Ghent in 1687.   The story may possibly relate to Catherine Howard, daughter of Philip Howard of Corby Castle, Cumberland, who went first to York Bar Convent in 1766, then to the Blue Nuns at Paris on July 5, 1770, when she was nearly fifteen years old.   She left on Sept. 24, 1771, to go to the Abbaye of Port Royale.   In 1776 she was married to John Gartside of Crumpsall Hall, near Manchester.

some very severe Expressions. What can I do? at last says [1] Sister Kitty, I put the Eggs on before I went to Mattins that they might be tender, but I think nothing *will* soften them for my Part.

We left these Ladies pleased with us, and We pleased with them;—when we returned to Dinner we found Mr Colebrook [2] & Mr Motteux ready to sit down to dinner with us; after that Ceremony we set off for the Boulevards attended by a young Roman Catholick that Mrs Strickland found to go with us. We were well diverted by an incomparable Harlequin not much taller than Queeney but very clever. On our Return we found our Gentlemen returned from the Theatre &

23 Octr continued
highly pleased with the Representation of Dido [3]—the French do beat us at acting Plays, at making Bread, at stuffing Cushions and at cutting Roads, but nothing is so false as the Notion of the French Police being so excellent as to prevent disturbance in the Streets. I have from my Window seen more Quarrels, Overturns, & Confusion in the Rue Jacob, where I have now lived a Month, than London will exhibit in a Year's walking the Street at decent Hours only—though here we meet a Soldier at every Turning too, & yet the coming out of Publick Places is attended with ten Times the Difficulty [that you find at] an English Theatre. turn over.

23 Octr continued
There is in Paris, as Count Manucci told us —who was very diligent too to pick up every Intelligence, especially to the Disadvantage of the French, there is a Place called the

---

[1] poor *crossed through*.   [2] See below, p. 183.
[3] *Didon*, a tragedy by Jean-Jacques le Franc de Pompignan, was first published in 1734.

Morgue [1] where all dead Bodies which have been found in the Night, drowned, crushed or assassinated, are carried every Morning to be owned & buried by their Friends. Here, says Manucci, are often to be found six or seven Corpses of a Morning, but seldom fewer than two.

The next Frenchman who dined with us after I had heard this horrible Story was Mʳ Le Roy, from whom I endeavoured to extract the Truth of it, but Mʳˢ Strickland unseasonably frighted the Man with Exclamations at the Barbarity of a Nation where such [2] Outrages existed, so that he would at last acknowledge but *one* human Being to be murdered every day throughout the Year in the elegant City of Paris.

24 Octʳ   This is a glorious Town to be sure ; the Women sit down in the Streets as composedly as if they were in a Convenient House with the doors shut ; I mean the ordinary Women always—such as sell Fruit &c. in the Corners of the Bridges, Streets, and so forth. The Ladies do not behave *quite* so grossly ; they only ask you to retire, & ask you before all the Gentlemen present, & at the Comedies they laugh & turn to the Men when an Obscene Jest is happily pointed out by the player. These Reflexions were broken by the arrival of our English Benedictines, who proposed taking us to see the King's Library. We saw it and we wondered, for the like did we never see : for Public Buildings, & single Strokes of Magnificence, surely France is the Nation, and Paris is the Town. The rest of the Morning was wasted at Mercer's Mantua Makers, &c. I had the Pleasure to hear Mʳ Thrale

---

[1] Morne *written above.*   [2] things *crossed through.*

offer me any Silk at any Price,[1] and had the Pleasure to feel myself contented with his Kindness & unwilling to put him to any further Expence. Three Gowns is all I carry over, for it was all I wanted. I came without one Silk Gown.

24 Oct. continu'd   We dined at home, the Librarian,[2] the two Monks & Monsr L'Abbé were our Company: besides Mr Swaine & a Mr Clayton, who is going to Turin, that came to see us in the Afternoon. For a Wonder we went no where at Night, so Mrs Strickland took the Coach I call mine & went to chat with a sick Friend, while the Gentlemen amused themselves with Mad[me] Boccages. I read the pretty Comedy which pleased me so much when I saw it at Fontainebleau, it does not read as it acts to be sure, but one can read it with Pleasure, though as the Merriment all arises from Situations, it makes its best figure on the Stage.

25 Oct[r]   We fooled away some more Money at the Palais Marchand, & then went to dine with the Monks of S[t] Edmund. We were to have come home at 4 that Queeney might attend her Dancing Master but the Fryars desired they might not lose our Company & that we would send for la Liever to their

---

[1] In a letter to Johnson dated "Streatham, 3 June" (1777?), Mrs. Thrale writes: "How kind you are to be thinking of my clothes & Queeney's! Mine are a plain White Silk which I bought in Paris of a colour peculiarly elegant—trimmed with pale Purple & Silver by the fine Madame Beauvais & in the newest & highest Fashion. My fair Daughter has no new Clothes, nor I see no Call, for we get no Tickets for the Chamberlains Box so we are to make amends by Ranelagh."—J.R.L., *Thrale-Johnson Letters*.

[2] Dr. Luke Joseph Hooke; see below, pp. 226-227.

House—we did so—& Niggey capered it away in the
Benedictine Monastery. At Night we saw Dido [1]—I
am not well enough to commend or criticise tonight—
I must absolutely go to bed. The Cold I have caught
now quite disables me.—Queeney keeps well.

26 :   Mademoiselle de Haut Cour [2] shall not go without that Praise she so justly deserves, because
I have got a shocking Cold; She is a lovely Actress,
has numberless Excellencies & but one Fault. The
French Players amaze me they are so very good—yet
to see a Woman [like this] turn aside after a Rant to
spit & hawk in a Corner, is a [Sight of such] grossness
that for the Moment one is tempted to detest her; wiping
the Sweat off their Faces too in Tragedy
is quite a common Trick with them, nor
can they conceive I suppose how greatly it
disgusts one. The Farce was Allegorical, not unlike
our Lethe,[3] & the Girl who played the principal Character was wonderfully pleasing—the Comic Actresses
are all in Gloves—the Tragic have their Hands uncovered—So much for Yesterday's *Evening* Entertainment : We were very happy with the Monks till Play
time—Father Librarian & I had a long Tête a Tête in
the Print Room, while Queeney danced in another of
the Apartments—Johnson staid there till it was time for

26 Oct^r
continued

---

[1] See above, p. 137.

[2] Raucoux *written above*. Françoise Clairien Raucourt (1753-
1815). Walpole, writing to the Hon. Henry Seymour Conway on
Nov. 12, 1774, says : " Mademoiselle de Raucoux I never saw till
you told me Madame du Deffand said she was *démoniaque sans chaleur !*
What painting ! I see her now."—*Letters*, vol. ix., p. 92.

[3] David Garrick's *Lethe*, of which the first version was published
in 1745.

the Fryars to go to Bed, & Killpatrick whom we had before seen at St Germains supped with us.

27 Octr[1]   Captn Killpatrick came [to] breakfast, and made us very good Glee : He is a Character as the Phrase is—Jockey, Buffoon, Fortune Hunter, & a friendly honest Creature as the Men call any body who makes them laugh over a Bottle, & is no Disgrace to the Company.—Kill : is a Man of a most unbounded Acquaintance, free Speech—& empty Purse—always studious to please & desirous to divert,—will buy you a Horse & see that you're not cheated. [Hang][2] Ye says Kill : if you thrust a spavin'd Jade down my Friend's Throat, I'll thrust my Whip down yours ye Dog.—He finds the way to Dr Johnson's heart by abusing the French, & knows how to flatter Baretti who defends them—but enough of Captain Killpatrick. The Abbé

27 Octr continued   came betimes to call us to see the Manufacture of Sêve China at Sêve where it is made. I was forced to buy a bit for a Specimen, because Mr Baretti would persist that their painting is superior to ours—Alas ! I know but too well that it is their Porcelaine—as to the mere Drawing & Colouring I [am sure][3] the Man at Chelsea[4] has the better of them —I would our Clay were as good. From hence we went forward to Belle Vue, the finest Situation I have hitherto seen in France—the House perfectly elegant ;[5]

---

[1] Oct. 26. The previous entries clearly refer to the evening of the 25th. See below, p. 147.

[2] Damn *crossed through*.   [3] know *crossed through*.

[4] William Duesbury (1725-86), the Derby china manufacturer, had bought the works and stock of the Chelsea manufactory in 1770.

[5] This house, destroyed during the Revolution, was built for Madame du Pompadour in 1748. Louis XV. added two new wings in 1756. Marie-Antoinette presented the house to the unmarried daughter of Louis XV. in 1775.

—it was inhabited by Madame Pompadour it seems, when in the plenitude of her Power—her Chapel is a very fine one, & there is a Hanging of one small Room worked wholly by herself in the Tambour—exceedingly pretty. From this charming Spot one has a glorious View of the Seine with its Islands, of Paris itself, of the Hills wch in France resemble Hampstead & Highgate in England, & are called Mont Martyre [1] & Mount Calvary,[2] Shaded at a small Distance by the Bois de Boulogne, a Wood which spreading like Norwood [over] a considerable Tract of Ground fills the Prospect and finishes it to wonderful Perfection. At Meudon, the next Place we saw, was only to be admired another catch of the same Country, to be despised there were some childish parterres with Turf cut in forms & Dwarf Hedges like a Desert Frame with Walls round the whole in the manner of old Fashioned Pye Crust. St Cloud is [in] a better Taste, more Shade & larger Trees, but all clipped & cut & forced into Forms perfectly unnatural. Here I saw some excellent Pictures too, particularly Cartons representing the Exploits of Jove by Giulio Romano which are of immense Value, & suffer'd to run to Ruin every day—a Rembrant too of great Magnitude with the Story of Eneas's filial Piety is going apace to Decay. The Busts in the Gallery, all Antiques, are very valuable. Johnson abuses the French for writing the names of [these] ancient Heroes in their own Language always & not in Greek or Latin. I certainly thought Alexander's Bust, for which it is supposed he sate himself—somewhat disgraced by having it written under—Alexandre le Grand—To-day we have made Acquaintance with two

27 Octr continued

---

[1] Montmartre.   [2] Mont Valérien.

new Folks, Sr Harry Goff[1] & a Mr Keene,[2] so M[rs]
Strickland will have Beaux about her, &
Queeney has [contrived to catch][3] Cold at
last after many fruitless Efforts—so She will
have the Pleasure of seeing me fret about her which She
passionately loves. I am terribly hoarse myself, & felt
my Throat so much swelled last Night that I was very
apprehensive I might be ill in earnest & troublesome;
which would be a bad Affair upon me who have enough
to do to make people like me as it is.—If I am sullen
here however I am perfectly ungrateful; for my Master
spares no Expence, nor M[r] Baretti no Trouble to keep
me in good humour. I have had a prodigious fine
Journey of it—yet am quite glad to hear we set out for
England on Wednesday. I wish Queeney's Cold was
well—I am so afraid of a Cough always.

28 Oct[r] [4]   We went nowhere to day but to the Great
Toy Shop called the Petit Dunkerque;[5]
I bought a Trinket or two, & longed for a Snuffbox of
exquisite beauty. At Night Stricky took one Coach &
paid Visits while the Men went to the Play—I was not
well enough to venture so M[r] Johnson sat at home
by me, & we criticized & talked & were happy in one
another—he in huffing me, & I in being huff'd.

27 Oct[r] continued

---

[1] Sir Henry Gough, afterwards Gough-Calthorpe. On June 16,
1796, he was created Baron Calthorpe of Calthorpe, co. Norfolk.

[2] Was this Henry Keene, the well-known Oxford architect?

[3] caught *crossed through.*

[4] Oct. 27; see above, p. 141.

[5] " D'une enseigne parisienne, *Au petit Dunkerque*, la ville de
Dunkerque étant rénommée pour la fabrication des bibelots en
ivoire."—Hatzfeld et Darmesteter, *Dictionnaire général de la langue
française.*

29 Oct[1]   This day I took final leave of my amiable
              Nuns at the Fossée.   Miss Canning promised
me her Correspondence, & thanked me a thousand
Times for my little present of Books—I had sent her
the Rambler—& Mrs Fermor the Rasselas; I kissed
['em] through the Wicket, and wished them most sincerely well.   Miss Fitzherbert has promised to send me
a Pair of Ruffles to take Care of for her Mama—I shall
be glad to see something from the House.   From hence
I waited on Madame de Barbançon[2] who lives on the
outside of their Convent while She is in Paris but is
grated up with prodigious Care—though I have myself
met her in her Equipage driving along the Streets of
Paris, & She has even left her Cards at this very Hotel,
for Mrs Strickland and me.   She is an agreeable Woman,
& I like her as well as when I saw her at Rouen : She
cannot write a Note however, for such a performance
sure was never seen as her Card of Compliments &c.
 Today I saw a Procession in the Church of S[t] Sulpice
—Priests, richly clothed in splendid Dresses, walked on
each Side a Banner of Red Velvet on which was
embroidered the resemblance of a Chalice filled with
Wine & crowned with the Glory.   Presently came the
Crucifix richly gilt & adorned with Jewels—then Priests
again—singing the Songs of Adoration, & some Men
playing on a Horn—after these four Reverend old
Priests bore a rich Red Velvet Canopy most beautifully
embroidered with Gold, over a curious Shrine in which
was kept the Sacrament of Bread[3] appearing through
the Glass Case in which it was contained—the Glory
round the Glass was all of Diamonds and the foot[4]

---

[1] Oct. 28 ; see above, p. 141.   [2] See above, p. 122.
[3] which *crossed through.*
[4] proportionably adorn *crossed through.*

ornamented in proportion to the rest of the Magnificence.
The Monks who followed were in a prodigious Number
—I counted till they came to 70, & then left off. They
walked three times round the Church stopping at every
4th: Altar when the Host was elevated & all the people
in the Church fell on their Knees except my Man Sam ;
whose Protestant Spirit boyling, he ran behind the door
to avoid the necessity of joyning in this Act of Worship.

29 Octr
continued
For my part I esteemed the Fellow though I
had no Intention to imitate him—they stopt
the Procession where I stood, & all those
who walked before the Sacrament turning back &
prostrating themselves before it—while every body
seemed to feel the Impulse of Devotion, I knelt down
too, & with my whole Heart repeated the Collect for
the *tenth* Sunday after Trinity.[1] So much for this Day
Adventures : We finished it at home, which did not
please Mrs Strickland—but as I have done nothing yet
since I came here purposely to please myself, I did venture to steal this one Afternoon to nurse Niggey's Cold—
as for my own I see it will plague me for a Week at least
—so I give it up.

30 Octr [2] I went again to St Sulpice where there
was another Procession of attendants upon
the Crucifix only—The Crucifix was not so rich a one
as that they carried Yesterday nor the Number of Priests
so considerable. From hence we drove to the Chapel
of the Invalides [3] which exceeds every thing for Beauty,

---

[1] " Let thy merciful ears, O Lord, be open to the prayers of
thy humble Servants ; and that they may obtain their petition make
them to ask such things as shall please thee."
[2] Oct. 29 ; see above, p. 141.
[3] Cole describes this at length, *Paris Journal*, pp. 147-151.

Taste & Elegance that has been shewn me in this great Town. We spent our Evening with Madame Bocages who heaped us with Favours & gave us each a Bouquet of Flowers, which She had herself brought from Verona. We were treated with Tea there, & when the old Lady found the Pot did not pour She very composedly bid her Footman blow in the Spout; which he was about to do but Mᵣˢ Strickland prevented him: Madame de Bocages however—jealous of the honour of her Tea Pot would examine into the Cause of its not pouring [1] —& finding somewhat in effect stick fast in the Spout She put the End into her Mouth & blew it away. Ah ça! cries She immediately, if this had been done sooner —the Pot would have pour'd fast enough You see.[2] This Evening Mᵣˢ Strickland & I parted; She goes home to her little Girl; Convent of poor Claires at Rouen tomorrow, & I set out with my Horses heads towards home on Wednesday next. We have I hope & believe been of mutual Use & Pleasure to each other. I have through her means made a more rational Figure where I have been, not staring about as I should have done a lone Woman with two or three Men about me, & She has seen many Places of publick Resort, in which She seems to have very great Joy; especially when She can get some Gentleman of Rank to attend her which with us She has seldom wanted. We have been long acquainted, but never lived much together till now, I think myself therefore particularly fortunate that She has proved as agreeable to all my Friends & to my Husband as to me—I should not absolutely have known what to have done without her, & my three Gentlemen are at

---

[1] Two or three indecipherable words *crossed through*.
[2] See below, p. 232.

last as sorry to part with her as I am.—Even Queeney loves her, & is grieved that She has left us.

31 Oct [1]   Here am I left alone as it were now I have
            lost my Companion whom I shall miss most grievously : I must think a moment how [I] shall contrive to amuse myself. Well! Queeney & I took a Run in the Luxembourg Gardens, a Turn through the Palais Marchand and a long Look at the Orleans Collection of Pictures wch delight me only more & more : I half cryed over some of them with mere delight—if ever was true Sublime seen—surely here it is [to be] found. Excellence of various kinds, & nothing but Excellence fills my heart with rapture ; one View of one Room in this House is [well] worth crossing the Seas for.—The Evening was spent at home.

31 Oct^r   [Here is some mistake in the date, for I
            hear *this* is the 31st of Oct^r *only*, I thought it was the 1st of Novr but on the 1st Novr it seems, we shall leave Paris.] I passed the Morning in the same Place—the Palais Royale, & took my leave of the Orleans Collection of Pictures perhaps—& most probably—for ever. I therefore staid among them three Hours & was treated with the Sight of many that are never shewn to common Observers—particularly those in the Bed-Chamber of the Duke of Chartres, who selected half a Dozen which he wish'd to open his Eyes on in a Morning ; among these was a Landskip by Rubens over his Chimney which for a Moment effaced that of Carracci from my Memory : the Judgment of Paris only filled the Scenery, but the Paysage was the principal part of the Picture—& such a Paysage ! I

[1] Oct. 30, see above, p. 141.

never saw anything to equal : Queeney made me observe
a mighty pleasing Incident in it ; Juno's Peacock pecking
the Leg of Paris for not bestowing the Apple on his
Mistress.[1]   A Mars & Venus by Titian,[2] a holy Family
by Corregio, a Landschape with Nymphs by Titian, a

31 Oct   Virgin & Child by Raphael, and a beautiful
            Portrait of a Woman full length by Titian
or Tintoret.

When we returned home to Dinner we had our
Friend Le Roy to dine with us, & that Mr Swale [3] who
has taken such a fancy to us.   The Gentlemen are gone
to the Opera & [I] sent Moll to see the Shew.   The
Streets of Paris are very entertaining to drive through ;
I had a long Prance over them this Morning—Coxcombs,
Religious Habits, Wenches with Umbrellas, Workmen
with Muffs, fine Fellows cover'd with Lace, & Old Men
with Woollen Wigs make a Contrast & Variety incon-

31 Oct   ceivable to a Londoner, who thinks all
            Monks & Nuns are shut up in Convents—
& have (sic) No Idea of a Sawyer working thro' a Block
of Marble with his Muff and Snuff Box lying by him &
his Dog to guard them.   Dogs indeed live very happily
here as it should seem—every body appears to me to
keep a Dog, & the smallest are in the highest Estimation

[1] This was acquired by Lord Kinnaird for 2000 guineas, and
afterwards, in 1824, was in the possession of I. Penrice, Esq., of
Great Yarmouth.   It is now in the National Gallery.

[2] Now in the Fitzwilliam Museum, Cambridge.   It is described
in the Catalogue as *A Gentleman playing the Guitar to His Mistress.*
For this and the other pictures in the Orleans collection, see also
Waagen, *Art Treasures of Great Britain*, vol. iii., pp. 485-503.

[3] Possibly one of the Swales of Swaledale, the old Yorkshire
family.   After Thrale's death Mrs. Thrale, writing to Fanny
Burney, describes a letter from Count Swale offering her marriage
(see Sotheby's *Sale Catalogue*, for May 5, 1930, lot 200).

—'Tis comical enough to see the gravest looking Gentlemen airing their Lapdogs in the Tuilleries or Luxembourg Gardens in a Morning, holding them for the most part in a little Red String for fear they should run away —I no longer think my Attention to Queeney so ridiculous. Horses however are as ill used with them as with us ; they strike 'em over the face & treat them with odious Cruelty—I hate the Embarras of Paris for that Reason more than the danger—Their Coachmen however are sufficiently dextrous. The lighting up of the Streets with a Lanthorn hung in the middle by a String is very despicable, & they themselves are ashamed on't.

1 Nov^r   We left Paris—where we have spent a Month of extreme Expence, some Pleasure & some Profit ; for we [have]¹ seen many People & many Things ; & Queeney has picked up a little French & a good deal of Dancing. The *Things* which struck me most in Paris are, the Chapel of the Invalides, the House of Monsr de St Julien, the Disposition of the Altars in St Roque's Church, & the Pictures at the Palais Royal. The *People* who have pleased me best were I think all Foreigners except old Monsr Le Roy the Mechanist & his Brother who has travelled into Greece, Asia &c. & is a pleasing Man enough, & vastly friendly with his Brother of whose Machines he seems very proud & very confident. They appear to intend trying their Fortune in England soon & applying to Parliament for the Reward appointed to those who discover the Longitude. We arrived in good Time at S^t. Denys where we cou'd not see the Treasure because it was a Holy-Day.

¹ *Not in MS.*

2 Nov[r]   We have now seen the Treasures of S[t]
            Denys [1] which appear to be very consider-
able.   The Altar is enriched with various precious
Stones, & round the Mitre of S[t] Hilaire are the finest
Pearls I think I ever saw.   An Antique Cup cut in Agate
struck me as eminently curious, & there was an Amethyst
in the Centre of a Cross of a wonderful Size ; We were
likewise shewn a very magnificent Ruby, & the Model
of Pitt's Diamond. [2]   The Buildings at S[t] Denys are
elegant, the Church, where the Treasures are, is adorned
with mighty beautiful Windows, & the Chapel belonging
to the Nuns' convent where Madame Louise, [3] Aunt to
the King of France, [is] retired—seems a very pleasing
Building—it was late last Night when we looked at it,
& heard the Nuns sing in the Choir.   In the Course of
the Day we drove forward to Chantilly [4] which exceeds
in Taste & Elegance all I have seen in France.   There is
the most beautiful Water in the most lavish Abundance
so that they are obliged to make something resembling
natural Cascades & Rivers to get rid of it besides seven

2 Nov.   Jet D'Eaus constantly playing in sight of
contind   the Windows, & large Canals with sharp
            Angles edged with Marble which however
are very Magnificent in their Way.   Here is a little
Village too on an Island that I fancy delights them much,
they think it in the English Style which is much prized

[1] They are described in Michel Félibien, *Histoire de l'Abbaye
Royale de St. Denys.*

[2] The diamond acquired in India by Thomas Pitt, an East India
merchant, and sold in 1717 to Philip, Duke of Orleans.

[3] Madame Louise Marie, the youngest daughter of Louis XV.,
was a Carmelite nun.   She was frequently involved in the political
intrigues of her father's reign.

[4] Here was the magnificent residence of Louis-Joseph de
Bourbon, Prince de Condé.

among them. Here is a Playhouse decorated with much Pomp & Stables of a Magnitude I had never seen before : a Kennel of 300 English Hounds & a Menagerie not valuable for the Rareties it contains, but for the Splendor & Convenience in which the Animals appear to live : the golden Vulture however had his Feet [1] broken off by the Frost.

2 Nov[r] continued   The Apartments within were extremely gay and rich, and their Summer houses, Dairy, &c. were all in proportion : upon the whole this is the most pleasing Mansion I have seen upon the Continent—& the Masters princely Conduct inclines one to be pleased with all that belongs to him.[2]

Anecdotes of the Prince of Condé.

His Gardener told us that when any Foreigners of the least distinction came hither during the Months of his Residence they were always invited to the Prince's Table, & I heard that some English Gentleman—Member of the House of Commons—coming to Chantilly too late to see a Play which he had hoped for, the Prince of Condé immediately ordered a new Representation that his Curiosity might be satisfyed. This is that Prince of Condé who having given 50 Louis D'Ors to his Son for Pocket Money during his Absence when the Boy was Nine Years old, at his return the Child produced them, saying, Papa, here is all your Money safe still.—Papa however, taking him gravely to the Window, threw the Money into the Street, saying to his Son—If you have neither Virtue to give away your Money, my Boy, nor Spirit to spend it ; always *do this*, that the Poor may at least have a *chance* for it.

---

[1] legs *crossed through*.   [2] See below, p. 196.

3 Nov^r   We left Chantilly—& after I have forgotten how many Posts arrived at Noyonne [1] where we saw a beautiful Church with the high Altar very curiously adorned: a Palm Tree all of Chas'd Silver spread its Boughs over the Tabernacle on which in the same Metal lay the Lamb of the Apocalypse: two Silver Angels hovering over him, & a third at the Top of the Tree seeming to hang out a very well enchased frame made something like a Lanthorn & inclosing a golden Chalice full of the Wine for the Sacrament—This Device was new to me at Noyonne. The Bishops Seat opposite the high Altar was ornamented by a fine Representation of the Virgin's Assumption in white Marble—the Church is called Notre Dame. Our Beds were good & our Lodging comfortable; Mr Thrale says the common People are hideously ugly & so they are: We set out in the Morning on the 4th for Cambray before it was Light so I remember but little of the Town—I rather think it was a bad one.—

4 Nov^r   brought us to Cambray as we wished before the Gates were shut. It seems a beautiful Town, the Streets spacious & populous—& the Buildings—I mean the public ones—promise by their external Appearance no small Entertainment. We are now returned to Flanders, & find all the Women wrapped in their long pieces of black Cloth again which they call [. . .] [2] The Beggars are still more numerous than in france, and the Butcher's Meat more plentiful— We have changed our soft Beds for clean ones that are

---

[1] The Cathedral at Noyon which was begun in the twelfth century, is, of course, one of the finest buildings in France of the Transition style.

[2] Name omitted.

much harder, & have lost the hexagonal Bricks & got
plain square ones—I mean [in] the Bed Chambers, for
here we have a decent Parlour as in England & floored
too, tho' not with inlaid Floors like the French, & we
have no Beds in our eating Room nor no Maid coming in
to turn it down whilst we are at Supper ; here are paper
Hangings too to my Chamber & a Blue & White Check
Bed, & it all looks much nearer home than France does,
[add to this that] [1] here is a Lock to the Door bearing
a distant resemblance to an English one, 'tis the 1st
I have seen since I left home.   I had forgot the Fryar
& the Nun ; they are grown so familiar to
me, but the Truth is Dr. Johnson had a
Letter from Father Prior at Paris to the
Confessor of the English Benedictine Nuns at Cambray.
We went to the Convent of Course, chatted with the
Lady at the Grate—She was a Sheldon [2] of Winchester
—& got Acquainted with the Confessor who came to
keep us Company at & after Supper at our Inn.   He
was a Mr Welch [3] from Westmorland & knew Mrs

4 Novr
continued

[1] *crossed through.*

[2] Dame Elizabeth Frances Sheldon (1720-1808), daughter of
William Sheldon, Esq., of the Manor of Lower Ditchford, co.
Warwick, and of the city of Winchester.   Her father's first wife,
Catherine, was the mother of two nuns, Catherine (died 1723), and
Mary (died 1756).   Dame Elizabeth was professed in 1740.   She
was imprisoned with the other nuns at the Revolution, and on being
released went to Woolton.   She died at Salford Hall.   Catholic
Record Society *Miscellanea*, VIII. ; *Records of the English Benedictine
Nuns at Cambrai (now Stanbrook), 1620-1793.* p. 14.

[3] Father Welch, or Welsh, " ended his life with the Nuns at
Cambray " on Aug. 20, 1790 (*ibid.*, p. 29).   When Cole was in
Paris in 1765 he was asked to dine with a Father Welch, the Prior of
the convent of English Benedictines.   Of the Prior he says : " He
was about the Age of 40, an handsome black Man, with a fresh
Colour, & 6 Foot high, & was just come to reside here, from a

Strickland's Name & Family full well as all the Roman Catholicks do. This Father Welch is a Man eminently handsome, but by some strange Chance, I have never yet seen an ill looking Man in a Religious Habit; I mean only Monks & Fryars—the Regular Priests, Abbés, &c. are poor Figures enough for the most part. Whether the Religious Habits are particularly becoming, or whether all the handsome Fellows take a fancy to put them on I know not—but from the Capucin at Calais to the Benedictine at Cambray I have seen none that did not give me Pleasure to look at them.

5 Nov[r] We quitted Cambray, but not till we had seen every thing that was recommended to our Inspection; the Cathedral here is very magnificent in its Ornaments, & the Face upon the Napkin is finer than I ever saw one done. We saw Fenelon's Monument [1] & Fenelon's Picture and Vestments for the Priests which exceeded in Dignity & Splendour all I had been shewn of that kind before. In the Church belonging to a Benedictine Convent we were entertained with a Sight of some curious deceptions by Gerard of Antwerp,[2] who has made such Imitations of Sculpture [as are] not to be discerned at two Yards distance from Alto Relievo; though I was prepared to expect them I could not believe it was them I was expecting; & one

Gentleman's Family in Cumberland, after an Absence of 13 years, when, he told me, he found the French People much altered both in their Religion & Morals. He shewed me his Apartments, up one Pair of Stairs, out of their Cloyster & near the Church, which were neat, small & convenient."—*Paris Journal*, p. 284.

[1] François de Salignac de la Mothe de Fénelon, Archbishop of Cambrai, 1651-1715.

[2] Martin Joseph Geeraerts, 1707-91, was born at Antwerp, and was distinguished for his grisaille painting, in imitation of bas-reliefs.

of our Servants refused Conviction till he had touched
them with the end of his Whip. I suppose they are
the most perfect Things of this kind in the World—
no description can do them Justice.

6 Novr We came last night in very good Time to
Douay, where the Prior at Paris had given
Mr Johnson another Letter to the Convent of English
Benedictines ; [1] he carried his Letter last Night & gave
me a very pleasing Account of the Monk to whom it
was directed. Here is an Inn without ever a Maid in
it ; the Waiter turns down the Beds, & does all other
Offices of a Chamber—but we do not eat in [our] Bed Room.
Mr Thrale & Molly say that the Gentlemen in this Town
walk about in Pattens, but as my Windows do not look
into the Streets I have not seen any—they use Para-
pluyes [as] at Paris. This Morning we went to Saint
Peters Church in the Town. It is of modern Architecture
elegant enough & expensively adorned. On the high
Altar stand two Arms cased in Silver with each a wooden
Hand to't—one is said to be St Sebastian's, the other
Saint George's, the Busts of these Saints in Silver stand
by them. The Parliament of Douay [2] came to hear
high Mass while we were examining the Church so we
had an Opportunity of seeing them & hearing the
Musick which consisted of a good Orchestra in the
Choir of Fiddles, Bassoons &c. What most shocked
me was that while every one else was paying the

---

[1] Cole describes a visit to the convent in 1765. *Paris Journal*,
pp. 18-20, 23-24.

[2] The Parliament of Flanders was transferred in 1714 by Louis
XIV. from Cambrai to Douai. In 1771 it received official notifica-
tion of its suppression, in place of a simple Council, but it was
reconstituted the following year and survived until the Revolution.

most profound Respect to the Sacrament & bowing to
the Altar where it stood—the Soldiers came
6 Novr strutting in with their Hats on in their Attendance upon the Parliament.   In the Afternoon we came to
Lisle [1] which is called le petit Paris.   Queeney had a
pain in her Stomach this Morning & Sam was Ill in
the same way this Afternoon ; I gave her some Rhubarb
& him some Ipecacuanha, & expect every body will
be well tomorrow.   Here are Rooms floored as in
England & washed too.   I have never seen a Mop till
today since I crossed the Channel.   The Chamber I
sleep in is a spacious one, & was sweet enough when
I chose it, but such a Stink was got into it at night as
I never smelt a worse but at Llanhriadr.[2]

6 Novr This Morning Mr Johnson had a mind to
continued   dispute with me concerning the High Mass
            we saw celebrating at Douay & whether
we might or might not have staid through the whole
Ceremony & seen the Elevation of the Host.   If you
had staid, says Baretti, you must have kneel'd.   I have
no Scruples, said I, I was willing enough to kneel.
Johnson said he would not have knelt on such an [3]
Occasion for the whole City of Douay.   I was not in
a humour to argue at that Moment, & besides I felt
a Fear lest his force of Reasoning might destroy my
Quiet, for I have kneeled two or three Times or more
at the Elevation since I have been upon the Continent
& am firmly perswaded that in so doing I was not dis-

---

[1] Lille.

[2] Johnson and the Thrales stopped at Dr. Worthington's house
at Llanrhaiadhr on the night of Sept. 8, 1774.   See A. M. Broadley's
Dr. Johnson and Mrs. Thrale, p. 247.

[3] *MS.* on.

pleasing to God; for those y^t: do *not* believe the real Presence of Christ in the Sacrament—think it highly proper to respect the Elements consecrated to represent his Death & Passion—are perfectly willing to fall on their Knees when a Publick Exhibition of them is made to People who thinking it the very Body of their Saviour adore in silence that God who sent his only begotten Son to redeem them. This Spirit is surely very different from [that wch prompts a man to the] doing it as a public Profession of his Faith in a Point which he does not believe, & [that too] for the sake of obtaining any temporal Riches or Honours: Such a Sin against the Allseer who knows our Hearts ought to be avoided doubtless even by the Endurance of Martyrdom, & such a one I hope I should not commit for the City of Douay nor for the whole World itself. However the Romanists make no public Profession of

6 Novr continued — their Belief in the real Presence at the Time the Host is elevated, neither do they kneel down themselves as an Act of Faith, but merely as an Act of Reverence: & when the Crucifix was carried round the Church in Procession at St Sulpice in Paris on the last of October—(I was there) every body, & me among the rest, fell on our Knees, though I suppose the simplest Beggar in the Place had more Wit [than] to imagine that Silver Image the Body of our blessed Saviour. Be this as it will—the Church of Rome does apparently and positively believe the Transubstantiation, & every days Service which is supposed Obligatory is the Ceremony of seeing the Priest repeat a very few Latin Prayers in a very low Voice preparatory to receiving the Sacrament which he does in both Kinds himself, many washings of the Hands &c. intervening to fill up the Time, & then elevates

the Host in presence of all the People who fall down on their Knees or Faces at the call of a little Bell which rings that no one in the Church may fail to know the Ceremony performing at that Altar & pay their Adorations accordingly.

7 Nov^r   We took a Fiacre for the Streets were dirty, & drove about the Town of Lisle to look for Entertainment—Our Fiacre was lin'd with Cafoy [1] & the Top laced with a very fresh good Gold Lace, but the Horses drew us by Ropes & Yoaks of the coursest kind covered with Sheepskin. There is in this City a Fashion I never saw before of Dogs drawing Carts with light Loads proportioned to their Strength. We were shewn the Magazine of Corn, a Building of great Capacity—I saw nothing in it but some Rice in one Corner. Mr Thrale indeed is always censuring their little Skill in Agriculture & says their Ground would produce vast increase if they knew how to make the full use of it. I am inclined to think their frequent Holydays may impede Labour very much—as for the Sabbath, I am sure they are [but] too willing to give that up to every sort of Business & of Pleasure. M^r Le Liever, Queeney's Dancing Master [at Paris] offered to attend her on Sunday Mornings, but upon All Saints Day his Scruples boyl'd amazingly.

We saw one very shewy Church where [there are] [2] these Pictures of the Souls in purgatory & a Money Box under the pictures with this Inscription :

7 Nov^r   Tronc pour les Ames
continued   qui sont en la purgatoire.

---

[1] " Some kind of fabric, imported in the 18th c."—O.E.D.
[2] *Not in MS.*

likewise an Image of the Virgin dressed up by some zealous Votary in a very fine gown studded with Stars & this Motto

> Je vous salue
> Brillante Aurore
> Etoile de la Mer.

The Virgin has another Statue in this Church with a Blue & Silver Gown on, & a large dress'd Hoop. Her Crown & Sceptre are of solid Silver, & the devotion most in fashion hereabouts is giving little Silver Hearts to any favourite Saint—some are quite hung round with them, & now & then a Silver Eye when the Votary has rec^d his Sight by Application to that Saint, or an Ear, if his hearing was restored to him any how uncommonly.[1] Mr Thrale says the Superstition of the

---

[1] More than two years later Mrs. Piozzi made the following entry in *Thraliana* : " When I myself was at Lille in Flanders in the year 1775 I walked with Mr. Johnson and Mr. Thrale round the great Church there, and in one of the Chapels I observed myself to stumble in an odd manner so as to give me uncommon Pain, and at the same time to excite strange ideas of Terror wholly unaccountable to me, who am neither timorous nor over delicate : I looked at the Altar-piece and saw it was the figure of an Angel protecting a boy about twelve years old, as it should seem, and somehow the child struck me with a Resemblance to my own, and alarmed me in an unusual manner. I prayed for the safety of my young ones and as I came out of the Chapel I asked an old Man to *whom* that Chapel was dedicated—he replied—to the Guardian Angel of children. I resolved to walk round the Church and go into every Chapel in it to see if I should stumble in them, I could not stumble, however, but when I returned with better spirits to the Children's Chapel I stumbled again and even hurt myself. The Impression it made alarmed me and as I could not rid myself of the uneasiness it caused, I told Mr. Johnson in the afternoon when Hester was gone to the play with her Papa : he bid me be careful not to encourage such Fancies and talking the thing through cleared my Head of it for a

Romish Church runs much higher in the Queens Dominions, & in every part of Flanders, than it does in France. To morrow we leave Lisle where we have seen some Appearance of Commerce, and nearer Approaches to London Manners than any where else; but they *will* grate their Windows.

8 Nov^r [I rose at 4 o'clock unnecessarily.] [1]

We reached Dunkerque by Dinner Time having missed the fine Prospect from Mount Cassell the Weather being grown coarse & rainy ; I had however great Pleasure in the Landlady, who having been bred at an English Convent spoke our Language quite readily. What has taken most of my Attention on this day's Journey is the new Phenomenon of Flemish Words written under the Signs, & the Peasants when one speaks French to 'em not understanding a word one says. This looks like being fairly in another Nation, & this gives me some Idea of the abrupt Changes which must be perpetually happening on the Continent when the

Time, soon after our return from abroad, however, I was dreadfully alarmed by my son's sudden Illness and Death, and though he continued ill but three Hours, this old Superstition haunted me all the while, the more perhaps as I had two days before, going down to dinner with Company, when he was perfectly well at School, heard something like a preternatural Voice (that of his Guardian Angel perhaps) call me by my name, but this I never mentioned to anyone, lest I should be suspected of Madness. But Mad I am not. I have the best health in the world, no Indigestion, no Headaches, no Vapours : no Change of Weather affects me, nor did even the loss of my only Son lay strong hold on my Heart as it was utterly impossible to avoid. My mind is an active whirligig mind, which few things can stop to disturb, and if disturbed it soon recovers its strength and its Activity."—Charles Hughes, *Mrs. Piozzi's Thraliana* (London, 1913), pp. 23-25.

[1] *In the margin of MS.*

Barrier of any Dominion is passed, & that of another Prince begins; & of this Sensation going merely to France gives one no Specimen, for when the Seas are crossed something new is expected—but while the Carriage drives on through a Country in appearance the same, to find Language changing suddenly—& in some sort Dress—gives the Mind another turn & is consequently pleasing. At Dunkerque Captain Fraser [1] waited on us very civilly (and) [2] desired us to dine tomorrow with his Lady & spend a Day in seeing the Fortifications & other Curiosities of the place: I was glad Mr Thrale promised to accept his Civilities—his Wife's Father & Mother [3] are my Neighbours at Stretham & they will be pleased to hear good News of their Daughter when I come home. The Captain says it is a horrible Road from hence to Calais, so there is another Reason to be glad of some breath first, especially as my Servant Sam is ill, & will by this means get rest before he has Difficulties to encounter.

8 Novr continued

[1] Andrew Frazer, afterwards lieutenant-colonel of engineers. In 1763 he was sent out as assistant to Colonel Desmaretz, the British commissary appointed to watch the demolition of the fortifications of Dunkirk in fulfilment of treaty obligations. In 1767 he succeeded Desmaretz, and remained in Dunkirk until 1778. In the British Museum are two of Frazer's reports: " A Description of Dunkirk," 1769 (*Add. MS.* 16593), and the " Report and Plans of Dunkirk," 1772 (*Add. MS.* 17779). There is among the MSS. of the *Chefferie* of Dunkirk a " Description historique et abregée de Dunkerque, depuis son origine en 646, jusqu'en l'année 1769, par monsieur Frazer, commissaire anglais." See also *D.N.B.*

[2] *Not in MS.*

[3] In 1773 Frazer had married Charlotte, daughter of Stillingfleet Durnford of the engineering department, and a granddaughter of Colonel Desmaretz.

9 Nov^r   Captain Fraser called on us at our Inn, breakfasted, & went with us to see the demolition of the Works : He seems a very intelligent Man, & appears to have collected all the Plans, Treaties, &c., which have any reference to his Business here ; he shewed us the torn Materials of which the Fortifications were once composed, & related an affecting Anecdote concerning the Man who erected them, & died with Grief at the Sight of the State they are now reduced to. He told us too of some odd Fellow I forget the Name—who wishing literally to trample upon France, sent for two of [the] Stones that had served [to] form Batteries here, & laid them at the Door of His House [in England] that he might tread on them every Time he went out or in. We dined with the Captain & Mrs Fraser, who made herself perfectly agreeable to me by her Civility & Attention—every day shews that Goodhumour will do without anything else ; & that everything else will not do without Goodhumour. I went with Mrs Fraser to a Convent of very pleasing Nuns ; Benedictines, English Women—the Lady Abbess Sr Harry Ingoldfield's [1] Daughter : they are 23 in Number, practise no Severities, go to Bed at 10 o'Clock & rise at 6—their Forehead Cloth is likewise put on

9 Nov^r   in a Manner more becoming than that of any Set of Religious I have yet seen. The Abbess is called Lady & Ladyship & wears a Gold Cross like Madame de Barbançon. I forgot to ask, but I fancy 'tis a Royal Abbaye [2]   What struck me as another

---

[1] Sir Henry Englefield, 6th baronet, of White Knights, Berkshire. He had two daughters, Ethelinda-Catherine and Teresa-Anne, who in 1782 married Francis Cholmeley, Esq., of Brandsby.

[2] This was a foundation made from Ghent in 1662, when Dunkirk was an English possession. Charles II. not only approved

Peculiarity was the Prioress— Mrs Berkely [1]—telling me that they said their Mattins of an Evening the last thing they did *to get them over.* There was a Mrs Sheldon here—related—but not Sister I think to the Nun I saw at Cambray—she is a Cousin of Mrs Strickland's, so we did not want for C^l at. I bought some Trifles of 'em, & they told me there was in this Town a Convent containing above forty poor Claires—Englishwomen among whom is another Mrs Vavasor—I was thinking all the Women of that Family were resolved upon Misery—there are two among my poor wretched Friends the Claires at Rouen ; but there is need enough of all their Prayers for their Nephew, Sr Walter,[2] who I am told is giving away his Property to some fine Strumpet at Paris as fast as he can.

9 Nov^r   How all these English Convents are sup-
continued ported is to me astonishing. I can now
            reckon ten of my own Knowledge for
Women only. Mrs Fraser entertained us with the greatest Kindness, & did all in her power to make the place agreeable to us ; it has been upon the whole a Day of no small Information or Amusement, perpetual Rain teized us a little in our Walks upon the Quay but we saw every thing at last. There was some French Company at the Captain's in the Afternoon to Tea & Cards, who seemed much diverted with the odd Appearance

of the foundation, but contributed generally toward the early expenses. After the Revolution the nuns first found a home at Hammersmith, and in 1863 moved to St. Scolastica's Abbey at Teignmouth in Devonshire.

1 Probably one of the Berkeleys of Spetchley, co. Worcester.

2 Sir Walter Vavasor, 6th baronet, of Haslewood, had succeeded to the title on April 13, 1766. He married in 1797 Jane, only daughter and heiress of William Langdale, Esq., of Langthorp.

of Johnson's Wig [1] & Queeney's Cap and refrained from laughing out with the greatest Difficulty—I have this Evening understood that Mrs Masterman was bred up at the Convent of English Dominican Nuns at Calais where I had so much Chat with the Superior, and where I intend to have more tomorrow or next Day when I get to Dessein's. The Road is said to be bad but we have been so often frighted with false *formidabilities* that I begin to laugh at them *now* as Mr Johnson has done all this while. Custom House Officers indeed I have a dread of yet, though a three Livre piece has hitherto silenced the most sullen, but at Dover we are threatened with sad brutal Fellows—Nous verrons.

10 Nov^r   Brought us safe to Calais; M^r & Mrs Fraser took a friendly leave of us early in the Morning at Dunkerque, and dismissed us in the kindest Manner—We stopt at Gravelines, where there is nothing curious to be seen but a Convent of Claires from which my Friends at Rouen are a Colony. We did not however try to see them. I knew it would be difficult if not impracticable: The Road was bad enough, but it served to carry [us] safe to Dessein's, & poor Sam seems happy that he is at least within Sight of England. I hope we shall be able to get him over tomorrow. Our Friend the Capuchin [2] is gone into the Country, but sent us his Respects by an agreeable Brother who brought Queeney a little Present of a Pincushion & entertained us with [a] good deal of

---

[1] Of Johnson's wigs Boswell writes: " His wigs, too, were much better; and during these travels in France, he was furnished with a Paris-made wig, of handsome construction."—*Life of Johnson*, vol. iii., p. 325.

[2] See above, p. 71.

Chat.   He would drink no Wine, & said he was not to taste any on Frydays & Saturdays from All Saints to Xmas, nor to eat Meat except on Sundays till Xmas Day.

Here I had the Mortification to find the things I sent by the Diligence cruelly mangled by injudicious Management [in the Carriage] & that fretted me.

11 Nov.   We returned to Dover with Captain Baxter, who was much disturbed by Fears lest we should lose the Tide & be obliged to sleep on Shipboard or hazard some chance—I never knew what—by coming on Shore in a Boat.   However we saved our Tide as the phrase is by 4 Minutes only, & all was to our wish. Queeney & Moll were Seasick again indeed but it will do them no harm.   [Sam: was too ill to be Seasick.] [1] The Weather was not good, but I kept the Deck from 12 at noon to near 6 at Night.—I have at last brought my Niggey safe home again to England—which I shall now love on more rational Grounds than ever I did yet—I see now that it is better than France.   I had this Morning a long Talk with a Dominican Nun at Calais—not M.rs Gray whom [2] I saw before—She has been [ill] ever since it seems & is not likely to live, but I picked up some Anecdotes of M.rs Masterman which I was very desirous of, from another Nun of the Name of Dale, an agreeable conversible Woman.

My Adventures are now at an End & so shall be my Journal

finished at Dover
Saturday—11.th: Nov.r 1775.

[1] *In the margin.*   [2] *MS.* who.

The only thing I saw which ought to have been mentioned, but was forgotten, is Compiegne ;[1] a Palace of the King of France which we stopt at between Chantilly & Noyonne ; it is uninhabited, & not very grand, but I have a Notion it is old—for one of the Cielings is like that in the best Parlor at Bachygraig[2] only ours is gilt. The Pictures of Martin Luther & John Calvin in the presence Chamber were what struck me most at Compiegne.

> The Things, we know, are neither rich nor rare
> But wonder how the D——l they got there.[3]

---

[1] Compiègne had always been a favourite residence of the Kings of France, but the present palace was built by Gabriel for Louis XV. on the site of a château of Charles V. The palace contained a small art gallery. It appears that Compiègne was the scene of a disagreement between Johnson and Mrs. Thrale (see below, p. 228).

[2] The ancestral home of Mrs. Thrale's family.

[3] Pope, Epistle to Dr. Arbuthnot, being the Prologue to the Satires, ll. 171-172.

DR. JOHNSON'S
FRENCH JOURNAL
1775

NOTE

Dr. Johnson must have had at least three note-books containing minutes of his French journey, of which only one appears to have survived. This small paper-book fell into the hands of Boswell, who printed the notes in his *Life of Johnson*. It is entitled "France 2" on the leather cover, and Johnson's observations cover the period from Oct. 10 to Nov. 5, 1775. The book consists of 17 leaves, the pages of text being numbered 1 to 29. There is the following note of Malone's inside the cover: "Delivered to Mr. Boswell by desire of Dr. Scott, July 21st 1787. Edmond Malone." William Scott, later Lord Stowell, was one of Johnson's executors. A later note adds: "Presented to the British Museum by the daughters of the late William Sharpe of 1 Highbury Terrace, from the collection of Samuel Rogers, the poet, their great uncle." The book is now "British Museum Additional MS. 35299."

DR. SAMUEL JOHNSON

From the Engraving by T. Cook, after the painting of Sir Joshua Reynolds

Oct. 10.   We saw the *Ecole Militaire*, in which 150
Tu.   young boys are educated for the army.
           They have arms of different sizes according
to the age; flints of wood.   The building is very large,
but nothing fine except the council room.   The French
have large squares in the windows; they [1] make good
iron palisades.   Their meals are gross.

We visited the observatory,[2] a large building of a
great height.   The upper stones of the parapet very
large, but not cramped with iron.   The flat on the top
is very extensive, but on the Insulated part, there is no
parapet.   Though it was broad enough, I did not care
to go upon it.   Maps were printing in one of the rooms.

We walked to a small convent of the Fathers of the
Oratory.   In the reading desk of the refectory lay the
lives of the Saints.

Oct. 11.   We went to see *Hôtel de Chatelet*,[3] a house
Wed.   not very large, but very elegant.   One of
           the rooms was gilt to a degree that I never
saw before.   The upper part for servants and their
Masters was pretty.

Thence we went to Mr Monville's, a House divided
into small apartments, furnished with effeminate and
minute elegance.—Porphyry.

---

[1] *MS.* the.   [2] infirmary *crossed through.*

[3] The hotel of the Duc de Châtelet.   Boswell, in error, wrote
" Chatlois."

The(nce) we went to S* Roque's Church, which is very large, the lower part of the pillars incrusted with marble. Three Chapels behind the high Altar. The last a mass of low arches. Altars, I believe all round.

We passed through *Place de Vendôme*, a fine square, about as big as Hanover Square, inhabited by the high Families. Lewis XIV, on horseback in the middle.

Monville is the son of a Farmer general. In the house of Chatelet is (a) room furnished with Japan, fitted up in Europe.

We dined with Bocage,[1] the Marquis Blanchetti, and his Lady—The sweetmeats taken by the Marchioness Blanchetti, after observing that they were dear. Mr. Le Roy, Count Manucci, the Abbe, the Prior, and Father Wilson, who staid with me, till I took him home in the coach.

Bathiani [2] is gone.

The French have no laws for the maintenance of their poor. Monk not necessarily a Priest. Benedictines rise at four, are at church an hour and half, at Church again half an hour before, half an hour after dinner, and again from half an hour after seven to eight. They may sleep eight hours. Bodily labour wanted in Monasteries.[3]

The poor taken to hospitals, and miserably kept. Monks in the convent fifteen : accounted poor.

Oct. 12.   We went to the Gobelines. Tapestry makes
Th.   a good picture, imitates flesh exactly. One
        piece with a gold ground. The Birds not exactly coloured. Thence we went to the King's

---

[1] See above, p. 110.   [2] See above, pp. 107-108.
[3] *MS*. Monastris.

Cabinet, very neat, not perhaps perfect. Gold ore.[1]
Candles of the candle tree. Seeds. Woods. Thence
to Gagni's [2] house, where I saw rooms nine furnished
with a profusion of wealth [3] and elegance which I
never have seen before. Vases. Pictures. The dragon
China, the lustre said to be of crystal and to have cost
3500L. The whole furniture said to have cost 125000L.
Damask hangings covered with pictures. Porphyry.
This house struck me. Then we waited on the Ladies
to Monville's. Capt. Irwin with us.[4] Spain. County
towns all beggars. At Dijon he could not find the way
to Orleans. Cross roads of France very bad. Five
soldiers. Woman.—Soldiers escaped. The Colonel
would not lose five men for the death of one woman.
The magistrate cannot seize a soldier but by the Colonel's
permission. Good inn at Nismes. Moors of Barbary
fond of Englishmen. Gibraltar eminently healthy; it has
beef from Barbary. There is a large Garden. Soldiers
sometimes fall from the rock.

Oct. 13.   I staid at home all day, only went to find
Fr.[5]   the Prior, who was not at home. I read
            something in Canus.[6] — *Nec admiror, nec*
multum laudo.

[1] *MS.* oar.

[2] See above, p. 112. Boswell has " Gagnier." J. W. Croker
in his edition suggests this was " Gagny, Intendant des Finances,
who had a fine house in the Rue de Varennes."

[3] *MS.* weath.

[4] " The rest of this paragraph appears to be a minute of what
was told by Captain Irwin."—*Boswell.*

[5] Th. *crossed through.*

[6] " Melchior Canus, a celebrated Spanish Dominican, who died
at Toledo, in 1560. He wrote a treatise *De Locis Theologicis*, in
twelve books."—*Boswell.*

Oct. 14.   We went to the house of Mr Argenson,[1]
Sat.   which was [2] almost wainscotted with looking
                glasses, and covered with gold.   The Ladies
closet wainscotted with large squares of glass over painted
paper.   They always place mirrours to reflect their rooms.

Then we went to Julien's,[3] the Treasurer of the
clergy.   30000L a year.   The house has no very large
room, but is set with mirrours, and covered with gold.
Books of wood here, and in (an)other library.

At D'Argensons I looked into the Books in the
Lady's closet, and in contempt shewed them to Mr. T.
—Prince Titi,[4]—Bibl. des Fées, and other books.   She
was offended, and shut up, as we heard afterwards, her
apartment.

Then we went to Julien Le Roy,[5] the King's Watch
maker, a man of character in his business, who shewed
a small clock made to find the longitude.—A decent
man.[6]

Afterwards we saw the palais [7] marchande,[8] and the
courts of Justice, civil and criminal.   Queries [9] on the
Sellette.[10]   This building has the old Gothick passages,
and a great appearance of antiquity.   Three hundred
prisoners sometimes in the gaol.

---

[1] Is this Marc-Antoine René de Paulmy, Marquis D'Argenson?
[2] glazed *crossed through*.   [3] St. Julien ; see above, p. 117.
[4] Cordonnier de Saint Hyacinthe published his *Histoire du
Prince Titi*, a fairy tale, at Paris in 1736.   Mr. A. Napier, in his
edition of Boswell's *Life* (vol. ii., p. 550), has discussed the suggestions of various editors as to the book here referred to by
Johnson.
[5] Evidently a mistake for Pierre Le Roy.   See above, p. 117.
[6] Minute and small *crossed through*.   [7] *MS.* plalais.
[8] See above, p. 114.   [9] *MS.* Queeries.
[10] " The *selette* was a stool on which the criminal sat while he
was *interrogated*—questioned by the court."—*Croker*.

Much disturbed—hope no ill will be.[1]

In the afternoon I visited Mr. Freron the Journalist.[2]
He spoke Latin very scantily, but seemed to understand
me. His house not splendid, but (of) commodious
size. His family, wife, son, and daughter, not elevated
but decent. I was pleased with my reception. He
is to translate my book which I am to send him with
notes.

Oct. 15.   At Choisi, a royal palace on the banks of
Sunday.   the Seine, about 7m. from Paris. The
           terrace noble along the river. The rooms
numerous and grand but not discriminated from other
palaces. [The Chapel beautiful but small.] China Globes,
inlaid table. Labyrinth. Sinking table.[3] Toilet tables.

Oct. 16.   The Palais royal very grand, large and lofty,
M.   a very great collection of pictures. Three
            of Raphael—two Holy Family—one small
piece of M. Angelo. One room of Rubens. I thought
the pictures of Raphael fine.

The Tuilleries Statues. Venus. Æn. and Anchises
in his arms. Nilus. Many more. The walks not open
to mean persons. Chairs at night hired for two sous
apiece. Pont tournant.[4]

Austin Nuns.[5] Grate. Mrs. Fermor, Abbess. She

---

[1] " This passage, which so many think superstitious, reminds
me of Archbishop Laud's Diary."—*Boswell.*

[2] " For a brief account of Fréron, father and son, see Carlyle's
French Revolution, part ii., bk. i., ch. 4."—*Birkbeck Hill.*

[3] See above, p. 118.

[4] " Before the Revolution, the passage from the garden of the
Thuilleries into the *Place Louis XV.* was over a *pont tournant,* a kind
of drawbridge."—*Croker.*

[5] See above, p. 120.

knew Pope, and thought him disagreeable. Mrs. . . .[1]
has many books, has seen Life. Their frontlet disagreeable. Their hood. Their life easy. Rise about
five; hour and half in Chapel, dine at ten, another
hour and half at Chapel, half an hour about three, and
half an hour more at seven. Four hours in Chapel.
A large garden. Thirteen pensioners. Teacher complained.

At the Boulevard saw nothing, yet was glad to be
there. Rope dancing, and farce. Egg dance.

N. Near Paris, whether on weekdays or Sundays,
the roads empty.

Oct. 17.   At the palais marchand.   I bought
T.

A snuff-box [2]	.	24L.	2	12	6
———	.	6			
Table book	.	15 [3]			
Scissars 3 p	.	18			
		63			

We heard the lawyers plead.

N. As many killed at Paris as there are days in the
year. Chambre de question.[4] Tournelle at the palais
marchande.[5] An old venerable building.

The Palais Bourbon belonging to the Prince of
Conde. Only one small wing shewn, lofty, splendid,
gold and glass. The battles of the great Conde are
painted in one of the rooms. The present prince a
Grandsire at thirty-nine.

[1] Name omitted. The lady was evidently Miss Canning; see
also pp. 120-121, 224.

[2] He gave a snuff-box to Miss Porter; see below, p. 221.

[3] Several words *crossed out*.   [4] The torture-chamber.

[5] That section of the parliament of Paris dealing with criminal
affairs.

The sight of palaces and other great buildings, leaves no very distinct images, unless to those who talk of them, and impress them. As I entered my Wife was in my mind.[1] She would have been pleased. Having now nobody to please, I am little pleased.

N. In France there is no middle rank.

So many Shops open that Sunday is little distinguished at Paris. The palaces of Louvre and Tuilleries granted out in lodgings.

In the palais de Bourbon, gilt globes of metal at the fire place.

The French beds commended.[2] Much of the marble, only paste.

The Colosseum [3] a mere wooden building, at least much of it.

Oct. 18. W.   We went to Fontainbleau, which we found a large mean town crouded with people. The forest thick with woods, very extensive. Manucci secured us Lodging. The appearance of the country pleasant. No hills, few streams, only one hedge. I remember no chapels nor crosses on the road, pavement still, and rows of trees.

N. Nobody but mean people walk in Paris.

Oct. 19. Th.   At Court, we saw the apartments,[4] the King's Bedchamber and council chamber extremely splendid. Persons of all ranks in the outward rooms through which the family passes.

---

[1] " His tender affection for his departed wife, of which there are many evidences in his *Prayers and Meditations,* appears very feelingly in this passage."—*Boswell.*

[2] See below, p. 224.   [3] See above, p. 95.

[4] *Altered from* appartments.

Servants and Masters. Brunet [1] with us the second time.

The Introductor came to us—civil to me. Presenting. I had scruples—not necessary. We went and saw the King and Queen at Diner.[2] We saw the other Ladies at Diner. Madame Elizabeth with the Princess of Guimené.[3] At night we went to a comedy. I neither saw nor heard—drunken women. Mrs. Th. prefered one to the other.

Oct. 20.   We saw the Queen mount in the forest.
Fr.   Brown habit, rode aside, one lady [4] rode aside. The Queens horse light grey—martingale. She galloped.[5]—We then went to the apartments, and admired them. Then wandered [6] through the palace—in the passages, Stalls and Shops. Painting in Fresco by a great master worn out. We saw the king's horses and dogs. The Dogs almost all English. Degenerate q.

The horses not much commended. The stables cool, the kennel filthy.

At night the Ladies went to the opera. I refused, but should have been welcome.

The king fed himself with his left hand as we.

Saturday   In the night I got ground. We came home
21   to Paris.—I think we did not see the chapel.
          Tree broken by the wind. The French chairs made all of boards painted.

---

[1] " Perhaps M. J. L. Brunet, a celebrated advocate of the parliament of Paris."—*Croker*.

[2] One or two sentences crossed through.

[3] See above, pp. 124-125.   [4] See above, p. 127.

[5] *MS.* galoped.   [6] *MS.* wanded.

N. Soldiers at the court of Justice. Soldiers not amenable to the magistrates. Dijon. Woman.[1]

Faggots [2] in the palace. Every thing slovenly, except in chief rooms. Trees in the roads, some tall, none old, many very young and small.

Womens saddles seem ill made. Queen's [3] Bridle woven with silver. Tags to strike the horse.

Sunday, Oct. 22. To Versailles, a mean town. Carriages of business [4] passing. Mean Shops against the wall. Our way lay through Sevre,[5] where the China manufacture. Wooden Bridge at Sevre in the way to Versailles. The Palace of great extent. The Front long. I saw it not perfectly. The Menagerie. Cygnets dark, their black feet, on the ground, tame. Halcyons, [or] gulls. Stag and Hind—young. Aviary very large, the net wire. Black Stag of China, small. Rhinoceros. The horn broken, and pared away which I suppose will grow. The basis I think, four inches cross. The skin folds like loose cloath doubled, over his body, and cross his hips, vast animal though young, as big perhaps as four Oxen. The young Elephant with his tusks just appearing. The brown Bear put out his paws. All very tame. The lion. The tigers I did not well view. The Camel or dromedary with two bunches, called the Highgeen [6] taller than any horse. Two Camels with one bunch. Among the birds was a Pellican who being let out, went to a fountain, and swam about to catch fish. His feet well webbed. He dipped his head, and turned his long bill sidewise. He caught two or three fish but did not eat them.

---

[1] See above, p. 171.   [2] *MS*. Fagot.   [3] *MS*. Queen.
[4] of burden *crossed through*.   [5] Seve *crossed through*.
[6] Boswell has " Huguin," with the note : " This epithet should be applied to this animal, with one bunch."

Trianon is a kind [of] [1] retreat appendant to Versailles. It has an open portico, the pavement and, I think, the pillars of marble. There are many rooms which I do not distinctly remember,[2] a table of porphyry about five feet long and between two and three broad, given to Lewis XIV. by the Venetian State. In the Council room almost all that was not door or Window was, I think, looking glass.

Little Trianon is a small palace like a Gentleman's house. The upper floor paved with brick. Little Vienne. The court is ill paved. The rooms at the top are [3] small, fit to sooth the imagination with privacy. In the front of Versailles are small basons of water on the terrace, and other basons, [I think], below them. There are [4] little courts.—The great Gallery is wainscotted with mirrors not very large but joined by frames. I suppose the large plates were not yet made. The play house was very large.[5] The Chappel I do not remember if we saw. We saw one Chappel, but I am not certain whether there or at Trianon. The foreign Office paved with bricks. The dinner half a Louis each, and I think a Louis over. Money given, at Menagerie, 3 Livres, elsewhere [6] 6 Livres.

Oct. 23.   Last night I wrote to Levet.[7] We went to
Monday.   see the looking glasses wrought. They
          come from Normandy in [cast] plates,
perhaps the third of an Inch thick. At Paris they are
ground upon a marble table, by rubbing one plate on

---

[1] Not in MS.   [2] A word *crossed through.*
[3] were *crossed through.*   [4] many *crossed through.*
[5] and *crossed through.*
[6] Boswell has " at palace " for " elsewhere."
[7] See below, p. 218.

another with grit between them. The various sands, of which there are said to be five, I could not learn. The handle by which the upper Glass is moved has the form of a wheel which may be moved in all directions. The plates are sent up with their surfaces ground, but not polished, and so continue till they are bespoken, lest time should spoil the surface, as we were told. Those that are to be polished are laid on a table covered with several thick cloaths, hard strained that the resistance may be equal, they [1] are then rubbed [with a hand rubber held down hard] by a contrivance which I did not well understand. The powder which is used last seemed to me to be iron dissolved in aqua fortis. They called it, as Baretti said, Mar de l'eau forte, which he thought was dregs. They mentioned vitriol and saltpetre. The [2] cannon ball swam in the quicksilver. To silver them. A leaf of beaten tin is laid, and rubbed with quicksilver to which it unites. Then more quicksilver is poured upon it, which by its mutual [attraction] [3] rises very high. Then [4] a paper is laid at the nearest end of the plate, over which the glass is slided till it lies upon the plate, having driven much of the quicksilver before it. It is then [I think] pressed upon cloaths, and then set sloping to drop the superfluous mercury. The slope is daily heightened towards a perpendicular.

In the way I saw the Greve, the Mayor's house, and the Bastile.

We then went to Sansterre,[5] a Brewer. He brews with about as much malt as Mr. T., and sells his beer at the same price though he pays no duty for malt, and

---

[1] it *crossed through*.   [2] Several words *crossed through*.
[3] Supplied by Boswell.   [4] *MS*. the.
[5] Antoine-Joseph Santerre.   He commanded the troops surrounding the scaffold when Louis XVI. was executed.

little more than half as much for beer. Beer is sold retail at 6p. a bottle. He brews 4000 barrels a year. There are seventeen brewers in Paris [of] whom none is supposed to brew more than he—reckoning them at 3000 each they make 51000 a year. They [1] make their malt, for malting is [here] no trade.

The moat of the Bastile is dry.

Oct. 24.   We visited the King's Library. I saw the
Tuesday.   Speculum humanae Salvationis [2] rudely printed with ink sometimes pale, sometimes black, part supposed to be with wooden types, and part with pages cut on boards. The Bible [3] supposed to be older than that of Mentz in 62, it has no date; it is supposed to have been printed with wooden types; I am in doubt; the print is large and fair in two folios. Another book was shewn me supposed to have been printed with wooden type, I think Durandi Sanctuarium [4] in 58. This is inferred from the difference of form sometimes seen in the same letter, which might be struck with different puncheons. The regular similitude of most letters proves better that they are metal. I saw nothing but the Speculum which I had not seen, I think, before.

Thence to the Sorbonne. The Library very large, not in lattices like the king's. Martene [5] and Durand's,

    [1] He *crossed through*.

    [2] Possibly the edition supposed to have been printed in Holland in or about 1470.

    [3] This may be either the 42-line Bible or the 36-line Bible, both of which were printed at Mainz before 1462.

    [4] Several editions of Durand's *Rationale divinorum officiorum* were printed in 1459.

    [5] Boswell, in error, has " Marbone." Martène (E.) and Durand (U.), *Thesaurus novus Anecdotorum*, etc. Paris, 1717, 5 vols., folio; also their *Veterum Scriptorum et Monumentorum*, etc. Paris, 1724-33, 9 vols., folio.

q. collection 14 vol. Scriptores de rebus Gallicis,[1] many Folios. Histoire genealogique of France,[2] 9 Fol. Gallia Christiana,[3] the first Edition 4, the last 12 Fol. The Prior and Librarian [4] dined [with us],[5] 1 waited on them home. Their garden pretty, with covered walks, but small, yet may hold many students. The Doctors of the Sorbonne are all equal, chuse those who succeed to vacancies. Profit little.

Oct. 25. I went with the Prior to St. Cloud, to see
W.   Dr. Hooke.—We walked round the palace, and had some talk. I dined with our whole company at the Monastery.[6] In the Library, Beroald, Cymon,[7] Titus,[8] from Boccace. Oratio Proverbialis,[9] To the Virgin from Petrarch.[10] Falkland to

---

[1] *Recueil des historiens des Gaules et de la France*, published by the Benedictines of S. Maur.

[2] *Histoire généalogique et chronologique de la maison royale de France, des pairs*, etc., by Père Anselme, continued by M. Du Fourny. 3rd edition, 1726-33.

[3] The first edition of this work by the brothers Sainte-Marthe was published at Paris in 1646 in 4 vols., folio. The first volume of the new edition is dated 1716, and twelve volumes had appeared before 1775.

[4] Probably Dr. Hooke; see below, pp. 226-227.

[5] Inserted by Boswell.   [6] *MS*. Monastry.

[7] [*Decamerone*.] *Mythica historia Joannis Boccaccii per P. Beroaldum de Italico in Latinum translata. In qua ostenditur exemplo cujusdam.* . . . *Cymonis*, etc. Leipsic, 1495 ?

[8] [*Decamerone*.] *Mythica historia J. Boccatij* . . . *de Tito romano* . . . *nuper per P. Beroaldū ex Italico in Latinum transversa.* Leipsic, 1495 ?

[9] Philippus Beroaldus, *Oratio proverbiorum*. Bologna, 1499; also an edition in 1500.

[10] P. Beroaldus, *Pœanes Beatæ Virginis ex Petrarcae pœmate in latinum conversi*. Editions of this work, together with his *Carmen de die dominicae passionis*, were printed at Bologna about 1481, Paris

Sandys.[1]   Dryden's preface to the third vol.[2] of Miscellanies.[3]

Oct. 26.   We saw the china at Sevre, cut, glazed,
Th.   painted.   Bellevue, a pleasing house, not
              great, fine prospect.   Meudon, an old Palace.
Alexander, in Porphyry, hollow between eyes and nose,
thin cheeks.   Plato and Aristotle.   Noble terrace over-
looks the town.   St. Cloud.   Gallery not very high nor
grand, but pleasing.   In the rooms, Michael Angelo,
drawn by himself.   Sir Thomas Moore, Des Cartes,
Bochart, Naudaeus, Mazarine.   Gilded wainscot, so
common that it is not minded.   Gough and Keene.[4]
Hooke came to us at the Inn.—A message from Drumgould.[5]

about 1495, and 1498 (two), and Heidelberg in 1500.   The *Pæanes*
were also printed at Paris in 1506.

[1] In George Sandy's *A Paraphrase upon the Psalmes of David*,
etc. (London, 1636), is a prefatory poem " To my Noble Frend,
Mr. George Sandys," signed " Faukland."   This was Lucius Cary,
2nd Viscount Falkland.

[2] The third volume of Dryden's *Miscellany Poems* appeared in
1693.   He wrote a Dedication to Lord Radcliffe.

[3] " He means, I suppose, that he read these different pieces
while he remained in the library."—*Boswell.*

[4] See above, p. 143.

[5] Johnson said to Boswell later :   " I was just beginning to
creep into acquaintance by means of Colonel Drumgould, a very
high man, Sir, head of *L'Ecole Militaire*, a most complete character,
for he had first been a professor of rhetorick, and then became a
soldier."—Boswell's *Life*, vol. ii., pp. 401-402.   Numerous variant
spellings of this soldier's name included Dromgould, Drom-
goole, Romgold, and De Romgold.   The Rev. William Cole met
him in 1765 (*Paris Journal*, pp. 63-69), and refers to him at length.
He writes :   " Mr. Dromgould was of good Irish Family drove
away from his Country by the Rebels in Oliver's Time, & ever since

27 Oct.[1] I staid at home. Gough and Keene and
Fr.   Mrs. S——'s Friend [2] dined with us. This
           day we began to have a fire, the weather is
grown very cold, and I fear, has a bad effect upon my
breath, which has grown much [3] more free and easy in
this country.[4]

Sat.   I visited the grand Chartreuse [6] built by
Oct. 28.[5] St Lewis. It is built for forty, but contains
           only twenty-four, and will not maintain
more. The Friar that spoke to us had a pretty apartment. Mr. Baretti says four rooms, I remember but
three. His books seemed to be French. His garden
was neat, he gave me grapes. We saw the place de
Victoire with the Statues of the King, and the captive
nations.
     We saw the Palace and Gardens of Luxembourg,
but the Gallery was shut. We climbed to the top
stairs. I dined with Colbrook,[7] who had much Company.

established in France. About 22 years ago, when Mr. Walpole was
before at Paris, he was acquainted with him."
     [1] 26 *crossed through.*
     [2] Mrs. Strickland's friend, Captain Killpatrick. See above,
p. 141.
     [3] freer *crossed through.*   [4] See below, p. 221.
     [5] *Altered from* 27.
     [6] The Carthusian house, formerly situated in the Rue d'Enfer,
and destroyed during the Revolution. Louis IX. installed five
monks of the order at Gentilly in 1257, and in 1260 laid the founda-
tion-stone of a magnificent church. In 1776 the Paris monks sold
to Louis XVI. twenty-two tableaux by Eustache Le Sueur, depicting
the life of St. Bruno, the founder of their order. These paintings
are now in the Louvre.
     [7] Croker identifies this with Sir George Colebrooke, but Mrs.
Thrale has Mr. Colebrooke (above, p. 137).

Foote,[1] Sir George Rodney,[2] Motteux, Udson, Taaf.[3] Called on the Prior, and found him in bed.

Hotel—a guinea a day. Coach 3 guineas a week. Valet de place, 3L. a day. Avant coureur a guinea a week. Ordinary diner 6L. a head. Our ordinary seems to be about five guineas a day. Our extraordinary expences, as diversions, gratuities, cloaths; I cannot reckon. Our travelling is [4] ten guineas a day.

White Stockens 18L. Wig. Hat.

Sunday, Oct. 29.   We saw the boarding School, the Enfans trouvés. A room with about 86 children in cradles, as sweet as a parlour. They lose a third; take in to perhaps more than seven [years old],[5] put them to trades, pin to them the papers sent with them. Want nurses. Saw their chapel.

Went to St. Eustatia,[6] saw an innumerable company

---

[1] Samuel Foote. Boswell writes: "It happened that Foote was at Paris at the same time with Dr. Johnson, and his description of my friend while there, was abundantly ludicrous. He told me that the French were quite astonished at his figure and manner, and his dress, which he obstinately continued exactly as in London;— his brown clothes, black stockings, and plain shirt. He mentioned that an Irish gentleman said to Johnson, ' Sir, you have not seen the best French players.' JOHNSON: ' Players, Sir! I look on them as no better than creatures set upon tables and joint-stools to make faces and produce laughter, like dancing dogs.'—' But, Sir, you will allow that some players are better than others ? ' JOHNSON: ' Yes, Sir, as some dogs dance better than others.' "—See Boswell's *Life*, vol. ii., pp. 403-404.

[2] The well-known admiral, afterwards raised to the peerage as Baron Rodney of Stoke Rodney.

[3] Was this Denis Taaffe, the Irish political writer and ardent nationalist ?

[4] about *crossed through*.   [5] Inserted by Boswell.

[6] " He means the well-known parish church of St. Eustache." —*Croker*.

of girls catechised, in many bodies, perhaps 100 to a Catechist. Boys taught at one time, girls at another. The Sermon ; the preacher wears a cap, which he takes off at the name—his action uniform, not very violent.

Oct. 30.   We saw the Library of St. Germain. A
Mond.   very noble collection. Codex Divinorum
           Officiorum, 1459,[1] a letter, square like that
of the Offices, perhaps the same. The Codex by Fust and Gernserheim.[2] Meursius,[3] 12 v. Fol. Amadis [4] in French, 3 v. Fol. Catholicon, sine colophone— but of 1460.[5] Two other editions, one by Lathomi, one by Badius.[6] Augustin. de Civitate Dei,[7] with[out] name, date, or place, but of Fust's square letter as it seems.

[1] *Rationale divinorum officiorum.*   Mainz : Fust and Schoeffer, 1459, folio.

[2] *Psalmorum codex.*   Mainz : Fust and Schoeffer, 1457 or 1459, folio.

[3] Meursius (Joannes), *Opera omnia.*   Florentiae, 1741-63, 12 vols., folio.

[4] Amadis de Gaula, traduit en françois.   Paris, 1543-48, 3 vols. out of 4, folio.

[5] Johannes Balbus de Janua, *Summa quae vocatur Catholicon.* Mainz : J. Gutenberg (?), 1460, 2 vols., folio.

[6] Boswell omits the last six words in the text but notes : " I have looked in vain into De Bure, Meerman, Mattaire, and other typographical books for the two editors of the *Catholicon,* which Dr. Johnson mentions here, with *names* which I cannot make out. I read ' one by *Latinius,* one by *Bœdinus.*' I have deposited the original MS. in the British Museum, where the curious may see it. My grateful acknowledgements are due to Mr. Planta for the trouble he was pleased to take in aiding my researches." We read the two names as " Lathmi and Badius." On July 4, 1494, Perrinus Lathomi, Bonifacius Johannis and Johannes de Villa vetera printed at Lyons an edition of the *Catholicon ;* and in 1510 Badius Ascensius also printed an edition at Lyons.

[7] Augustinus, *De civitate Dei.*   Mainz : Schoeffer, 1473, folio.

I dined with Col. Drumgould, had a pleasing after-noon.

Some of the books of St. Germain's stand in presses from the wall like those at Oxford.

Oct. 31.   I lived at the Benedictines, meagre day.
Tues.   Soup meagre, herrings, eels, both with sauce. Fryed fish. Lentils, tasteless in them-selves. In the library, where I found Maffeus Historia Indica ; [1] Promontorium flectere, to double the cape. I parted very tenderly from the Prior and Friar Wilkes.[2]

Maitre es Arts 2 y. Bacc. Theol. 3 y. Licentiate 2 y. Doctor Th. 2 y. in all 9 years. For the doctorate three disputations, major, minor, Sorbonica. Several colleges suppressed, and transferred to that which was the Jesuites' College.

Nov. 1.   We left Paris. St. Denis a large town, the Church not very large, but the middle Isle is very lofty and aweful. On the left are chapels built beyond the line of the wall which destroy the symmetry of the sides. The Organ is higher above the pavement than I have ever seen. The gates are of brass. On the middle gates is the History of our Lord. The painted windows are historical, and said to be eminently beauti-ful. We were at another church belonging to a Convent, of which the portal is a dome ; we could not enter further, and it was almost dark.

Nov. 2.   We came this day to Chantilly, a seat be-Thurs.   longing to the Prince of Conde. This place is eminently beautified by all varieties of waters starting up in fountains, falling in cascades,

---

[1] G. P. Maffei, *Historiarum Indicarum libri xvi.* Many editions between 1588 and 1637.

[2] See below, p. 224.

running in streams, and spread in lakes. The water seems to be too near the house. All this water is brought from a source or a river three leagues off, by an artificial canal,[1] which [for] one league is carried underground. —The House is magnificent. The cabinet seems well stocked, what I remember was the jaws of a hippopotamus, and a young hippopotamus preserved, which however is so small that I doubt its reality. It seems too hairy for an abortion, and too small for a mature birth. Nothing was in spirit, all was dry. The dog. The Deer. [The ant bear, with long snout.] The Toucan, long [broad] beak. The Stables were of very great length. The Kennel had no scents. There was a mockery of a village. The Menage had few animals.[2] Two Fausans [3] or Brasilian weasels, spotted, very wild. There is a forest, and, I think, a park. I walked till I was very weary, and next morning felt my feet battered and sore with pains in the toes.

[1] Of *crossed through*.

[2] Boswell notes : " The writing is so bad here, that the names of several animals could not be decyphered without much more acquaintance with natural history than I possess.—Dr. Blagden, with his usual politeness, most obligingly examined the MS. To that gentleman, and to Dr. Gray, of the British Museum, who also very readily assisted me, I beg leave to express my best thanks." Dr. Charles Blagden (1748-1820), of whom Johnson said : " Blagden, sir, is a delightful fellow," was elected Secretary of the Royal Society in 1784, and knighted in 1792.

[3] Boswell notes : " It is thus written by Johnson, from the French pronunciation of *fossane*. It should be observed, that the person who showed this Menagerie was mistaken in supposing the *fossane* and the Brasilian weasel to be the same, the *fossane* being a different animal, and a native of Madagascar. I find them, however, upon one plate in Pennant's *Synopsis of Quadrupeds*."

Nov. 3.   We came to Compiegne, a very large town
Fryday.   with a royal palace built round a pentagonal
        court. The court is raised upon vaults,
and has, I suppose, an entry on one side by a gentle rise.
Talk of painting.[1] The church is not very large, but
very elegant and splendid. I had at first great difficulty
to walk, but motion grew continually easier. At night
we came to Noyon, an Episcopal City. The Cathedral
is very beautiful, the pillars alternately Gothick and
Corinthian. We entered a very noble parochial Church.
Noyon is walled, and is said to be three miles round.

Nov. 4.   We rose very early, and came through St.
Sat.   Quentin to Cambray not long after three.—
        We went to an English Nunnery, to give
a letter to Father Welch [2] the Confessor, who came to
visit us in the evening.

Nov. 5.   We saw the Cathedral. It is very beautiful,
Sunday.   with chappels on each side. The Choir
        splendid. The Balustrade in one part brass.
The Neff very high and grand. The altar Silver as far
as it is seen. The vestments very splendid.—At the
Benedictines Church—— [3]

---

[1] See below, p. 228.   [2] See above, p. 153.
[3] Here Johnson's note-book ends; the book in which he
continued his account is now lost.

MRS. PIOZZI'S
FRENCH JOURNEY
1784

NOTE

In July, 1784, Mrs. Thrale was married to her second husband, Gabriele Piozzi, and on Sept. 5 of the same year they were at Dover preparing to set out upon a Continental tour. They did not return to England until March, 1787. Mrs. Piozzi kept an account of the journey in two large quarto note-books, one of which bears on the leather cover the title " Italian Journey," and the other the title " German Journey." The first note-book contains a description of their passage through France, and of their stay in Italy up to their departure from Milan on Sept. 22, 1786. The second book begins with an entry made on Sept. 22, 1786; its contents include notes made at Verona, Trent, Munich, Vienna, Dresden, Berlin, Hanover, and Brussels; and it ends with an entry made at Brussels early in March, 1787.

Mrs. Piozzi later wrote up her account in seven folio note-books, and then re-wrote it with numerous modifications and alterations. The work in its final form was printed in 1789 in two volumes, with the title *Observations and Reflections made in the course of a journey through France, Italy, and Germany.* All the above manuscripts were acquired by the John Rylands Library from Mrs. R. V. Colman at the same time as the *French Journal.* We are now printing from the original note-book Mrs. Piozzi's account of her journey through France on the way to Italy. It will be found that this contains much that is not found in the printed version of 1789. On the other hand, we have given in the footnotes a number of interesting passages, found in the printed version, which were not in the original note-book, but were added by Mrs. Piozzi from memory or from other notes. The manuscript of Mrs. Piozzi's " Italian Journey," here used, is now " J.R.L. English MS. 618."

MRS. PIOZZI'S FRENCH JOURNEY, 1784

Dover. Sunday 5 Sept[r] 1784

LAST night I arrived at this Place in Company with my dear Husband & faithful Maid,—having left my Daughters reconciled to my Choice, (all at least except the eldest who parted with me cooly, not unkindly :) and my Friends well pleased with my leaving London I fancy, where my Stay perplexed 'em, and entangled their Duty with their Interest.

I am setting out for the Country which has produced so many People & Things of Consequence from the foundation of Rome to the present Moment that my Heart swells with the Idea, and I long to leap across intermediate France. The Inn here is execrable, we came late last Night & put up at the wrong house. There never was a Coach & six at the Door till now I dare say—ours is a very elegant one, and M[r] Piozzi is on all Occasions kindly attentive to my being accomodated in every possible Respect.

Calais 7: Sept[r] I write from my Bed to which I am at length arrived after a passage of twenty Hours— a Thing scarce known between two Coasts of seven Leagues distance [from each other ;] and in such lovely Weather, that we never lost Sight either of France or England : the Truth is, we had no Wind at all ; & the Flights of Shaggs & Shoals of Maycril both uncommon at this Season, made us little or no Amends for the Tediousness of a Night passed on Shipboard. Seeing the Sun both rise and set was however a new Idea gained to me, who had never such an Opportunity before : it confirmed to me the Truth of that Maxim which tells us, that the human Mind must have something left to supply for itself on the Sight of all Sublunary Objects. When my Eyes have watched the rising or setting Sun amidst a crowd of intervening Trees—my Imagination painted the full View finer than I found it— and if the Sun itself cannot satisfie the cravings of Fancy, let us be sure that nothing earthly *can* satisfy them ; and let us *set our Affections* as directed by Scripture, on *that Place where only true Joys are to be found.*—Pious Reflections remind one of a Nunnery ;[1] I went to see my old Acquaintance the Dominican Nun as soon as I was refreshed from my Fatigue : She had forgot me though, & even

[1] The printed version (pp. 2-3) has : " Pious reflections remind one of monks and nuns ; I enquired of the Franciscan Friar who attended us at the inn, what was become of Father Felix, who did the duties of the quête, as it is called, about a dozen years ago, when I recollect minding that his manners and story struck Dr. Johnson exceedingly, who said that so complete a character could scarcely be found in romance. He had been a soldier, it seems, and was no incompetent or mean scholar : the books we found open in his cell, shewed he had not neglected modern or colloquial knowledge ; there was a translation of Addison's Spectators, and Rapin's Dissertation on the contending Parties of England called Whig and Tory. He had likewise a violin, and some printed music, for his entertainment. I was glad to hear he was well, and travelling to Barcelona on foot by orders of the superior.

" After dinner we set out to see Miss Grey, at her convent of Dominican Nuns ; who, I hoped, would have remembered me, as many of the ladies there had seized much of my attention when last abroad : they had however all forgotten me, nor could call to mind how much they had once admired the beauty of my eldest daughter, then a child, which I thought impossible to forget." See above, pp. 71-72.

after I told the name of my first Husband, did not recollect it. One is always more important in one's own Opinion than in reality—but no one is of Importance to a Nun; who is or ought to be employed on other Speculations. When the great Mogul showed his Splendour to a Dervise . . . shall you not often be thinking of me in future, said the Emperor? perhaps I might, replied the Religieux, if I was not always thinking on God.

Well! I bought some Toys to send my younger Daughters in England, & took my Leave of the Lady, who was pleased to find that I had married a Roman Catholick.

The Women spinning at their Doors [here], or making Lace, or employing themselves in some Manner, is particularly pleasing to a British Eye; yet I do not recollect observing it when I was over last: Industry without Bustle, and any Appearance of Gain without Fraud, comforts one('s) Heart, but all the Profits of Commerce scarce make amends to a truly delicate Mind, for the Noise and Brutality of an English Port.[1] Custom-

[1] The printed version (pp. 4-6) then has: "I looked again for the chapel, where the model of a ship, elegantly constructed, hung from the top, and found it in good preservation: some scrupulous man had made the ship, it seems, and thought, perhaps justly too, that he had spent a greater portion of time and care on the workmanship than he ought to have done; so resolving no longer to indulge his vanity or fondness, fairly hung it up in the convent chapel, and made a solemn vow to look on it no more. I remember a much stronger instance of self-denial practised by a young lady of Paris once, who was enjoined by her confessor to wring off the neck of her favourite bullfinch, as a penance for having passed too much time in teaching him to pipe tunes, peck from her hand, etc. —She obeyed; but never could be prevailed on to see the priest again.

"We are going now to leave Calais, where the women in long

house Examiners and the Impositions practised on Travelling Families filled up the rest of this Day : yet I slept
well through the Night, and hear with Pleasure that
this Morning we are to go to Boulogne, a Place I
never yet saw—a *Refugium Peccatorum* for our Runaway
Wretches it is ; but one always wishes to *see* something
new, & to *relate* something old : for example it was
comical in Miss Ashe speaking of D[r] James,[1] who
loved profligate Conversation dearly—That Man should
set up his Quarters across the Water (said She)—Why
Boulogne would be a Seraglio for him. The Length
of the Passage took off from that Surprize one feels on
being suddenly transported from one Race of Mortals
to another—I observed my Maid was not at all astonished
at the difference of Dress & Manner—Why should she ?
We were twenty or twenty two hours on our Passage,
and might easily have been carried much further.

white camblet clokes, soldiers with whiskers, girls in neat slippers,
and short petticoats contrived to show them, who wait upon you
at the inn ;—postillions with greasy night-caps, and vast jack-boots,
driving your carriage harnessed with ropes, and adorned with
sheep-skins, can never fail to strike an Englishman at his first
going abroad :—But what is our difference of manners, compared
to that prodigious effect produced by the much shorter passage
from Spain to Africa ; where an hour's time, and sixteen miles
space only, carries you from Europe, from civilization, from
Christianity. A gentleman's description of his feelings on that
occasion rushes now on my mind, and makes me half ashamed to
sit here, in Dessein's parlour, writing remarks, in good time !—
upon places as well known as Westminster-bridge to almost all
those who cross it at this moment ; while the custom-house officers
intrusion puts me the less out of humour, from the consciousness
that if I am disturbed, I am disturbed from doing *nothing*." See
above, p. 171.

[1] Probably Dr. Robert James (1705-76), the physician, an old
friend of Dr. Johnson. See Birkbeck Hill, *Letters*, vol. i., p. 211 *n.*

Montreuil 9: September Thursday We passed thro' Boulogne yesterday, but saw nothing of it except the Situation, which is beautiful;—The Fish was very fine too, I had forgotten the plenty of Game at every Inn, but my Maid will not easily forget the French Cuisine: I never saw a Creature so enjoy herself. We are indeed all of us but too happy. Last Night coming in late, [however], I broke my Fool's Pate against a Water Windlis (*sic*), and frighted myself and my Husband for nothing at all. The Country we passed thro' yesterday was a wretched one.

Thin Herbage in the plains & fruitless Fields &c.[1]

Their Wheat Harvest is not yet got in, and will I fear scarce pay the reaping this Year: Summer is come so late that scarce any profit can be derived from it, tho'

---

[1] The printed version (pp. 7-8) has : " The cattle too are miserably poor and lean ; but where there is no grass we can scarcely expect them to be fat : they must not feed on wheat, I suppose, and cannot digest tobacco. Herds of swine, not flocks of sheep, meet one's eye upon the hills ; and the very few gentlemen's seats that we have passed by, seem out of repair, and deserted. The French do not reside much in private houses, as the English do ; but while those of narrower fortunes flock to the country towns within their reach, those of ampler purses repair to Paris, where the rent of their estate supplies them with pleasures at no very enormous expence. The road is magnificent, like our old-fashioned avenue in a nobleman's park, but wider, and paved in the middle : this convenience continued on for many hundred miles, and all at the king's expence. Every man you meet, politely pulls off his hat *en passant ;* and the gentlemen have commonly a good horse under them, but certainly a dressed one.

" Sporting season is not come in yet, but I believe the idea of sporting seldom enters any head except an English one : here is prodigious plenty of game, but the familiarity with which they walk about and sit by the road-side, shews they feel no apprehension." See above, pp. 75, 129.

it affords much Pleasure : like a Life the early part of
which has been languish'd [out] in Sickness . . . so
that when Health *does* come, too little Time remains for
any considerable Work, and all that's left is spent naturally enough—in Enjoyment.

The Girl who waits on us here at Montreuil entertained me very much with her prattle, when complaining
of our Courier's Behaviour. " *Il parle sur le haut Ton,*"
says I, " *Mademoiselle, mais il a bon cœur.*"—"*Ouyda,*"
replied She (pertinently enough), " *mais c'est le Ton qui
fait le Chanson.*"

Amiens—   We left this place (Montreuil), and drove
Fryday   thro' a vile Country to Amiens, where we
Morning   came too late to see the Church, & whence
10: Sept: we ran too early to see anything ; but as
             I had been there before, I cared the less.
From Amiens to Chantilly we drove thro' some Vineyards, and found things more smiling than we had seen
them. The Grapes clustring on the Tops of Apple
Trees and mingling their Fruits have an exquisitely
pretty Effect, and I see that the Rage for Lombardy
Poplars is as great here as in England : Every Gentleman's House has long Walks of them planted about it
—and one sees by their Size that all are young Plantations.
We have run cursorily over the Palace & Gardens here
at Chantilly this Evening—it was new to neither of
us, yet lovely to both. The Cabinet is very fine for a
private Collection, but the Quadrant on the Globes was
rusted I observed, & the Orrery [1] broken & out of all
Condition : The Laboratory too wanted much repair.[2]

[1] Planetarium.

[2] A fuller account of the house is given in the printed version
(pp. 10-12), together with several anecdotes of the Prince of Condé.
See above, pp. 150-151.

Every Penny Book tells of the Tame Fish & the great Stables ; but if those are really Carp that eat out of one's Hand I cannot guess the reason of their Colour—it seems as if they were grown white with Age.

Chantilly.   Fryday Evening 10.

Chantilly Sat: Morning. 11: Sept^r	The excessive Heat of the Weather made the Inn more odious, and the Gardens more tempting : I rose early and ran out of Doors to sit by the Waterfalls which are very lovely indeed.

All the Tricks that Money can play with a beautious & copious River may be seen at Chantilly ; & so well are they managed, that I am still at a Loss whether our Rage for renouncing all Endeavours of Art in order to do more honour to Nature is not carried too far in England.—A Jet d'Eau is a sweet Thing on [1] a hot day, let the Nature-mongers say what they will.

Paris Sat: Night 11.	We are arrived this Instant at Peace & Paris—my Bones ache with jumbling on the Stony Roads, and I am truly shaken to

pieces—it was time for me to put in, as the Sailors say, and refit. Our Lodging (In the Quartier d'Angleterre) is elegant & comfortable, but here is a burning Sun that even the Italians shrink from, & that tans one's Skin to a Parchment.

Sunday Morn: 12 Sept^{r.}	I have been to St Sulpice [2] where I well remembered the large Shells that contain the holy Water, and the brass Canopy that over-shadows the high Altar ; I received

---

[1] *MS.* in.

[2] The printed version (pp. 11-12) only has : " I was pleased to go over the churches again too, and re-experience that particular sensation which the disposition of St. Rocque's altars and ornaments alone can give."

Letters from Susan & Sophia that comfort, charm, and delight me ; none from the eldest Lady tho', who is either sick or sullen—God send it may be the latter, for every thing is better than Illness.   A Letter from dear M[r.] James [1] too, telling me of many Treacheries acted by the Maid that I have so long confided in, and at last brought away from England with me, mistaking her for a Treasure.   Lord of thy Mercy what a World is this ! but were we not to pass thro' it . . . we could not arrive at a better.   In the Evening my Husband showed me the new Square called the Palais Royal, whence the Duc de Chartres [2] took away all the fine high Trees, which having stood for Centuries, it was a Shame to touch with an Ax, and accordingly the people were as angry as Frenchmen can be, when the Folly was first committed. The Court had however Wit enough to convert the place into a sort of Vauxhall, with Tents, Fountains &. a Colonade of Shops and Coffeehouses surrounding it on every Side ; and now they are all happy & contented, and *Vive le Duc de Chartres !*

Monday	The Cold & Tepid Baths here are charming,
Morning	well kept ; and I enjoy them vastly after
13 Sept[r]	travelling so far in such hot and sunny
	Weather ; This Place indeed seems cal-

culated for Enjoyment ; and if I am not careful, my

---

[1] George James, the portrait painter.   This letter is not among those of James to Mrs. Piozzi which survive among the Rylands Piozzi MSS.   James may have painted Queeney's portrait, for in a letter of June 9, 1785, he writes : " I am much flattered that the Italians should like Miss T's picture—the young Lady's beauty & her English dress no doubt claims great share of the admiration—that pretty white throat."

[2] Afterwards known as Philippe Égalité.   After a fire in 1781 he had constructed a new Palais Royal.

Husband's Indulgence, my past Afflictions, wch give additional Relish to present delights; the numberless Comforts w^{ch} [offer themselves], & utter Absence of Anxiety from my present Situation, together with that recovered flow of Spirits that new-found health inspires, will go near to make me a Sensualist: but I hope not; yet if it has always been found difficult to pass with a Mind unpolluted from great Poverty to sudden Abundance, how much more should those be on their Guard who are transported like me from Misery to Enjoyment, from corroding Sorrow to soft Tranquillity?

14-15-16. Nothing has occurred worth noting in my Book:—nothing that as Hamlet says " *Give me my Tablets*—meet it is I set it down " [1]—except general reflections on the difference of Manner between this Nation and that I left behind, a Difference so great that all one meets with expresses the strong Contrast, & evinces the *Natural* Aversion which London & Paris must for ever bear to each other. . . . The Behaviour of the Shopkeepers which at first Sight contradicts all one hears of the *fawning Parisian*, the *supple Gaul* as our Satirists call them, shews to my Mind more than any other Part of their Conduct the peaceful Tenour of a Life which loves not to be broken in upon for the sake of obtaining Riches, which when gotten must end in the Pleasure of counting them. A French man who should make his Fortune tomorrow by Trade, would be no nearer Advancement in Society or Situation— Why then should he solicit by Arts he is too lazy to delight in the Practice of, that Opulence which [w^d] afford so slight an Improvement of his Comforts? He lives as well as he wishes, he goes to the Boulevards

[1] " My tables, meet it is I set it down."—*Hamlet*, I., v. 107.

every Night, treats his Wife with Lemonade, and holds up his Babies by Turns to see Harlequin or hear the Jokes of Merry Andrew. Was he to recommend his Goods like the London Shopkeepers with studied Eloquence and attentive Flattery—he could not hope like them that his Flattery might one Day be listened to by a Lady of more Birth than Riches when employed on a different Subject; he could not hope like them that the Eloquence he now bestows on the Decorations of a Hat, or the Varnish of an Equipage, may one day serve to torment a Minister, or obtain a Charge of honour for his Son. The Mercer at Paris shows you few Silks —*vous devez choisir* is all he thinks of saying; then takes out his Snuff-box, and Yawns fatigued by your Enquiries.

Precluded from all possibility of Adventure, the Frenchman leads a gentle humble Life; he envies not the Greatness he never can obtain, but either wonders delightedly, or diverts himself philosophically with [yᵉ] Sight of that Splendor which excites Envy in the Englishman, & often occasions Suicide from Disappointments which these People never can feel. Like Eunuchs in a Seraglio they are contented to promote the Pleasure of their Prince, nor sigh for Enjoyments from which an irremeable Boundary divides them. They see at the beginning of their Lives how that Life is to end; and trot quietly down the Avenue, while we watch [wᵗʰ solicitude] the Turns of our *Serpentine* Walk, that is ever presenting either to Sight or Expectation, some Change and Variety in the prospect.[1]

---

[1] The printed version (pp. 16-18) has : " Reflections must now give way to facts for a moment, though few English people want to be told that every hotel here, belonging to people of condition, is shut out from the street like our Burlington-house, which gives a general gloom to the look of this city so famed for its gaiety : the

17 Septr This is my eldest Daughter's Birthday, who
1784. enters now on the last Year of her Minority :
May God protect & bless her ! We spent
this Day in Company with the Conte Turconi, who made
me a hundred Compliments which I valued the more
as I respect his Abilities exceedingly : he is a Milanese
Nobleman, but chuses to inhabit Paris, and enjoy that
Liberty which no Place but a populous City can afford :
he politely offer'd us his Seat in the Neighbourhood of
Milan to reside in. We have had some other Italians
dine with us . . . two of them the Marquess Trotti &

streets are narrow too, and ill-paved ; and very noisy, from the
echo made by stone buildings drawn up to a prodigious height,
many of the houses having seven, and some of them even eight
stories from the bottom. The contradictions one meets with
every moment likewise strike even a cursory observer—a countess
in a morning, her hair dressed, with diamonds too perhaps, a dirty
black handkerchief about her neck, and a flat silver ring on her
finger, like our ale-wives ; a *femme publique*, dressed avowedly for
the purposes of alluring the men, with not a very small crucifix
hanging at her bosom ;—and the Virgin Mary's sign at an alehouse
door, with these words,

Je suis la mere de mon Dieu,
Et la gardienne de ce lieu.

I have, however, borrowed Bocage's Remarks upon the English
nation, which serve to damp my spirit of criticism exceedingly :
She had more opportunities than I for observation, not less quick-
ness of discernment surely ; and her stay in London was longer
than mine in Paris.—Yet, how was she deceived in many points !

" I will tell nothing that I did not *see ;* and among the objects
one would certainly avoid seeing if it were possible, is the deformity of the poor.—Such various modes of warping the human
figure could hardly be observed in England by a surgeon in high
practice, as meet me about this country incessantly.—I have seen
them in the galleries and outer-courts even of the palace itself, and
am glad to turn my eyes for relief on the Duke of Orleans's pictures ;
a glorious collection ! " See also above, pp. 93-94.

his Governor, an Ex-Jesuit, are going to visit England,
I will send some letters by them; when they return
to Milan, I shall hear something of my Daughters perhaps; The Abate Bochetti's [1] not unlike a polished
Professor from Oxford or from Cambridge, [I] liked
him very well : he seemed not ashamed of his Religion
or Profession in this Land, & this Time of Infidelity ;
& will take care of his amiable Charge, a rich young
Nobleman sent out to see the World before he *can* understand it, like our Youths of Quality, who run to Italy
with a travelling Tutour just in the same Manner—&
I trust with just the same Success.   I never saw any
but this worth caring what became of them, except
dear Lord John Clinton,[2] & *that* was a *good* Boy, but he
died.

[1] The great-grandson of the Marquis Trotti, the Marquis
Malvezzi de' Medici (whose mother was a Trotti di Bentivoglio), is
preparing Trotti's journal of his travels for publication.   Trotti
and Buchetti remained friendly with the Piozzis for many years.
In Oct., 1787, Trotti wrote from Lisbon to Mrs. Piozzi about
a recent journey through England and Wales.   It was Trotti who
prevailed on Piozzi to make a tour of North Wales.   In 1791 on a
visit to England, during which Trotti and Buchetti were for a time
guests at Streatham Park, the marquis appears to have fallen in love
with Harriet Lee, the authoress.   Numerous letters between Mrs.
Piozzi and Mrs. Pennington relate to this romantic attachment,
which, however, was not of lasting duration.   There is among the
Rylands MSS. a letter from Trotti to Mrs. Piozzi as late in date
as June 14, 1803.

[2] In an entry in *Thraliana*, made at Bath in 1780, Mrs. Thrale
writes : " I have picked up an agreeable acquaintance here in Lord
John Clinton, second Son to the Duke of Newcastle ; I thought
at first he was in love with Hester by his close attention to me, but
I believe he was only seized with the present rage young Men have
of following *a woman of sense*, as they phrase it.—The pretty girls
are so empty, no Society please me but *a Woman of Sense*.   A lucky

18 Sep^{tr} 1784. This is Dr Johnson's Birthday : may God give him many & happy returns of it ; we used to spend these two Days in Mirth & Gayety at Streatham : but Pride & Prejudice hindered my longer Residence in a Place wch indeed had lost its Charms for me. I am Happier at this Moment than I have been these Two & Twenty Years.

1784 19 Septr Sunday On this Day all Paris, and ourselves amongst the Rest, assembled to see The Two advent-urous Brothers *Robert*, and a certain Monsieur Charles,[1] their Friend I fancy, mount up in the Air in a sort of flying Chariot, shaped like a Pleasure Barge ; and suspended to a Balloon filled with in-flammable Gas by a Netting which enclosed the Top, & supported the Vehicle, that hung at the Bottom in a Manner better described by Drawing than Writing & which is in fine described in five Hundred Drawings dispersed all over England & France. What struck me even more than the Sight of Human Creatures floating in the Air, was the Order & Decorum kept among us who were on the Ground—I have seen ten Times the Bustle and ten Times the Difficulty at a crouded play-house in London, than the Parisians made when all the

Folly at least, nor should I call it such but that I conclude it affecta-tion in this Boy ; However it may be genuine perhaps as he thinks it is."—Charles Hughes, *Mrs. Piozzi's Thraliana*, pp. 30-31. Lord John, who was an M.P., died in 1781. He was the *fourth* son of the Duke of Newcastle.

[1] Jacques-Alexandre-César Charles, the well-known French physicist and experimentalist, who first proposed the use of hydrogen gas for balloons. He had superintended the work of the brothers Robert on a balloon sent up from the Champ de Mars on Aug. 26, 1783. Mrs. Piozzi's printed journal adds that Pilâtre de Rosier, another famous balloonist, conducted the flight.

City was gathered together.   Nobody was hurt, nobody
was frighted—nobody was even *incommoded :* some Comforts must then be confessed to result from a despotic
Government.

My Republican Spirit boyl'd a little indeed on
Monday or Tuesday when I went to petition Mon-
seigneur de Calonne for the Things detained by the
Customhouse at Calais : his Politeness at last however,
& the Sight of others performing the same Act of
Humiliation, reconciled me in some Measure to the
Idea of being sent from Subaltern to Subaltern to intreat
the Remission of a Law either just or unjust :—if just,
no Solicitation ought to be suffered ; if unjust nothing
can be more grating than the Obligation to solicit : &
I who have lived only where the Laws are irrevocable,
must be excused some feeling on so awkward an Occasion.

I went to see my old Friends the Austin Nuns at the
Fossée [1] one Morning ; & found them all alive, & well,

---

[1] The printed version (pp. 20-22) has : " Mean time I have
stolen a day to visit my old acquaintance the English Austin Nuns
at the Fossée, and found the whole community alive and cheerful ;
they are many of them agreeable women, and having seen Dr.
Johnson with me when I was last abroad, enquired much for him :
Mrs. Fermor, the Prioress, niece to Belinda in the Rape of the
Lock, taking occasion to tell me, comically enough, ' That she
believed there was but little comfort to be found in a house that
harboured *poets ;* for that she remembered Mr. Pope's praise made
her aunt very troublesome and conceited, while his numberless
caprices would have employed ten servants to wait on him ; and
he gave one ' (said she) ' no amends by his talk neither, for he
only sate dozing all day, when the sweet wine was out, and made
his verses chiefly in the night ; during which season he kept himself
awake by drinking coffee, which it was one of the maids business
to make for him, and they took it by turns.'

" These ladies really live here as comfortably for aught I see
as peace, quietness, and the certainty of a good dinner every day

& not the least altered : I told them again how much happier they lived, than we who bustled in the World ; & once more promised them to come to their Convent if my Husband used me ill. . . .[1] I had told them so before, when married to Mr Thrale : they laughed & said they saw no sign of my Disposition towards a *Nunnery* by my chusing to enter again into the married State, but acknowledged I had not been in haste.

I have seen the Gobelins again, & think the Manufactury improved since I visited it last : the Colouring more harmonious, & the Drawing more correct : The beautiful Church of St Roque is as elegant as ever, & the Symmetry of the Invalides produced the same Effect as when I saw it first.

The Pictures in the palais Royal like every thing which is truly excellent, rise upon Acquaintance : never did I feel my Heart so full with Pleasure at any Exhibition : but the want of Language to express one's Delight helps to oppress one ; The Italians who were

can make them. Just so much happier than as many old maids who inhabit Milman Street and Chapel Row, as they are sure not to be robbed by a treacherous, or insulted by a favoured, servant in the decline of life, when protection is grown hopeless and resistance vain ; and as they enjoy at least a moral certainty of never living worse than they do to-day : while the little knot of unmarried females turned fifty round Red Lion Square *may* always be ruined by a runaway agent, a bankrupted banker, or a roguish steward ; and even the petty pleasures of sixpenny quadrille may become by that misfortune too costly for their income.—*Au reste*, as the French say, the difference is small : both coteries sit separate in the morning, go to prayers at noon, and read the chapters for the day : change their neat dress, eat their little dinner, and play at small games for small sums in the evening ; when recollection tires, and chat runs low."

[1] The dots here and below are Mrs. Piozzi's.

with me, all acknowledged the Magnificence and good Choice of the Collection.   I believe there is nothing to be compared with it on this Side the Alps; & indeed our Friends confessed that Italy itself could not shew at *one View* such a Constellation of Excellence.   I shall let loose however in this Journey the Fondness for Painting which I was forced to suppress while Dr. Johnson lived with me, & ridiculed my Taste of an Art his own Imperfect Sight hindered him from enjoying.[1]   The Parisians however are not thinking about Pictures or Poetry; they are all wild about a wretched Comedy called *Figaro*[2] full of such Wit as we were fond of in Charles the Second's Reign; all Indecent Merriment, & gross Immorality mixed however with Satire as if Sir George Etherege & Johnny Gay had clubbed their Ingenuity to divert & corrupt their Auditors : The King has desired the Queen it seems not to go to it.—The Authour is Mr de Beaumarchais, & possesses so entirely the favour of the Public, that the Women weare Fans with Verses on 'em out of his Comedy as they did by the Beggars Opera in London 40 Years ago. —I have not been at a Theatre myself, but the Conte Turconi (no contemptible Judge of such matters) gave me the Acc^{t.} which I see confirmed by daily Experience. Tomorrow then adieu to Paris ! and let us try to make pleasure out of the various Scenes which present them-

---

[1] See also p. 228.

[2] *Le Mariage de Figaro*, by Pierre Augustin Caron de Beaumarchais.   This brilliant comedy had been accepted by the Théâtre Français in Oct., 1781, but the first public performance did not take place until April 27, 1784.   Louis XVI. was acutely aware of the dangerous influence likely to be exerted by this play, the presentation of which was one of the most important events leading up to the French Revolution.

selves upon the Route to Lyons.   One ought to be
imbued wth Whalley's [1] Notions in the Country, &
Johnson's in the Town, to make a perfect Traveller:
—I will add that one should possess Dr Burney's [2]
Style [in the Closet], when one sits down to write either
of Landskip, Sciences, or Life.

Paris	I must add before I finish the Memoirs
24 Sept^r	made in this City that the Aerial Travellers
1784	are found at Bethune having follow'd the

Direction of the Wind for fifty Miles distance: no Method of guiding the Machine has however
been hitherto discovered.—I saw the Speaking Figure
again this Eve^g & am still more amazed—She eats
Sugar Plums now d'une très bonne grace. [3]

25 Sept^r	We left Paris, & put into the Coach for
1784.	our Entertainment a Book recommended by
	Goldoni [4] & which afforded us Amusement

[1] Dr. Thomas Sedgwick Whalley, poet and traveller, lived much
upon the Continent.   He was a friend of Mrs. Piozzi.

[2] Dr. Charles Burney had published the accounts of his journeys
on the Continent; see *The present state of music in France and Italy*,
London, 1771, and *The present state of music in Germany, the Netherlands and the United Provinces*, 2 vols., London, 1773.

[3] The second half of the eighteenth century was the age of
automata. Perhaps the most famous was the chess player of
Wolfgang von Kempelen, who also constructed a speaking figure.
See also *Wolfgang von Kempelen Mechanismus der menschlichen Sprache,
nebst der Beschreibung Seiner Sprechenden Maschine*, Wien, 1791.

[4] The printed version (pp. 19-20) has : " The famous Venetian
too, who has written so many successful comedies, and is now
employed upon his own Memoirs, at the age of eighty-four, was a
delightful addition to our Coterie, *Goldoni*.   He is garrulous, good-
humoured, and gay ; resembling the late James Harris of Salisbury
in person not manner, and seems justly esteemed, and highly, by
his countrymen."

from the French Fanfaronnades it contained. The
Author [1] gained the Prize which the Academy of Berlin
promised to whoever wrote best on a Subject of Belles
Lettres : this Gentleman judiciously chose to give
reasons for the universality of the French Language
and has been so gaily insolent to ev'ry other Nation
in his Pamphlet, that I trust some will praise, many will
reply, and all will soon forget him. I confess myself
so seized on by his sprightly Impertinence, that I wished
at the moment for Leisure to translate, or Wit to answer
him ; but the want of one *solid Thought* by which to
recollect his Existence, has cured me, and I now see he
was deliciously cool & sharp, like the ordinary Wine
of the Country I am passing thro' ; but [w^ch] having
no *Body*, can neither keep its little Power long, nor use
it while fresh to any desirable Effect. The Country is
really beautiful & the Inns detestable much beyond what
I had any Idea of : whether Travellers never use the
proper Words, or whether Words mislead the Readers
to think of *them* instead of the Things described I know
not, but I had formed no adequate Notion of the magnificent River called the Yonne with Cattle grazing on
its Banks—those Banks clothed with a Verdure scarce
equall'd by any thing we see from Richmond Hill ;
The Vineyards covering the rising Grounds, and young
Wheat ornamenting the Valleys below, while clusters
of aspiring Poplars, or single Walnut Trees spreading
their ample & well-formed Shade seem to be placed
on purpose to attract one's Notice, & inspire poetical
—perhaps pedantic Ideas. M^r· Piozzi once made an

[1] In the *Nouveaux Mémoires de l'Académie Royale des Sciences
et Belles-Lettres, 1774* (Berlin, 1776), pp. 520-552, is the treatise
"*Observations générales sur la Grammaire et les Langues,*" by M.
Thiebault.

Observation which I then thought too slightly of, &
now perhaps remember only because 'twas his :—that
the so-much-praised Verdure of England was too *Mono-
tone :* [1] I now see the Discernement which prompted
that Observation ; the Variety of Greens exhibited in
a French View may well spoyl the Eyes of Foreigners
for an English one : few Things have delighted me more
than to see the Caerulean Willow, the gloomy Beech,
the Golden Walnut, & the Silver Theophrastus sweetly
disposed as if by Brown [2] or Shenstone [3] in a Landschape
worthy a Nation of immense Extent, uniting all the
Sublimity which a wide Expanse conveys to the human
Mind, with all the Beauty that Cultivation can offer or
Fertility can bestow. Every Town one sees scattered
about these lovely Hills & Plains however, shews on
a nearer Approach misery the more mortifying as less
expected by a Spectator, who pays at Night by lodging
in Wretchedness & Dirt, for the Pleasures he has
enjoyed in the Day Time, derived from an Appearance

[1] The printed version later (p. 32) has : " That among the gems
of Europe our island holds the rank of an *emerald*, was once suggested to me, and I could never part with the idea ; surely France
must in the same scale be rated as the *ruby ;* for here is no grass,
no verdure to repose the sight upon, except that of high forest
trees, the vineyards being short cut, and supported by white sticks,
the size of those which in our flower gardens support a favourite
carnation ; and these placed close together by thousands on a hill
rather perplex than please a spectator of the country, who must
wait till he recollects the superiority of their produce, before he
prefers them to a Herefordshire orchard or a Kentish hop-ground."

[2] Lancelot (" Capability ") Brown revived the natural style of
landscape gardening. He laid out gardens both at Kew and
Blenheim (see *D.N.B.*).

[3] William Shenstone, the poet, laid out his domain of the
Leasowes in a style of rural elegance which attracted many visitors
and aroused envy and admiration.

14

of Elegance & Wealth. . . . Elegance the Work of
Nature . . . not of Man . . . and Opulence . . . the
Gift of God, and not the Result of Commerce. The
French do really seem the idlest People one can conceive
to exist, as their Motto to the Arms they are so proud
of expresses it . . . *they toil not, neither do they spin.*
Poverty therefore forces its way among them, though
their Climate is such as would tempt other Dispositions
to improve its Blessings, but *Content, the Bane of Industry* [1]
as Mandeville calls it, renders them happy with what
Heaven has unsolicited shaken into their Lap, and
perhaps the Spirit of blaming such Behaviour may be
less pleasing to Him who gives than the Behaviour
itself. Let us not however suppose them acting from
Principle : . . . I never thought so little Religion could
be tolerated in a Xtian Country : They leave their little
wretched Shops open on a Sunday, & forbear neither
Pleasure nor Business on account of the Sabbath. The
Crucifixes & Madonnas which us'd when I was last on
the Continent to meet my Eyes perpetually . . . are
strangely diminished in Number, & those that are still
standing, will not be here long ; for nobody repairs
them which the Weather ruins.

Our good Protestants may [therefore] shortly travel
from Calais to Lyons, unoffended by the Recollection
of him who dyed to save them.

These Reflexions are interrupted by my Arrival on
the Banks of the Rhône, and Oh how beautiful are its
Banks ! how gloriously rapid its Course !
30 Sept
ember   here seems [likewise] to be something *doing,*
the Sight of which is ever sure to please, and
which I have not seen these last five & twenty Days.

[1] Bernard Mandeville, *The Grumbling Hive* (1705), l. 388, reprinted in *The Fable of the Bees* (1714).

Letters from my Daughters too have contributed to make me see every Thing wth good Humour, & tho' my Health is not all I could hope for, I have little even [on] *that* Side to give me just Cause of Complaint.   Our Apartments here are elegant & comfortable, and we shall take a Week's rest before we pass the Mountains.

L'Hotel de la Croix de Malthe affords good Accomodation within, and a very good agreable View from its Windows . . . they say we have many English Families in the House with us, but I mean not to make enquiries after *them*, the Baths I am told of attract my Attention much more ; and a Dip in this delightful River will surely have some Effect on one's Fancy, as well as one's Constitution.   The view of it by Moon light with its magnificent Bridge and useful Mills, makes one wish for the Pencil of Vanderneer,[1] which alone could do Justice to an Assemblage so truly Picturesque.   The Manufactures at Lyons too deserve a Volume, and I shall scarce give them a Page, though nothing at London or Paris can compare with the Beauty of these Velvets, and the Art necessary to produce such an Effect, while the wrong Side is smooth . . . not struck thro' like the Tapestry at the Gobelins, which at last does not exceed the hangings made here for the Empress of Russia's Bed Chamber.   A Screen for the Grand Signor also was shewn me. . . . He would I fancy have been contented with Richness in his Furniture, but Mr Pernon has added Taste to it, and sunk the Urn made of red Velvet in a Gold Back Ground very cleverly.   It is observable that the more People advance in Elegance, the less they value Splendour ; for Distinction is at last all which mortal Man seems to pant after ; when Necessity is

[1] Aert van der Neer, 1604-77.

once supplied, & Convenience contented ; and as soon
as we have found means to make ourselves eminent for
matters of Taste, we scorn those who can only be dis-
tinguished by their Riches.—Let me now vindicate the
French manner of laying out their Gardens again : we
passed a Day or two at some of the Villas which adorn
the Environs of this City, & I saw with Pleasure the
Shade formed by the Junction of fine old Trees in the
South of France, tho' I should disapprove them at a
Gentleman's Seat in Lancashire to be sure, where the
Sun should be call'd in, not shut out ; & where a large
Piece of Water is wanted to repose the Eye upon, not a
Fountain to murmur in one's Ears, & cool one with the
Sound . . . but where the Rhône is navigable up to
the Doors of a Man's house, I see not but 'tis rational
enough to form Jet d'Eaus of the superfluous Water,
and to walk under the Shade of meeting Oaks on a hot
day.   The Hospitality [1] here is such, & [such] the

[1] The printed version (pp. 33-34) has : " We were not a very
numerous company—from eighteen to twenty-two, as I remember,
morning and evening ; but the ladies played upon the pedal harp,
the gentlemen sung gaily, if not sweetly after supper : I never
received more kindness for my own part in any fortnight of my
life, nor ever heard that kindness more pleasingly or less coarsely
expressed.   These are merchants, I am told, with whom I have
been living ; and perhaps my heart more readily receives and
repays their caresses for having heard so.   Let princes dispute, and
soldiers reciprocally support their quarrels ; but let the wealthy
traders of every nation unite to pour the oil of commerce over the
too agitated ocean of human life, and smooth down those asperities
which obstruct fraternal concord.

" The Duke and Duchess of Cumberland lodge here at our hotel ;
I saw them treated with distinguished respect to-night at the
theatre, where à force de danser, I actually was moved to shed many
tears over the distresses of Sophie de Brabant.   Surely these pantomimes will soon supplant all poetry, when, as Gratiano says, ' Our

Luxuries of the Table, that I counted 36 Dishes today where we dined, and 24 where we supped, and we were not a *very* numerous Company, every thing was serv'd in Silver at both Houses, and nobody talked of the peculiar Opulence of the Masters: they were of the Bourgeois Rank too I believe, and I saw little Difference between the Splendour of an Entertainment given by a Rich Tradesman in London or Lyons, except such as arose from the mere Difference of Custom & Manners. The Duke & Duchess of Cumberland lodge in our Hotel here, & are exceedingly kind to M^r. Piozzi & myself— they are going to pass the Winter She says at Aix en Provence, & mean judiciously to make the Journey by Water, at once enjoying the Beauties of the Rhône & its Banks—& avoiding the wretched Inns they must meet with in going by Land.

Tomorrow we set out for the Mountains of Savoy, we shall get to their feet that Even^g. I am told.

words will suddenly become superfluous, and discourse grow commendable in none but parrots.' "

Henry Frederick, Duke of Cumberland, a younger brother of George III. of England, had alienated the King in 1771 by his marriage with Mrs. Horton (daughter of Lord Irnham). It is *Lorenzo* in *The Merchant of Venice* (Act III., sc. v., 42-45) who says: " How everie fool can play upon the word, I thinke the best grace of witte will shortly turne into silence, and discourse grow commendable in none onely but Parrats."

APPENDIX

APPENDIX

I

LETTERS RELATING TO DR. JOHNSON'S FRENCH TOUR

THERE are a few letters from and to Dr. Johnson which relate to his French journey. On September 14, 1775, in a letter to Boswell, Johnson wrote, " I shall not very soon write again, for I am to set out to-morrow on another journey." [1] Soon afterwards Boswell discovered that this was " no less than a tour to France with Mr. and Mrs. Thrale." From Calais Johnson sent a letter to his humble friend, Mr. Robert Levet, the " obscure practiser in physick amongst the lower people," who " had an apartment in his house, or his chambers, and waited upon him every morning, through the whole course of his late and tedious breakfast." The letter revealed a little of their plans. [2]

> " To Mr. Robert Levet.
>
> > " Sept. 18, 1775. [3]
> > " Calais.
>
> " Dear Sir,
>
> " We are here in France, after a very pleasing passage of no more than six hours. I know not

---

[1] Boswell's *Life*, vol. ii., p. 384. [2] *Ibid.*, p. 385.
[3] On this day at Calais Johnson composed a prayer. It was, he says, " Composed at Calais, in a sleepless night, and used before the morn at Nôtre Dame, written at St. Omers." *Prayers and Meditations, composed by Samuel Johnson, LL. D.*, published by George Strahan (London, 1785), also see Birkbeck Hill, *Johnsonian Miscellanies*, vol. i., pp. 1-124.

when I shall write again, and therefore I write now, though you cannot suppose that I have much to say. You have seen France yourself.[1]   From this place we are going to Rouen, and from Rouen to Paris, where Mr. Thrale designs to stay about five or six weeks.   We have a regular recommendation to the English resident, so we shall not be taken for vagabonds.   We think to go one way and return another, and for (? see) as much as we can.   I will try to speak a little French ; I tried hitherto but little, but I spoke sometimes.   If I heard better, I suppose I should learn faster.   I am, Sir,

" Your humble servant,

" SAM JOHNSON."

More than a month later Levet received another letter from Paris :

" To Mr. Robert Levet.

" Paris, Oct. 22, 1775.

" Dear Sir,

" We are still here, commonly very busy in looking about us.   We have been to-day at Versailles.[2]   You have seen it, and I shall not describe it.   We came yesterday from Fontainbleau, where the Court is now.   We went to see the King and Queen at dinner, and the Queen was so impressed by Miss, that she sent one of the Gentlemen to enquire who she was.[3]   I find all true that you have ever told me of Paris.   Mr. Thrale is very liberal, and keeps us two coaches, and a very fine table ; but I think our cookery very bad.   Mrs. Thrale got into a convent of English nuns, and I talked with her through the grate,[4] and I am very kindly

---

[1] Levet, early in life, was a waiter at a coffee-house in Paris. Boswell's *Life*, vol. i., p. 243, *n.* 3.
[2] See above, p. 177.   [3] See above, p. 125.
[4] On October 16, see above, p. 173.

Madame très honorée

Puisque, pendant que je me trouve chez vous, il faut passer, tous les jours, plusieurs heures dans une solitude profonde, dites moi, si vous voulez que je vogue a pleine abandon, ou que je me contienne dans des bornes prescrites. S'il vous plait, ma très chere maitresse que je sois casé a hazard. La chose est facile. Vous vous fatiguez de la garde de notre ami, Si je ferai de Mais, si ce n'est trop d'esperer que je puisse être digne, comme auparavant, des soins et de la protection d'une ame si aimable par sa douceur, et si venerable par son elevation, accordez moi, par un petit ecrit, la connoissance de ce que m'est permis, et que m'est interdit. Et s'il vous semble mieux que je . demeure dans un certain lieu, je vous supplie de m'epargner

Facsimile of part of a Letter from Dr. Johnson to Mrs. Thrale
in the John Rylands Library.

used by the English Benedictine friars.[1] But upon the whole I cannot make much acquaintance here; and though the churches, palaces, and some private houses are very magnificent, there is no very great pleasure after having seen many, in seeing more; at least the pleasure, whatever it be, must some time have an end, and we are beginning to think when we shall come home. Mr. Thrale calculates that, as we left Streatham on the fifteenth of September, we shall see it again about the fifteenth of November.

"I think I had not been on this side of the sea five days before I found a sensible improvement in my health. I ran a race in the rain this day, and beat Baretti. Baretti is a fine fellow, and speaks French, I think, quite as well as English.

"Make my compliments to Mrs. Williams; and give my love to Francis [2]; and tell my friends that I am not lost.

"I am, dear Sir,

"Your affectionate humble, etc.,

"SAM. JOHNSON."

While in Paris Johnson received a letter [3] from Boswell, dated October 24, 1775, announcing the birth of his son Alexander. Boswell was eagerly looking forward to an account of the journey. He writes:

"Shall we have *A Journey to Paris* from you in the winter? You will, I hope, at any rate be kind enough to give me some account of your French travels very soon, for I am very impatient. What a different scene have you viewed this autumn, from that which you viewed in autumn 1773!"

[1] See below, p. 222.
[2] Francis Barber, Johnson's black servant.
[3] Boswell's *Life*, vol. ii., pp. 386-387.

On November 16, after his return from France, Johnson replied, congratulating Boswell on the birth of the young Laird,[1] and adding :

"Paris is, indeed, a place very different from the Hebrides, but it is to a hasty traveller not so fertile of novelty, nor affords so many opportunities of remark. I cannot pretend to tell the publick any thing of a place better known to many of my readers than to myself. We can talk of it when we meet."

Several other letters written by Johnson on the same day (November 16) survive. To Dr. Taylor at Ashbourne [2] he writes :

"I came back last Tuesday from France. Is not mine a kind of life turned upside down ? Fixed to a spot when I was young, and roving the world when others are contriving to sit still, I am wholly unsettled. I am a kind of ship with a wide sail, and without an anchor. . . . Let me particularly know the state of your health. I think mine is the better for the journey. The French have a clear air and fruitful soil, but their mode of common life is gross and incommodious, and disgusting. I am come home convinced that no improvement of general use is to be gained among them."

To Edmund Hector [3] he writes :

"On Tuesday I returned from a ramble about France, and about a month's stay at Paris. I have seen nothing that much delighted or surprised me. Their palaces are splendid, and their churches magnificent in their structure, and gorgeous in their ornaments, but the city in general makes a very mean appearance. . . . the Queen was so

[1] Boswell's *Life*, vol. ii., p. 387.
[2] Birkbeck Hill, *Letters*, vol. i., pp. 368-369.
[3] *Ibid.*, p. 369. Hector, of Birmingham, was Johnson's old schoolfellow.

pleased with our little girl, that she sent to enquire who she was."

In a later letter to Hector, dated March 7, 1776, he says of France : [1]

"I saw something of the vintage, which is all I think that they have to boast above our country, at least, it is their great natural advantage. Their air, I think, is good, and my health mended in it very perceptibly."

Another letter, dated November 16, 1775, was to his stepdaughter, Miss Lucy Porter, at Lichfield. He writes : [2]

"This week I came home from Paris. I have brought you a little box, which I thought pretty ; but I know not whether it is properly a snuff-box, or a box for some other use. I will send it, when I can find an opportunity. I have been through the whole journey remarkably well. My fellow-travellers were the same whom you saw at Lichfield, only we took Baretti with us. Paris is not so fine a place as you would expect. The palaces and churches, however, are very splendid and magnificent, and what would please you, there are many very fine pictures ; but I do not think their way of life commodious or pleasant."

Miss Porter did not reply immediately, and in December Johnson sent her another letter [3] expressing the fear that winter has laid hold on her fingers and hinders her from writing. He later adds :

"When I was in France, I thought myself growing young, but am afraid that cold weather will take part of my new vigour from me. Let us, however, take care of ourselves, and lose no part of our health by negligence."

[1] Birkbeck Hill, *Letters*, vol. i., p. 378.
[2] Boswell's *Life*, vol. ii., pp. 387-388.   [3] *Ibid.*, p. 388.

Several friendships formed during the French visit were maintained. Count Manucci came over to England early in the following year and was often in Johnson's company, while the relations established with the English Benedictine monks of Paris resulted in more than one visit from members of the order. On May 22, 1776, Johnson [1] wrote to Mrs. Thrale :

> "While I was holding my pen over the last period, I was called down to Father Wilks the Benedictine, and Father Brewer, a Doctor of the Sorbon, who are come to England, and are now wandering over London. I have invited them to dine with me tomorrow. Father Cowley is well ; and Mrs. Strickland is at Paris. More than this I have not yet learned. They stay, I think, here but a little time."

On June 8 he wrote : [2]

> "Of the monks I can give no account. I had them to dinner, and gave each of them the *Political Tracts*, and furnished Wilkes with letters, which will, I believe, procure him a proper reception at Oxford."

One of the above letters [3] survives. It is addressed to the Rev. Dr. Adams, Master of Pembroke College, Oxford :

Sir,

> The Gentleman who brings this is a learned Benedictine, in whose monastery I was treated at Paris with all the civilities which the Society had means or opportunity of shewing. I dined in their refectory, and studied in their library, and had the favour of their company to other places, as curiosity led me. I therefore take the liberty of recommending him to you, Sir, and to Pembroke

---

[1] Birkbeck Hill, *Letters*, vol. i., pp. 401-402.
[2] *Ibid.*, pp. 406-407. [3] *Ibid.*, p. 402.

college, to be shewn that a lettered stranger is not
treated with less regard at Oxford than in France,
and hope that you and my fellow collegians,[1] will
not be unwilling to acknowledge some obligations
for benefits conferred on one who has had the
honour of studying amongst you.

I am, Sir,

Your most humble servant,

Sam : Johnson.

May 29, 1776.

In 1777 the Prior of the convent visited England
with a companion. In a long letter to Johnson dated,
probably incorrectly, September 18,[2] Mrs. Thrale writes :

" I have got some News that will please you
now ; here is an agreeable Friend come from Paris,
whom you were very fond of when we were there :
the Prior of our English Benedictine Convent,
Mr. Cowley—I did not know him again ; so much
was he altered by the change of Dress. How capri-
cious and absurd one is always ! I feel longing to
call him *Father* Prior now ; and upon the Continent
my Scruple hindered (me)[3] from using an Ap-
pelation clearly and absolutely prohibited by our
blessed Saviour's own Words in the Gospel. The
same Objection however would again return if
I was out of England again ; but here, where one

---

[1] Johnson was entered as a commoner of Pembroke College
on October 31, 1728.

[2] H. L. Piozzi's *Letters to and from the late Samuel Johnson, LL.D.*
(London, 1788), vol. i., pp. 373-378. The date on the copy of this
letter evidently sent to the printers (and now in Manchester)
appears to have been altered from September 23. There is another
letter, unprinted, dated September 18, among the Thrale-Johnson
letters in the John Rylands Library, to which Johnson's letter of
September 20 (Birkbeck Hill, *Letters*, vol. ii., pp. 34-37) seems to
be the answer. Johnson appears to have replied to the letter
cited above on September 25 (*ibid.*, pp. 39-40). Numerous letters
were passing between Johnson and Mrs. Thrale about this time.

[3] Not in MS.

knows such Words carry no Meaning of more serious Import, I long to call him *Father* Prior for Fondness. He enquires much for you ; & says Wilkes is very well, No. 45 as they called him in the Convent. A Cell is always kept ready for your use, he tells me ; so when your cruel Mistress turns you out, no harm will come of it ; and when Mr. Thrale dismisses me, I am to take Refuge among the Austin Nuns, & study Virgil with dear Miss Canning.

"Mr. Cowley is as pleasant Company as ever :— We asked Lord Mulgrave to meet him, and *he* said a Thing so like a Thing of your saying, that I will repeat it directly. We talked of England and France —The Beds are softer there than here, quoth my Master. Softer if you will, but not so clean, Sir, replied the Prior.—No, No, dirty enough to be sure confess'd Mr. Thrale, but exceeding soft. Why then, interrupts Lord Mulgrave, one may infer—that a Hog in England lives just like a Gentleman in France I find—so there let the Parallel rest. Now was not that Speech quite in the Spirit of our dear Mr. Johnson ?—I think it will be carried about the Town for yours sometime. . . . Our Paris Friends are melancholy I hear, and Madame de Bocages laments her State of low Spirits ; is there any Foundation for the Idea prevalent among us that we are the only Nation where Hypocondriac Diseases are frequent ? and that the French are almost wholly free ? You are not willing to believe with the Herd in that particular I dare say, yet when a Man is sick you are always sending him to the Continent,—I never can think for what ; —he had [1] better dye at home ; and the Foreigners only get a Notion of England's being unwholesome by seeing such consumptive looking Creatures come out of it as flock to Nice, Montpellier, &c. I dare say they think we are all so ; and you may

---

[1] Always *crossed through*.

remember the French Ladies wondering at my healthy Looks—which I shall never get again."

In what is evidently an answer to this letter,[1] written on September 25, Johnson says :

"I am glad that the Benedictines found you at last. Father Wilkes, when he was amongst us, took Oxford on his way. I recommended him to Dr. Adams, on whom he impressed a high opinion of his learning : I am glad that my cell is reserved. I may perhaps some time or other visit it, though I cannot easily tell why one should go to Paris twice. Our own beds are soft enough."

In an earlier undated and unprinted letter [2] to which a known letter of Johnson's dated September 22 is evidently the answer, Mrs. Thrale writes :

"Your friend Levett came here yesterday, unluckily we dined out ; Father Prior too from the Paris Benedictines and another Monk came here to dinner, but Abbess & Armstrong managed very prudently & pleased them all."

A further instance of Johnson's relations with the Benedictines is given by Boswell [3] in the following account of a conversation at Dilly's [4] on April 15, 1778 :

"JOHNSON. 'O! Mr. Dilly—you must know that an English Benedictine Monk at Paris has translated *The Duke of Berwick's Memoirs*, from the original French, and has sent them to me to sell. I offered them to Strahan, who sent them back with this answer : "That the first book he

1 Birkbeck Hill, *Letters*, vol. ii., pp. 39-40.
2 J.R.L., *Thrale-Johnson MSS.*
3 Boswell's *Life*, vol. iii., p. 286.
4 Two brothers, Edward and Charles Dilly, carried on business as booksellers in the Poultry, London. Charles carried on tne business on the death of his brother in 1779, and among many other works, published Boswell's *Tour to the Hebrides*, and Boswell's *Life of Johnson*.

had published was the *Duke of Berwick's Life*, by which he had lost : and he hated the name."— Now I honestly tell you, that Strahan has refused them : but I also honestly tell you, that he did it upon no principle, for he never looked into them.' DILLY. 'Are they well translated, Sir ? ' JOHNSON. 'Why, Sir, very well—in a style very current and very clear. I have written to the Benedictine to give me an answer upon two points—What evidence is there that the letters are authentick ? (for if they are not authentick they are nothing ;) —And how long will it be before the original French is published ? For if the French edition is not to appear for a considerable time, the translation will be almost as valuable as an original book. They will make two volumes in octavo ; and I have undertaken to correct every sheet as it comes from the press.' Mr. Dilly desired to see them, and said he would send for them. He asked Dr. Johnson if he would write a Preface to them. JOHNSON. 'No, Sir. The Benedictines were very kind to me, and I'll do what I undertook to do ; but I will not mingle my name with them. I am to gain nothing by them. I'll turn them loose upon the world, and let them take their chance.' "

In 1779 the translation appeared in two octavo volumes.[1] A footnote to the advertisement of the original editor states : " The original Editor of the Memoirs is said to be Mr. Hooke, a Doctor of the Sorbonne, and son of the gentleman of that name, who wrote the Roman History." The French edition of the work had been published at Paris in 1778. Luke

[1] The full title was *Memoirs of the Marshal Duke of Berwick. Written by himself. With a summary continuation from the Year 1716, to his Death in 1734. In two volumes. To this work is prefixed a Sketch of an historical Panegyric of the Marshal, by the President Montesquieu ; and explanatory Notes, and original Letters relative to the Campaign in Flanders, in 1708, are subjoined. Translated from the French.* The work was printed by T. Cadell, London.

Joseph Hooke, D.D., son of Nathaniel Hooke, was librarian of the Mazarin Library and was, as we have seen, visited by Dr. Johnson[1] at St. Cloud in 1775.

Finally, less than six months before his death, Johnson was evidently in correspondence with the Prior of the English Benedictines at Paris, for the following passage occurs in a letter[2] of July 11, 1784, to his friend Dr. Adams :

> " I have now received the collations for Xenophon, which I have sent you with the letters that relate to them. I cannot at present take any part in the work, but I would rather pay for a collation of Oppian, than see it neglected ; for the Frenchmen act with great liberality. Let us not fall below them.
>
> " I know not in what state Dr. Edwards left his book. Some of his emendations seemed to me to (be) irrefragably certain, and such therefore as ought not to be lost. His rule was not (to) change the text, and, therefore, I suppose he has left notes to be subjoined. As the book is posthumous some account of the Editor ought to be given.
>
> " You have now the whole process of the correspondence before you. When the Prior is answered, let some apology be made for me.
>
> " I was forced to devide (sic) the collation, but as it is paged, you will easily put every part in its proper place."

The Prior may have acted as the intermediary. Johnson's " convivial friend," Dr. Edward Edwards, of Jesus College, Oxford, had been preparing an edition of Xenophon's *Memorabilia*, and among the manuscripts collated for this purpose were several in the King's Library at Paris. The edition was published posthumously in 1785 with a preface by the Rev. Henry Owen, rector of St. Olave, Hart Street, London. The

[1] See above, p. 181.
[2] Birkbeck Hill, *Letters*, vol. ii., pp. 409-410.

collation of Oppian referred to appears to have been required for an edition by Belin de Ballu, of which, in 1786, one volume was published at Strasbourg.[1]

References to the French journey, or arising out of the journey, are not, however, numerous among the letters of Johnson or of Mrs. Thrale. One interchange remains, however, to be mentioned. In a letter [2] dated May 1, 1780, Johnson writes:

> " The exhibition,[3] how will you do, either to see or not to see! The exhibition is eminently splendid. There is contour, and keeping, and grace, and expression, and all the varieties of artificial excellence. The apartments were truly very noble. The pictures, for the sake of a sky light, are at the top of the house; there we dined, and I sat over against the Archbishop of York. See how I live when I am not under petticoat government."

The reply [4] to the letter, which was written by Mrs. Thrale on May 9, begins with a passage which appears to reveal a little irritation:

> " When did I ever plague you about Contour & Grace and Expression? I have dreaded them all three since that hapless day at Compeigne, when you teized me so, and Mr. Thrale made what I hoped would have proved a lasting Peace; but French Ground is unfavourable to Fidelity perhaps, & so now you begin again: after having taken five Years breath you might have done more than this.—Say another Word, and I will bring up afresh the History of your Exploits at St. Denys, & how cross you were for nothing—but somehow

[1] Birkbeck Hill, *Letters*, vol. ii., p. 410, *n*. 1. The collation from Oxford does not seem to have been received.

[2] *Ibid.*, pp. 150-151.

[3] The Royal Academy was holding its Exhibition at Somerset House for the first time.

[4] Piozzi's *Letters*, vol. ii., pp. 116-117.

or other our Travels never make any part either
of our Conversation or Correspondence."

Mrs. Thrale discreetly makes no reference to the
events at Compiègne in her French journal,[1] but she
reveals, as we have seen, a little of the difference which
arose at St. Denys.[2]

II

DR. JOHNSON AND MISS FRANCES REYNOLDS

In the *Recollections of Dr. Johnson*, first published by
J. W. Croker from various MSS. in the handwriting
of Miss Frances Reynolds, youngest sister of Sir Joshua,
and a close friend of Dr. Johnson, several passages
occur relating to Johnson's French tour.[3] Miss
Reynolds writes :

"It is with much regret that I reflect on my
stupid negligence to write down some of Dr.
Johnson's Discourses, his observations, precepts,
&c. A few short sentences only did I ever take
any account of in writing, and these I lately found
in some old memorandum pocket-Books of ancient
date, about the time of the commencement of my
acquaintance with him. Those few indeed, relating to the character of the French, were taken
viva voce the Day after his arrival from France, Novr.
14, —75, intending them, I find, for the subject of
a letter to a Friend in the Country.

"Also from the same motive perhaps I wrote
down a long narration which Mr. Baretti gave of

[1] But see above, p. 166.   [2] See above, p. 88.
[3] Miss Reynolds's MSS. were then in the possession of the
Rev. John Palmer, grandson of her sister, Mary. Later the
papers descended to Lady Colomb of Dronquinna, Kenmare,
granddaughter of the Rev. John Palmer. Lady Colomb lent them
to Dr. Birkbeck Hill. It is from Hill's edition that the following
quotations are taken, see *Johnsonian Miscellanies* (Oxford, 1897),
vol. ii., pp. 250-300.

some Paris inn adventures &c. related probably the next Day, which is verbatim as he spoke it with an intermixture of French phrases." [1]

Later she gives the following account of a conversation in which Dr. Johnson took part, and also an account received by her from Baretti : [2]

" JOHNSON. ' The French, Sir, are a very silly People, they have no common life. Nothing but the two ends, Beggary and Nobility.'

" ' Sir, they are made up in every thing of two extremes. They have no common sense, they have no common manners, no common learning, gross ignorance or *les belles lettres.*'

" A LADY. ' Indeed even in their dress, their fripary [3] finery and their beggarly coarse linnen. They had I thought no politeness. Their civilities never indicated more good-will than the talk of a Parrot, indiscriminately using the same set of superlative phrases as *à la merveille !* to every one alike. They really seem'd to have no expressions for sincerity and truth.'

" JOHNSON. ' They are much behind-hand, stupid, ignorant creatures. At Fountainblue [4] I saw a Horse-race, everything was wrong, the heaviest weight was put upon the weakest Horse, and all the jockies wore the same colour coat.'

" GENTLEMAN. ' Had you any acquaintance in Paris ? '

" ' No, I did not stay long enough to make any. I spoke only Latin, and I could not have much conversation. There is no good in letting the French have a superiority over you every word you speak.

[1] *Johnsonian Miscellanies* (Oxford, 1897), vol. ii., pp. 286-287.
[2] *Ibid.*, pp. 289-292.
[3] The curious spelling of Miss Reynolds is followed throughout in the quotations. She spells Baretti in three ways.
[4] They saw this race before the visit to Fontainebleau. See above, pp. 98-101.

" ' Barreti was sometimes displeased with us for not likeing the French.'

" LADY. ' Perhaps he had a kind of partiality for that country, because it was in the way to Italy, and perhaps their manners resembled the Italians.'

" JOHNSON. ' No, he was the showman, and we did not like his show; that was all the reason.' "

FROM MR. BARRETI

A lady observed that Dr. Johnson had said that Madam De Bo-age [1] was a poor creature.

" BARRETI. ' Yes, because he hated her before he saw her, for the lady Mrs. Strickland, who went with us from Diepe [2] to Paris, being introduced to Madam D . . . e (by a letter she carried) told her, that le grand Johnson, l'homme le plus savant de toute l'Angleterre, was come to Paris, and Mr. Barretti. " Oh Barretti, Barretti, that I have heard so much of, and I have wish'd so much to see; bring me, bring me Baretti, je vous en prie." '

" Mrs. S . . . D. ' Et le grand Johnson aussi ? '

" M. D. ' Je ne me soucie de qui que ce soit d'autre, pourvu que vous m'amenez Barretti. Je lis actuellement son livre, son voyage d'Espagne,[3] et je suis variment [sic] impatiente d'en connoitre l'Auteur. Mais je vous prie de faire mes compliments à tous, et à Madame Thrale en particulier. Je serai très aise de voir toute cette bonne compagnie.'

" ' Mrs. S . . . d on her return (continued Barretti) said something of Madame D . . .'s impatience to see me in Johnson's hearing; and finding her quite indifferent about him he took such an antipathy to her, that he went with reluctancy to

---

[1] Madame Du Boccage.

[2] They do not appear ever to have visited Dieppe. Mrs. Strickland joined the party at Rouen. See above, p. 78.

[3] *A Journey from London to Genoa, through England, Portugal, Spain and France*, London, 1770.

visit her, and never could be prevailed upon to go a second time ' ;[1] which perhaps was not to be wondered at, for the Ladies and Barretti on going one Day to drink tea with her, she happen'd to produce an old chaina teapot, which Mrs. S . . . d, who made the tea, could not make pour. ' Soufflez, soufflez, Madame, dedans,' cry'd Madame D . . . e, ' il se rectifie immédiatement ; essayez, je vous en prie.' The servant then thinking that Mrs. S . . . d did not understand what his lady said, took up the teapot to le rectifier, and Mrs. S . . . d had quite a struggle with him to get it from him ; he was going to blow into the spout ! Madame D . . . e all this while had not the least idea of its being any impropriety, and wonder'd at Mrs. S . . . d's stupidity. She came over to the table, caught up the tea-pot, and blew into the spout with all her might, then finding it pour, she held it up in tryumph, and repeatedly exclaim'd, ' voilà, voilà, j'ai regagné l'honneur de ma Théière.' She had no sugar-tongs, and said something that shew'd she expected Mrs. S . . . d to use her fingers, to sweeten the cups. ' Madame je n'oserois.' ' O mon Dieu, quel grand quan quan les Anglois font de peu de chose ! '[2]

"This however could not have prejudiced Dr. Johnson against the lady, for, as I apprehended Barretti, it happen'd a few days before they left Paris !

---

[1] This account of Baretti's does not seem to agree with the facts, for Johnson and Madame Du Boccage evidently met on several occasions. See above, pp. 91, 102, 106, 110, 118, 139, 146, etc.

[2] See above, pp. 102, 146. Johnson's account, according to Boswell, was as follows : " The French are an indelicate people, they will spit upon any place. At Madame ——'s a literary lady of rank, the footman took the sugar in his fingers, and threw it into my coffee. I was going to put it aside ; but hearing it was made on purpose for me, I e'en tasted Tom's fingers. The same lady would needs make tea à l'Angloise. The spout of the tea-pot did not pour freely ; she bad the footman blow into it."—Boswell's Life, vol. ii., p. 403.

"On telling Mr. Barretti of the proof that Johnson gave of the stupidity of the French, in the management of their Horse-Races, that all the Jockies wore the same colour coat dye he said 'that was like Johnson's remarks, he could not see.' But it was observed that he could enquire.

"'Yes, it was by the answers he received that he was misled,' for he ask'd, 'What did the first jockey wear?' Answer, 'Green.' 'What the second?' 'Green.' 'What the third?' 'Green'; which was true but then the greens were all different greens, and very easily distinguish'd.[1] Johnson was perpetually making mistakes; so, on going to Fountainblue when we were about three-fourths of the way, he exclaimed with amazement that now we were between Paris and the King of France's Court, and yet we had not mett one carriage coming from thense, or seen one going thither! on which all the company in the coach burst out laughing, and immediately cry'd out, look, look, there is a coach gon by, there is a chariot, there is a post-chaise. I dare say we saw a hundred carriages at least, that were going to, or coming from, Fountain-blue.[2]

"It was mention'd with surprise to Mr. Barretti that Dr. Johnson should not have seen any Play but that one he saw at Fountainblue. 'Oh yes, he was at two or three.' 'Indeed he said he had not, and we know that he never tells an untruth.' B. 'Yes, I very well remember that he straddled over the Benches to come near some person, à la Comédie Française.'

"Baretti on his return from France seem'd full of animosity against Johnson, merely, I believe, from a false conceit of his own importance."

[1] Mrs. Thrale's account, however, agrees with Johnson's See above, p. 101.
[2] Here again Baretti at least exaggerates. See above, p. 118.

A comparison of the accounts by Baretti, Boswell and Mrs. Thrale of the various events described above strengthens the impression that little reliance should be placed upon many of Baretti's assertions.

III

GIUSEPPE BARETTI AND MRS. THRALE (PIOZZI)

THE most embittered of all the attacks on Mrs. Piozzi were made by Queeney Thrale's former tutor, Baretti. His enmity is fully revealed in his Strictures, published in the European Magazine,[1] *On Signora Piozzi's publication of Dr. Johnson's Letters*, and in his marginal notes in his copy of Mrs. Piozzi's work.[2] It may be said at once that such new evidence as is forthcoming, taken from sources which include Boswell's newly published papers and several unpublished letters from Baretti himself, tends to discredit very largely several of his assertions.

In the margin of the Thrale-Johnson Letters, against the letter of June 4, 1776, Baretti writes :

" On this day I quitted Streatham without taking leave, perfectly tired with the impertinence of the Lady, who took every opportunity to disgust me, unable to pardon the violent efforts I had made at Bath to hinder her from giving tin-pills to Queeney. I had by this time been in a manner one of the family during six years and a half,[3] teaching Queeney Spanish and Italian from morn to night, at her earnest desire originally, and Johnson's, who had made me hope originally that Thrale would at last give me an annuity for my pains ; but, never receiving a shilling from him

---

[1] *European Magazine*, vol. xiii., pp. 313, 393 ; vol. xiv., p. 89.
[2] Baretti's copy of Mrs. Piozzi's *Letters to and from the late Samuel Johnson, LL.D.*, is now in the British Museum.
[3] A characteristic exaggeration. Actually the time was under three years.

or from her, I grew tired at last, and on some provocation from her, left them abruptly."

Mrs. Thrale entered in her diary [1] under July 6, 1776, the following account :

> " This day is made remarkable by the departure of Mr. Baretti, who has, since October, 1773, been our almost constant inmate, companion, and, I vainly hoped, friend.   On the 11th of November, 1773, Mr. Thrale let him have 50*l*. and at our return from France 50*l*. more, besides his clothes and pocket-money ; in return to all this, he instructed our eldest daughter—or thought he did—and puffed her about town for a wit, a genius, a linguist, etc. At the beginning of this year 1776, we purposed visiting Italy under his conduct, but were prevented by an unforeseen and heavy calamity : that Baretti, however, might not be disappointed of money as well as of pleasure, Mr. Thrale presented him with 100 guineas, which at first calmed his wrath a little, but did not, perhaps, make amends for his vexation. . . ."

On May 10, 1776, he had written to his brothers [2] that the proposed Italian visit had been abandoned owing to the death of Thrale's son, and that the Thrales had gone away in an effort to find distraction from their grief. Of Thrale he adds :

> " Before starting he gave me a hundred guineas, and there is an end of all the benefits I had expected to reap from him, if we had taken the journey ; and here I am no better off than before.   Perhaps they will think of going abroad again next year ; but each year that passes means another gone, and I grow old apace and the evils of age are overtaking me all too soon."

[1] See Hayward's *Autobiography*, vol. i., p. 105.
[2] The translation is that of Lacy Collison-Morley in his *Giuseppe Baretti* (London, 1909), p. 293.

More interesting is the evidence of Boswell, who certainly would not go out of his way to make misstatements on the Thrales' behalf. On Monday, April 8, writing up in London his journal for Tuesday, March 26, he records certain remarks of Dr. Johnson : [1]

> " He said Mrs. Thrale did not like Baretti, nor Baretti her. But he was the best teacher of Italian that she could have for her daughter, therefore she kept him the house. Baretti was well entertained and well paid, therefore he staid in the house. He lived there as at an Inn. I suppose he meant, gave value for what he got, and did not mind whether the Landlady liked him or no."

By far the most serious of the charges brought by Baretti against Mrs. Thrale concerned her behaviour as a mother. He accuses her of being responsible for the deaths of her two sons, Ralph and Harry. Of the younger son Ralph, born on November 8, 1773, he writes in a marginal note :

> " He died within the year of the inoculated small-pox, during which the mother used to wash him in cold water in consequence of her great skill in physick."

Ralph died at Brighton, aged one year and eight months, on July 13, 1775, and the following extracts are taken from the correspondence, both published and unpublished, of Dr. Johnson and Mrs. Thrale. On May 4, 1775, at Streatham, Mrs. Thrale had given birth to a daughter, Frances Anna, and shortly afterwards it was decided to send Ralph, her next youngest child, who was evidently not strong, to Brighton. On June 7, from Streatham,[2] she wrote :

---

[1] *The Private Papers of James Boswell from Malahide Castle, in the Collection of Lt.-Colonel Ralph Heyward Isham*, vol. xi. (1931), p. 202.
[2] J.R.L., *Thrale-Johnson Letters.*

" Ralph is gone. The other Children are well.
. . . Mrs. D'Avenant [1] has coaxed me to go down
with her for one Week to see her Sister at Lewes,
& bathe Mrs. D'Avenant in the Sea for her health,
we are to *leave our Husbands* at home, I shall see the
Child's Situation—so that is an Inducement."

On June 10 Johnson replied : [2]

" I am glad that Ralph is gone ; a new air may
do him good. I hope little Miss promises well."

On June 16 Mrs. Thrale wrote : [3]

" They say Ralph mends. I long to go see,
but Mrs. D'Avenant is not yet stout enough to
travel so far."

On June 19, from Lichfield, Johnson replied : [4]

" I hope it is very true that Ralph mends, and
wish you were gone to see him, that you might
come back again."

On June 29 Mrs. Thrale wrote : [5]

" The Time is absolutely fixed for our going
to Brighthelmstone, and on Tuesday next the
4th of July we set out, and on Saturday the 8th
or Monday the 10th at farthest—we return. Mrs.
D'Avenant indeed does not go ; her Husband's
Relations grow more & more tyrannical, and will
not let her stir but strictly where they please ; however as I longed to see Ralph, and my Master has
somewhat particular to say to Scrase,[6] and I would
wish to see what Condition the House is in against
we go all together in September : he has promised

---

[1] Mrs. Thrale's cousin, Hester Salusbury Cotton, had married
Corbet D'Avenant, who took his mother's name and was created
a baronet in 1786 as Sir Corbet Corbet.
[2] Birkbeck Hill, *Letters*, vol. i., p. 328.
[3] J.R.L., *Thrale-Johnson Letters*.
[4] Birkbeck Hill, *Letters*, vol. i., p. 334.
[5] J.R.L., *Thrale-Johnson Letters*.   [6] A Brighton solicitor.

to drive me down (if I will take little Jack) and give me a dip in the Sea : we must be at home by the 10th."

On July 1 Johnson wrote from Ashbourne : [1]

" This I suppose will go after you to Sussex, where I hope you will find every thing either well or mending. You never told me whether you took Queeney with you ; nor ever so much as told me the name of the little one. Maybe you think I don't care about you."

On July 3 Mrs. Thrale replied : [2]

" I go to Sussex to-morrow Morning : I so little think of leaving Queeney behind that I forgot to say She went with me : This Post has brought me disagreeable Accounts of poor Ralph : he has had another Struggle with his Teeth it seems, a Fever & Diarrhea but is mending again."

On July 6 Johnson wrote : [3]

" I still hope good of poor Ralph ; but sure never poor rogue was so troubled with his teeth. I hope occasional bathing, and keeping him about two minutes with his body immersed, may promote the discharge from his head, and set his little brain at liberty."

In an undated letter from Brighton which was clearly delayed in the post, for Mrs. Thrale returned to Streatham on July 7, and the letter bears two post-marks " 10 JY " and " 11 JY," she wrote : [4]

" This poor unfortunate Child will dye at last. The Matter which discharged from his Ear was it seems a temporary Relief, but that was all over

---

[1] Birkbeck Hill, *Letters*, vol. i., p. 341.
[2] J.R.L., *Thrale-Johnson Letters*.
[3] Birkbeck Hill, *Letters*, vol. i., p. 344.
[4] J.R.L., *Thrale-Johnson Letters*.

when I came down & the Stupor was returned in a most alarming Manner : he has however violent fits of Rage—proceeding from Pain I guess—just as Lucy & Miss Anna had. Kipping says the Brain is oppressed of which I have no doubt : What shall I do ? What shall I do ? has the flattery of my Friends made me too proud of my own Brains ? & must these poor Children suffer for my Crime ? I can neither go on with this subject nor quit it. . . . I opened the Ball last Night —tonight I go to the Play : Oh that there was a Play or a Ball for every hour of the four & twenty ! Adieu ! my head & my heart are so full I forgot to say how glad I shall be to see you."

Mrs. Thrale returned to Streatham on July 7. Her next letter to Johnson is headed " Streatham, Saturday 9 : July," but July 8 was on a Saturday.[1] She wrote :

" I came home very late last Night and found your sweet Letters all three lying on the Table : I would not have come home at all but Mr Thrale insisted on it—so I have left this poor Child to dye at Brighthelmstone : Doctor Pepys says he will write every Post & Kipping too. What signifies their writing ? What signifies anything ? The Child will die & I fear in sad Torments too—he is now exactly as Lucy was. The discharge at the Ear stopping on a sudden, they bathed him exactly as you would have bid them yourself—by Bromfield's advice indeed but all to no purpose : they are now blistering away about the Ear, Head & Neck, & if he should give them time to do all they intend he will have a Fontanelle cut in his Arm. " Now it is not the Death of this Boy that affects me so ; he is very young, & had he lived would probably have been a greater Misfortune to me : but it is the horrible Apprehension of losing the others by the same cruel Disease that haunts my

[1] J.R.L., *Thrale-Johnson Letters.*

affrighted Imagination & makes me look upon them with an Anxiety scarce to be endured. If Hetty tells me that her Head achs, I am more shocked than if I heard she had broken her Leg. . . . Pray tell me if your Relation Mr Flint [1] has all his Children alive? there was a sweet little Girl among them very like my poor Lucy—& afflicted with Headachs: do enquire whether She be living or no: I took an Interest in her from the Resemblance, & was not without many Apprehensions for her Life. I have forgotten her name if it was not Lucy—I think it was."

The next letter sent by Mrs. Thrale [2] is dated " Streatham, Tuesday, 11 July ":

" I have dismal Letters from Pepys and Kipping too, though the Doctor has some faint hopes, probably for want of Experience in the Disorder. He cuts a Seton in the Neck. Young Practitioners in Physick as in Life will try to do something, Old Practitioners in both know that there is little to be done, and so relinquish Hope too soon perhaps. I am pleased that Ralph is in the hands of Pepys. Kipping the Apothecary of the Place lost one Child by this Disorder and has one alive who is an Ideot."

Meanwhile Mrs. Thrale had been complaining because Johnson had not been writing, and Johnson in a letter written on July 11, said: [3]

" I am sure I write and write, and every letter that comes from you charges me with not writing."

This letter with several others, appears to have reached Mrs. Thrale on July 12. Johnson had been reflecting

---

[1] Johnson and the Thrales visited Flint at Ashbourne in August, 1774. See A. M. Broadley's *Dr. Johnson and Mrs. Thrale*, p. 222.
[2] J.R.L., *Thrale-Johnson Letters*.
[3] Birkbeck Hill, *Letters*, vol. i., p. 345.

that had he money enough he would travel, and Mrs.
Thrale replied : [1]

> " At present the last paragraph of your last long
> letter is much in my head—& Mr. Thrale say'd,
> when we read it together, that you should not
> travel alone if he could once see this dear little
> Boy quite well, or see me well perswaded (as many
> are) that nothing ails him."

Later she added :

> " I said I would write nothing of Family
> Matters but here is a Letter from Sussex come, that
> will make me write of nothing else. The Child
> is very bad I am sure, but I had better go and see,
> for the suspense is terrible, and these nasty Posts !
> " The Illness of this Boy frights me for all the
> rest ; if any of them have a Headach it puts me in
> an agony, a broken Leg would less affect my peace.
> —So many to have the same Disorder is dreadful :
> What can be the meaning of it ? Sophy complained
> yesterday but I hope it was on purpose to fright me."

Ralph died on July 13. The posts must have been
very bad, for Johnson only replied to the above letter
on July 15 and he heard of the child's death on July 20.
On July 13, in reply to the letter of July 7, he had
written : [2]

> " Poor Ralph ! I think what they purpose to
> do for his relief is right, but that it will be efficacious
> I cannot promise. Your anxiety about your other
> babies is, I hope superfluous. Miss and Harry
> are as safe as ourselves ; they have outlived the
> age of weakness ; their fibres are now elastick, and
> their headachs, when they have them, are from
> accidental causes, heat or indigestion. If Susy

[1] J.R.L., *Thrale-Johnson Letters* ; also see Piozzi's *Letters*, vol. i.,
pp. 268-272.
[2] Birkbeck Hill, *Letters*, vol. i., p. 348.

had been at all disposed to this horrid malady, it would have laid hold on her in her early state of laxity and feebleness. That native vigour which has carried her happily through so many obstructions to life and growth, will, I think, certainly preserve her from a disease most likely to fall only on the weak. Of the two small ladies it can only be said, that there is no present appearance of danger; and of fearing evils merely possible there is no end. We are told by the Lord of Nature, that 'for the day its own evil is sufficient' . . . Mr. Flint's little girl is alive and well, and prating, as I hope yours, my dear Lady, will long continue."

On July 15, in reply to the letter of July 12, he had written : [1]

"Your concern for poor Ralph, and your resolution to visit him again, is too parental to be blamed. You may perhaps do good; you do at least your duty, and with that we must be contented; with that indeed, if we attained it, we ought to be happy : but who ever attained it? . . . To your anxiety about your children I wrote lately what I had to say. I blame it so little, that I think you should add a small particle of anxiety about me."

Mrs. Thrale was again at Streatham on Tuesday, July 18,[2] and wrote :

"I am once more returned home from my melancholy Expedition to Brighthelmstone, and finding there five children well, have resolved to be thankful to God and chearful among my Friends again till new Vexations arise. Baretti has been very good, and taken Care of my little ones like a Nurse while I was away, & has not failed writing to me &c. & I am sorry I was so peevish with him."

[1] Birkbeck Hill, *Letters*, vol. i., p. 351.
[2] J.R.L., *Thrale-Johnson Letters*.

Johnson wrote on July 20 as follows : [1]

" Poor Ralph ! he is gone ; and nothing remains but that you comfort yourself with having done your best. The first wish was, that he might live long to be happy and useful ; the next, that he might not suffer long pain. The second wish has been granted. Think now only on those which are left you. I am glad that you went to Bright-helmstone for your journey is a standing proof to you of your affection and diligence. We can hardly be confident of the state of our own minds, but as it stands attested by some external action ; we are seldom sure that we sincerely meant what we omitted to do."

On July 21, in his answer to the letter of July 18, he wrote this passage : [2]

" You and B——i are friends again. My dear mistress has the quality of being easily reconciled, and not easily offended. Kindness is a good thing in itself ; and there are few things that are worthy of anger, and still fewer that can justify malignity."

In view of the survival of Mrs. Thrale's letter to which this was the reply, and which was far from provocative, the following note on the above passage by Dr. Birkbeck Hill is interesting : [3]

" Baretti, describing Mrs. Thrale by the word which gave Mrs. Jonathan Wild such just offence, says that she ' has suppressed the letter that made Johnson write these idle words, therefore I cannot even have a guess at their meaning.' "

We will now give in full a letter from Baretti to Mrs. Thrale, when Ralph was just over eight months old, showing how at this time he wrote to the lady who was later to be so seriously accused by him : [4]

---

[1] Birkbeck Hill, *Letters*, vol. i., p. 353.
[2] *Ibid.*, p. 355.   [3] *Ibid.*, p. 355, *n.* 2.
[4] J.R.L., *Baretti-Thrale Letters.*

"London Aug^st 13. 1774.

" Honoured Madam.

" Ralph, I am sure, cares not a farthing whether his attendants write to you about him, or not. He has a couple of very white teeth in his mouth, and smiles often that people may see them, and write about them, or Let it alone, just as they list. He has had no fever, nor is at all likely to have any. I gave a kiss to his ruby lips for you : what would you have more ? However, if you have a mind he should have more than one, please to come and give them yourself, as we begin to be weary of your absence, and will go no longer through so fatiguing a work as that of kissing the rogue.

" But let us speak of his eldest brother, who delighted in the thought of telling himself to you, and the rest of the travelling folks, the most lamentable, but beautiful, story of the son of a Duke giving a very handsome black-eye to the son of a Squire ; and that fine Gentleman that good Mrs. Thomas makes so much of (how do you call him ?) has spoilt his game by anticipating the account of it. Well ! I have been to see Harry this very morning at school, and by what I have there heard both from him and from the usher, there is not the least hope of ever getting a good whipping, as Harry is [1] resolved not to deserve it these fifty years to come, and has taken his Bible-Oath, I think, to be the very best Boy of them all, be the consequence what it will.

" As to Susan and Popey,[2] they are as fine Girls as eyes can wish to see. I saw them on thuesday in the afternoon, and had a run with them to the end of the garden. In short, Madam, be very easy, for every child both at Streatham and Kensington is well ; nay every body else, Belle [3] included,

---

[1] is *crossed through*. [2] Sophia.
[3] A spaniel which had belonged to Mrs. Thrale's mother. It was not a favourite of Dr. Johnson's. See Piozzi, *Anecdotes*, p. 164.

whom I stroak'd on the back as I went up to the Nursery.

"Beg of the Ladies, Madam, not to bewitch Mr Johnson, and make him unfaithful to his Mistress; for I know she cannot conveniently spare him, as such a slave is not easily to be met with any where in this sublunary world.[1] Besides, should they run away with him, how could I ever starve him in that Land of poverty and famine, called Italy, where I intend to lead him next year? Miss Reynolds will give you a plat de son métier when you come back, for the kind Letter you wrote her. Faith, you threw her in a transport of joy; and for a while she will not be able to bear any Lady being compared to you, not only for goodness, kindness, generosity, and all that; but not even for beauty. Let this make you very warm, in case summer should begin to go off in your Northern Latitude.

"But I must have a few words with Queeney.

"Ditemi un poco, furfantella mia cara? L'avete voi trovata da voi medesima quell' allegoría dell' andar solcando un mar crudele d'Italiano, o ve l'ha suggerita la Mamma? Il Cavaliere Reinolds m'ha voluto scommettere Cento ghinee contro cinque, che voi non potete ancora avere tanto ingegno. Se avessi scommesso, avrei Io vinto o perso? Fatemi il favore di dirmelo a risposta o in Italiano o in Inglese. E quì notate, anima mea, che io non pretendo voi accresciate il tesoro di Lingua che avete; bastandomi che conserviate quello che possedete, perchè, rispetto all'accrescerlo, questa sarà mia cura al vostro ritorno. Addio, gioja, addio zaffíro, addio rubino, addio topazio mio rilucente! Dio vi mantenga sana, e vi rimandi il più presto che sarà possibile al vostro

"affettuosissimo Servidore

"e Maestro

"GIUSEPPE BARETTI."

---

[1] MS. wora.

Another charge brought by Baretti concerned the death of Harry Thrale, who died after an illness of a few hours only on March 23, 1776. On March 25 Dr. Johnson wrote condoling with Mrs. Thrale upon the death of her only surviving son. Baretti made the following note on this letter : [1]

" Here our Madam has sunk the letter to which this is an answer. Did she own in it that she herself poisoned little Harry, or did she not ? I think she suppressed that particularity, and attributed his death to convulsions, or some other complaint of that kind, as Johnson seemed the remainder of his life ignorant of the accident that caused the boy's death, and I would not tell him lest his attachment to her should make him discredit my words, and of course cause a serious quarrel between us."

This charge is further developed by Baretti in his article in the *European Magazine*. Angered by a passage in a published letter of Mrs. Thrale's to Johnson, dated May 3, which he suggests is a fabrication, he relates an incident which occurred soon after Mrs. Thrale, Miss Thrale, and he went to Bath on March 29, 1776 : [2]

" We had been in Bath but a day when, on arrival of the post, Madam proved so very wise as to shew me a letter from Dr. Jebb, afterwards Sir Richard, in which she was pretty bluntly reprimanded for her playing the physician with her children, and earnestly entreated at the same time to forbear giving her daughter what he termed tin-pills. . . . In the act of giving me the Doctor's letter to read, See, see, said Madam with a pert promptitude that always formed one of her chief characteristicks, see what fools these physicians are ! They presume to know better how to manage children than the mothers themselves !

[1] Birkbeck Hill, *Letters*, vol. i., p. 381, *n*. 1.
[2] *European Magazine*, vol. xiii., p. 315.

" On my receiving in this odd manner this odd
piece of information about Madam's private doings
in her medical capacity, and hearing such a mad
comment on a letter that I thought very wise and
very timely, my bile suddenly rose to such a degree,
that I am sure I uttered my indignation in the most
severe terms, and swore that she would soon send
the daughter to keep company with the son, if she
gave her any more of her damn'd pills."

The following evidence relating to Mrs. Thrale's
activities during the month or so after Harry's death
reveals something of the malicious nature of Baretti's
statements.

In the first place Mrs. Thrale did not suppress any
letter of hers informing Johnson of Harry's death, for,
as Boswell notes, the news reached Johnson in a letter
from Mr. Thrale's clerk. This letter concluded: [1]

" I need not say how much they wish to see you
in London."

Johnson reached London on March 29, and, on
visiting the Thrales, found the coach at the door ready
to take Mrs. Thrale, Queeney, who was not well, and
Baretti to Bath. Boswell [2] thought Johnson was hurt
because he was not asked to go with them, but there is
no evidence of this in Johnson's letters to Mrs. Thrale
on March 30, April 1, and April 4. [3] Nor is there any
sign of friction in the following reply from Mrs. Thrale : [4]

" BATH 1 : April.
" 1776.

" My Dear Sir

" Shall I beg you to tell Mr Boswell that I feel
myself but too much affected by his Friendship ;
Yours has been long the best Cordial to my Heart,
it is now almost the only one. I cold bathe here,

[1] Boswell's *Life*, vol. ii., p. 469.   [2] *Ibid.*, vol. iii., p. 6.
[3] Birkbeck Hill, *Letters*, vol. i., pp. 382-387.
[4] J.R.L., *Thrale-Johnson Letters.*

& endeavour all I can to excite appetite, & force Attention; I owe every Thing to Mr. Thrale's indulgent Tenderness, and will bring him home the best wife I can: how has it happened that everybody has been so kind?

"My dear Queeney will be spared me, I see She will; if by patient endurance of the great Calamity I forbear to provoke further Punishment from Heaven—her Danger has shewn me I have still something left to lose. Pray for her perfect Recovery Dear Sir, or you never more will have any Comfort of your

"Faithful & Affectionate friend

"Hester L: Thrale."

On Easter Sunday, April 7, Mrs. Thrale was back again in London, for on that day Boswell was at St. Paul's where he heard an excellent discourse by Mr. Winstanley. He remarks: [1]

"Mrs. and Miss Thrale were also here. I had written a few lines of condoleance to Mrs. Thrale on her son's death,[2] when I arrived in town with Dr. Johnson. She seemed in tender grief today, and said to me, 'What we have been now about is the true comfort.'"

Very soon after her return to London the proposed journey to Italy by the Thrales, Johnson and Baretti was definitely postponed, to Boswell's great regret and Baretti's intense disappointment. In his journal, under Friday, April 5, Boswell records: [3]

"I introduced the intended Tour of Italy which Mr. and Mrs. and Miss Thrale and Dr. Johnson were to make, and on which they were

---

[1] *The Private Papers of James Boswell*, etc., vol. xi., pp. 231-232.
[2] Boswell had written to Mrs. Thrale on March 29, 1776. His letter is printed by Birkbeck Hill. See *Letters*, p. 383, *n*. 5.
[3] *The Private Papers of James Boswell*, etc., vol. xi., p. 226.

to set out early in April. At Beauclerc's on Wednesday Evening it was mentioned, and Beauclerc said that Baretti, who was to go with them would keep them so long in the little towns of his own country that they would not have time to see Rome. I repeated this today to put them on their guard. Dr. Johnson was angry. Said he: 'we do not thank Mr. Beauclerc for supposing that we are to be directed by Baretti,' and he desired Thrale to go to Jackson (the all-knowing) and get from him a Plan for seeing the most in the time that they had to travel. 'We must, to be sure,' said he, 'see Rome, Naples, Florence, and Venice, and as much more as we can.' Thrale appeared to me to have some difficulty about going, and I feared that he might lay aside the design if he was not hurried away. I therefore pressed their setting out speedily, for I was very desireous that Dr. Johnson should see Italy and give us his grand remarks."

Thrale evidently soon made up his mind not to go, though Boswell and Baretti were pressing. On Tuesday Johnson sent Mrs. Thrale a note : [1]

" April 9, 1776.

" Mr. Thrale's alteration of purpose is not weakness of resolution ; it is a wise man's compliance with the change of things, and with the new duties which the change produces. Whoever expects me to be angry will be disappointed. I do not even grieve at the effect, I grieve only at the cause.

" Your business for the present is to seek for ease, and to go where you think it most likely to be found. There cannot yet be any place in your mind for mere curiosity. Whenever I can contribute to your tranquility, I shall readily attend, and hope never to add to the evils that may oppress you. I will go with you to Bath, or stay with you at home.

[1] Birkbeck Hill, *Letters*, vol. i., pp. 387-388.

" I am very little disappointed. I was glad to go to places of so much celebrity, but had promised to myself no raptures, nor much improvement: nor is there any thing to be expected worth such a sacrifice as you might make.

" Keep yourself busy, and you will in time grow cheerful. New prospects may open, and new enjoyments may come within your reach. I surely cannot but wish all evil removed from a house which has afforded my miseries all the succour which attention and benevolence could give. I am sorry not to owe so much, but to repay so little. What I can do, you may with great reason expect from,

" dearest Madam,

" your most obliged and most humble servant

" SAM: JOHNSON."

Mrs. Thrale replied the same day : [1]

" Tuesday.

" Every day every hour makes me more happy in your Friendship—it ought to take up a larger part of my Mind than I can just now afford it—nothing however out of my own Bosom is half so dear to my Heart as that is. I went to Streatham today, & left Baretti trying to perswade Mr. Thrale to go *somewhere* on the Continent—we should look so ridiculous he said—I hope our dear Master has more Wit however than to be bullied or coaxed out of a Resolution which his own good Sense originally suggested & Your Judgment has confirm'd in a Letter which is such a proof of Benevolence as I have not met before. I cannot tell you how much I am your obliged Friend Servant &c.

" H: L: THRALE.

---

[1] J.R.L., *Thrale-Johnson Letters*.

" They are just come home, my master holds his purpose & Baretti teizes no more; Mr Thrale says he has behaved well enough upon the whole, and that as he says he has been at some Expense on the Occasion, that Matter shall be made straight to him.

"Mr. Thrale has seen your Letter & shed Tears over the reading it—they are the first he has shed. —I can say no more. You dine at our House tomorrow. Jackson is put off."

Six days later (April 15) Johnson and the Thrales went to Bath. Johnson had to return to town on May 3 to assist his friend, Dr. Taylor of Ashbourne, in some legal business. He expected to rejoin the Thrales at Bath, but Dr. Taylor's business delayed him, and the Thrales returned to London at the beginning of June.

The letter which caused such annoyance to Baretti was written by Mrs. Thrale immediately on Johnson's return to London.[1] It is dated May 3,[2] which is obviously wrong, since Johnson only left Bath on that night about eleven o'clock. It was probably written a day or so later. The Italian journey was clearly looked upon as only postponed. Mrs. Thrale was very disturbed on account of Queeney's state of health but for which, she says, she would have persuaded Mr. Thrale to persist in his intentions of travelling. She recalls Johnson's kind letter of April 9 :

" Baretti said, you would be very angry because this dreadful event made us put off our Italian journey, but I knew you better. Who knows even now that 'tis deferred for ever? Mr. Thrale says, he shall not die in peace without seeing Rome, and I am sure he will go nowhere that he can help without you."

[1] J.R.L., *Thrale-Johnson Letters;* also see Piozzi, *Letters,* vol. i., pp. 316-319.
[2] " Bath " is added in a later hand.

She also recalled how kind every one had been to her in distress, but then added the offending passage :

"Baretti alone tried to irritate a wound so very deeply inflicted, and he will find few to approve his cruelty."

Baretti was bitterly disappointed because the Italian journey was postponed, notwithstanding his strenuous denials of this when later he was making his violent attacks on Mrs. Piozzi. His letters to his brothers which survive, and have been printed,[1] show how eagerly he had been looking forward to, and making preparations for, the journey, and Boswell relates how on April 10, 1776, when the resolve not to go that year to Italy was referred to, Baretti left the room.[2]

In the months that followed it is not surprising that a man of Baretti's passionate nature, labouring under a sense of grievance, was sullen and captious and liable to violent outbursts of temper. It is probable that Mrs. Thrale showed Baretti a letter from Dr. Jebb,[3] that Jebb warned her against giving Queeney physic, and that Baretti worked himself up into a furious rage. There is, however, every reason to believe that Mrs. Thrale had only done what she considered best for her daughter. She was not ashamed of her actions or she would not have shown the letter to Baretti, nor did she resent Dr. Jebb's advice, for in May she is found sending Dr. Jebb to attend to her other children. Finally, several letters written by Baretti himself in May, though sullen and captious enough in tone, reveal how anxious Mrs. Thrale was about her children's welfare. Mr. and Mrs. Thrale and Queeney were at Bath, Baretti was in London, when the two youngest Thrale girls, living in Kensing-

---

[1] See L. C.-Morley, *Giuseppe Baretti and his Friends*, pp. 285 ff.
[2] *The Private Papers of James Boswell*, etc., vol. xi., p. 233.
[3] Dr. Richard Jebb was created baronet in 1778. He was friendly with Mrs. Thrale after Thrale's death, and is found paying calls at her house.

ton, caught the chicken-pox. We give his first letter in full : [1]

" LONDON, Saturday 11th May 1776.[2]

" I told you, Madam, that both your Girls are well, and do you think I would have told you a fib ? I saw them, and Mrs. Wilton saw them, and, though Mrs. Cumings told us that Susan had had what they call the chicken-pox, we could scarcely find one mark left on her face, neck, arms, or hands ; and indeed I wonder'd at hearing such news, for I had seen her four or [3] five days before, and she was also then in the most perfect health. In short Susan is as well as Popey, and Popey as well as Susan ; and if you will make yourself inhumanly uneasy, I have nothing to say but that your imagination runs into inhuman ebullitions for nothing at all. The day before yesterday I saw Mannucci at Mr· Johnson (*sic*), and they agreed to set out together for Bath on Monday or Tuesday next. This is all the news I have for the present ; and begging of you to show yourself upon occasion, if not a stout Philosopher, at least a resigned Christian, in fact, as you can often show yourself in talk, I am most respectfully

" Your most humble

" and most obedient Servant

" JOSEPH BARETTI."

[1] J.R.L., *Baretti-Thrale Letters*.
[2] Johnson also visited the children on May 11. He writes : " That you may have no superfluous uneasiness, I went this afternoon to visit the two babies at Kensington, and found them indeed a little spotted with their disorder, but as brisk and gay as health and youth can make them. I took a paper of sweetmeats and spread them on the table. They took great delight to shew their governess the various animals that were made of sugar ; and when they had eaten as much as was fit, the rest were laid up for tomorrow."—Birkbeck Hill, *Letters*, vol. i., p. 393.
[3] *MS*. of.

On the following day he wrote : [1]

"Madam, here I am at 8 o'clock and pretty well tired with my walk from Kensington, where I could not go yesterday, nor the day before as I proposed, on account of the weather. I need not tell you that both the Girls are as brisk and alert as can be, and I heard that you made D[r] Jebb smile by sending him to them who have both more health than they know what to do with. Popey read a few lines to me, but she would have managed an Orange better than her book ; However there is no retrogradation at all. Susan mimicks Queeney in her bashfulness ; but there is no great harm in that. Mrs. Cummings would, she told me, have written to you this very night, but as she has nothing to say, and as I told her I intended to come straight home and write, so she begg'd I would give you her respects instead of doing it with her own pen."

And again on Friday, May 17 : [2]

"Madam, on Monday next M[r.] Wilton will go to execute your commands. To-morrow I will go to Kensington again, merely to keep you quiet by telling you as an eye-witness that the little things are well. I have heard yesterday that D[r] Johnson is still in town, and I thought him with you ever since Monday or Tuesday night with Mannucci. Had I imagined he would loiter here so long, I would have gone to take possession of his room at Bath, and stay with my good Queeney for a week, as I begin to grow impatient at her absence ; but one never can guess at the motion of irregular bodies."

On July 6 Baretti left the Thrales. Johnson sent an account to Boswell : [3]

[1] J.R.L. *Baretti-Thrale Letters.*   [2] *Ibid.*
[3] Boswell's *Life*, vol. iii., p. 96.

"Baretti went away from Thrale's in some whimsical fit of disgust, or ill-nature, without taking any leave. It is well if he finds in any other place as good an habitation, and as many conveniencies."

Later some sort of reconciliation took place. Baretti says they met again at a house near Beckenham four years later, but the remainder of his statement shows that his dates were hopelessly inaccurate.[1] The house referred to was Beckenham Place, the home of John Cator, a timber-merchant, who was for a time M.P. for Ipswich. Cator was friendly with the Thrales, and afterwards acted as Thrale's executor. In 1781 when Thrale was becoming more and more ill, his desire to go to Italy became strong. Baretti in a marginal note to his Piozzi *Letters* writes of Thrale:

"He thought of going to Italy, and spoke of it incessantly, and would have me with him, and desired me to keep ready : but he had recompensed me so *generously* for attending him to Paris, and I had so much trouble on that journey that I always put him off when he harped upon that string : besides, Mrs. Thrale would not go because of Piozzi."

Mrs. Thrale looked at the matter differently :[2]

"Baretti should attend, I think ; there is no man who has so much of every language, and can manage so well with Johnson, is so tidy on the road, so active too to obtain good accommodations. He is the man in the world, I think, whom I most abhor, and who *hates* and *professes* to *hate me* the most ; but what does that signifie ? He will be careful of Mr. Thrale and Hester whom he *does* love —and he wont strangle *me*, I suppose. Somebody we *must* have. Croza would court our daughter, and Piozzi could not talk to Johnson, nor, I suppose,

---

[1] *European Magazine*, vol. xiii., p. 395.
[2] Hayward, *Autobiography*, vol. i., p. 132.

do one any good but sing to one,—and how should we *sing songs in a strange land?* Baretti must be the man, and I will beg it of him as a favour. Oh, the triumph he will have! and the lyes he will tell!"

The Italian journey never took place, however. In the morning of April 5, 1781, Thrale died suddenly of a stroke of apoplexy.

Later in the year we find the widow contributing, unwillingly it is true, to the support of her avowed enemy. In a letter to Johnson, dated "Sunday, 18 Nov.," she writes:[1]

> "M[r.] Cator called yesterday indeed, and gave such a deplorable Account of Baretti as shocked me, & produced the five Guineas which I always meant to give him through your hands. He is in the Country with M[r.] Cator who sollicits for him very diligently, & contributes ten Guineas a Year: he would I think have fain perswaded me to make my five ten; but if one is to do *all one can do* for a professed Enemy—how does one deserve to have a Friend? I thought five enough. You however are the Person who is expected to relieve his Distress, and you are to ask the King to give him a pension I think;—it puts me in mind of M[rs.] and Miss Morris."[2]

Early in the following year the King granted Baretti a small pension of eighty pounds a year.

On Nov. 24, 1781, Johnson wrote to Mrs. Thrale from Ashbourne:[3]

> "Piozzi, I find, is coming in spite of Miss Harriet's prediction, or second sight, and when *he*

[1] J.R.L., *Thrale-Johnson Letters.*
[2] A Miss Morris, "daughter to a particular friend of his," begged to see Dr. Johnson on his death-bed so that he might give her his blessing. Boswell, who had the account from his own brother, Thomas David, says: "The Doctor turned himself in the bed, and said, 'God bless you, my dear!' These were the last words he spoke." Boswell's *Life*, vol. iv., pp. 417-418.
[3] Birkbeck Hill, *Letters*, vol. ii., pp. 238-239.

comes and *I* come, you will have two about you that love you; and I question if either of us heartily care how few more you have."

A week later, Dec. 1, 1781, Baretti wrote to Piozzi asking him to give a manuscript to Queeney. This manuscript, entitled *Easy Phraseology for the use of Young Ladies who intend to learn the colloquial part of the Spanish Language, by Joseph Baretti*,[1] was a Spanish translation of the Italian work printed in 1775. The translation had apparently been given to Queeney on January 3, 1780, since reborrowed and was now being returned.

Baretti was not apparently at enmity with Piozzi at first. On March 12, 1784, he wrote to his friend, Don Francesco Carcano:[2]

"I am not surprised at Piozzi's not having thought it advisable to give you any account of me, though he could have done so, as we had several talks just when he was hastening his departure. But I have quarrelled with a mad widow, who is in love with him, and the fact of my not speaking too well of her has not made him particularly well-disposed towards me."

Four years later, in 1788, Baretti in the pages of the *European Magazine* was with incredible coarseness to attack " the frontless female, who goes now by the mean appellation of Piozzi, La Piozzi, as my fellow-countrymen term her, who has dwindled down into the contemptible wife of her daughter's singing master."

[1] The manuscript and note are now in the possession of Lord Lansdowne. See his *Johnson and Queeney*, pp. xiv-xv.
[2] This translation is given in L. Collison-Morley's *Guiseppe Baretti and his Friends*, p. 335.

INDEX

A

Abbess, servant, 225.
Actors and actresses, 78, 96, 98, 123, 126, 137, 140, 184.
Adam Library, the R. B., 10.
Adams, Dr. W., 222, 225, 227.
Addison, J., 192.
Africa, 2.
Agriculture, French, 74 f., 88, 129, 158, 195 f., 209 f.
Alchemist, The, 80.
Alexander the Great, 142, 182.
Alexandre, Mlle., 110.
Amadis de Gaula, 185.
America, 81.
America, South, 112.
Amiens, 74 ff., 79, 108, 196.
Angelo, M., 173, 182.
Anselme, P., 181.
Antwerp, 154.
Araciel, Marquis, 35 f.
Aristotle, 182.
Armstrong, servant, 225.
Arras, 73 f., 79.
Artois, Comte d', 98, 101, 125.
—, Mme. d', 101, 125.
Ashbourne, 238, 240, 256.
Ashe, Miss, 194.
Asia, 2.
Astley, Philip, 99.
Athens, 116.
Augustine, St., 185.

Austin Nuns, English, 120 ff., 134 f., 144, 173 f., 204 f., 218, 224.
Automata, 207.

B

Bachygraig, 14, 166.
Badius Ascensius, 185.
Bagot, Dr., 38.
Balbus, J., 185.
Balloons, 203 f., 207.
Ballu, B. de, 228.
Baltic, 2.
Banks, Sir Joseph, 2.
Barbançon, Mme. de, 81, 122, 144, 162.
Barbary, 171.
Baretti, G., 57 ff., 231 ff., *passim.*
—, accusations by, 234-57.
—, gift to, 256.
—, Johnson's idea of, 58 f., 236.
—, kindness of, 242.
—, letters from, 244 f., 253 f.
—, *Marginalia* of, 3, 4, 27, 234 ff, 246.
—, notes on tour by, 231 ff.
—, payments to, 235 f.
—, scholarship of, 57 ff.
—, writings of, 59 ff., 257.
Bariatinski, Prince, 128.
—, Princess, 128.
Barrett, Mrs. C., 48.

Barry, Mrs., 79.

Bartolommeo, 113.

Basket-work, French, 100.

Bastille, 179 f.

Bath, 22, 64 f., 119, 202, 246 f., 251, 253 f.

—, Red Lion Square, 93, 205.

Bathyani, 103, 106 f., 108, 170.

Baxter, Capt., 70, 165.

Beaumarchais, P. A. C. de, 206.

Beauvais, Mme., 139.

Beckenham Place, 255.

Beds, in France, 75, 77 f., 116 ff., 152 f., 175, 224 f.

Beer, brewing, 179 f.

Belinda, 120, 204.

Belle, spaniel, 244.

Belle Vue, 148, 182.

Belot, Mme., 78.

Benedictine Monastery, Douai, 155.

—, Dunkirk, 162 ff.

—, Ghent, 136, 162.

—, Paris, 97, 170, 186, 219, 222, 225 ff.

—, prior of, see Cowley.

—, Rouen, 82, 85.

Berghem, N. P., 113.

Berkeley, Mrs., prioress, 163.

Berkeleys of Spetchley, the, 163.

Berlin, 190.

Beroaldus, P., 181.

Berry, Miss M., 51.

Bertinazzi, C. A., see Carlini.

Berwick, Memoirs of the Duke of, 225 ff.

Besançon, 122.

Besborough, Lord, 76.

Béthune, 207.

Bible, 38, 180.

Birds, 111 f.

Blackheath, battle of, 7.

Blagden, Dr. C., 187.

Blanchetti, Count, 110, 118, 170.

—, Countess, 91, 94, 102, 110, 118, 170, 201.

Blenheim House, 76, 209.

Blue Nuns, English, 104 ff., 134 ff.

Boccaccio, G., 181 f.

Boccage, Mme. du, 64, 78, 91, 94, 101 ff., 106, 110, 118, 139, 146, 170, 201, 224, 231 f.

—, —, teapot of, 146, 232.

Bochart, S., 182.

Bois de Boulogne, 142.

Boswell, Alexander, 219 f.

—, James, inaccuracy of, 43 ff.

—, —, journals of, 50.

—, —, Life of Johnson, passim.

—, —, private papers of, 236, 248, 252.

—, —, Tour to the Hebrides, 225.

—, T. D., 256.

Boulevards, 91, 116, 123, 174.

Boulogne, 195.

Bourbon, Hôtel de, 123, 127.

—, Louis-Joseph de, see Condé, Prince of,

Bowood, 51.

Bozzi and Piozzi, 46.

Bradkirk Hall, 105.

Brand, John, Popular Antiquities, 135.

Brazil, 112.

Bread, French, 137.

Brewer, Father, 222.

Brighthelmstone, see Brighton.

Brighton, 72, 236 ff.

Brill, P., 113.

Bristol, Bishop of, see Gray, Dr. Robert.

British Museum, MSS. in, 111, 168, 185.

Broadley, A. M., Dr. Johnson and Mrs. Thrale, 37, 69, 240.

Bromfield, Dr., 239.
Brooke, Mr., 112.
Brown, Rev. J., 93.
—, L., 209.
Brunet, M. J., 176.
Brussels, 190.
Brynbella, 64.
Buchetti, abate, 202.
Buffon, J. L. Leclerc, comte de, 111.
Bure, G. F. de, 185.
Burlington House, 93, 200.
Burney, Dr. C., 36, 38, 207.
—, Fanny, see D'Arblay, Mme.
Butler, Lady E., 37.
Byron, Admiral the Hon. J., 60.
—, Hon. Mrs., 37, 60 ff.
—, —, letters to, 61 f.

C

Calais, 70 ff., 74, 79, 164, 191 ff., 210, 217.
Cambridge, 37 f.
—, Fitzwilliam Museum, 148.
—, Trinity College, 38.
Canning, Miss, 120, 144, 174, 224.
Canterbury, 69.
Canus, M., 171.
Carcano, Don F., 257.
Carlini, 109.
Carlisle, Bishop of, 48.
—, Duke of, 103.
Carlyle, Thomas, 173.
Carracci, Annibale, 103, 147 f.
Carriages, dearth of, 118.
Cary, Lucius, Viscount Falkland, 181 f.
Castle Howard, 103.
Castle street, 45, 92.
Catholicon, 185.
Cator, J., 255 f.

Celibacy, 121.
Cellini, B., 127.
Cervantes, 16.
Cesaresco, Countess Evelyn Martinengo, 51.
Chambers, Sir Robert, 10.
Chantilly, 150 ff., 166, 186 f., 196 f.
— playhouse at, 151.
Chapel Row, 205.
Chapman, R. W., 49 f.
Chappelow, Rev. L., 38.
Charles II, of England, 162.
— V, of France, 166.
— X, of France, 91, 125.
Charles, J. A. C., 203.
Charlotte, Sophia, Queen of England, 48.
Chartres, Duc de, 98, 147, 198.
Chartreux, Grand, 4, 183.
Châtelet, Hôtel de, 169.
Chatsworth House, 76.
Chelsea china, 141.
Chesterfield, Lord, 51.
Child, Sir Richard, 107.
Choisy, 96, 118 f., 173.
Cholmeley, F., 162.
Cholmondeley, Hon. Mrs., 107.
Christchurch, 73.
Cid, Le, 96.
Clares, see Poor Clares.
Clayton, Mr., 139.
Clerk, Sir Philip Jennings, 37.
Clinton, Lord John, 201 f.
Cloyne, Bishop of, 93.
Club, the, 6.
Cobb, J., 120.
Cole, Rev. W., Paris Journal of, 70, 97, 104, 145, 153, 155.
Colebrook, Mr., 137, 183.
Colisée, 95, 102 f., 173.
Collect, 145.
Collier, Dr. A., 15 f.

Colman, Mrs. R. V., 68, 190.
Colomb, Lady, 229.
Combermere, 15.
Comedy, Italian, 106, 109.
Commerce, influence of, 212.
Compiegne, 165, 188, 228.
Condé, Prince of, 107, 150 f., 174, 186 f., 196.
Conway, W. A., 39 f.
—, Hon. H. S., 98, 102.
Cookery, French, 70, 103, 114 f., 130, 195, 218.
Cooling, see Cowley.
Corby Castle, Cumberland, 136.
Corneille, P., 96.
Correggio, 148.
Corsini, Cardinal, 35.
—, Prince, 35.
Cotterell, Admiral, 45.
—, Charlotte, see Lewis, Mrs.
—, Fanny, 45 f.
Cotton manufacture, 106.
Cotton, Hester Maria, 15.
—, Hester Salusbury, 237.
—, Lady, 15.
—, Sir Lynch Salusbury, 96.
—, Robert, 96.
—, Sir Thomas, 15.
Cowley, Father, prior of English Benedictines, Paris, 98, 110, 153, 155, 170, 181, 184, 186, 222 ff.
Cowper, Lord, 35, 37.
—, Lady, 35.
Coypel, A., 115.
Cranbourne Alley, 92 f.
Croker, J. W., 119, 172 f., 176, 184.
Cromwell, O., 182.
Croza, 255.
Crumpsall Hall, nr. Manchester, 136.
Crusoe, Robinson, 123.

Cumberland, Duchess of, 212 f.
—, Duke of, 212 f.
Cummings, Mrs., 77, 253 f.
Cunningham, P., 93.
Curios, 113, 116, 150, 171.
Customs officers, 193 f., 204.

D

Dale, Mrs., 165.
D'Arblay, Mme., 13, 22, 25, 36, 48, 56, 66, 148.
D'Argenson, M., 116, 118, 172.
Darmsteter, 143.
D'Aubenton, L. J. M., 111.
D'Avenant, Corbet, 237.
—, Mrs., 237.
Decamerone, 181.
Deerhurst, Lord, 37.
Deformity, in France, 94, 124, 126 f., 152, 201.
Delap, Dr. J., 39 f.
Della Crusca, see Merry, Robert.
Denbigh, 14.
Derby china, 141.
Des Cartes, R., 182.
Desmaretz, Colonel, 161.
Dessein, innkeeper, 70, 164, 194.
Devonshire, 44.
Didon, 137, 140.
Dieppe, 231.
Dijon, 171, 177.
Dilly, C., 225 f.
—, E., 225 f.
Dodd, Dr. W., 38.
Dogs, 148 f., 158, 176.
Dominican nuns, Calais, 71, 164, 192 f.
Douai, 72, 104.
—, Parliament of, 155.
—, St. Peter's Church, 155 f.
Dover, 3, 58, 69 f., 165, 190 f.

Dover, inn at, 191.
Dows, Gerard, 113.
Dresden, 190.
Dress, 70, 75, 94, 96, 100, 124, 126, 128.
Drumgould, Colonel, 182 f., 186.
Drummond, James, 32.
Dryden, J., 102, 182.
Du Barri, Mme., 119.
Dudley, Lord, 37.
Duesbury, W., 141.
Du Fourny, 181.
Dumouriez, C. F., 54.
Dunkirk, 160 ff.
Duppa, R., 69.
Durand, U., 180.
Durey de Meynières, see Belot.
Durnford, Stillingfleet, 161.
—, Charlotte, see Frazer, Mrs.

E

Eccard, J. E., 91.
Ecclesiastes, 30.
École Militaire, 169, 182.
Edwards, Dr. E., 227.
—, G., 112.
Elizabeth, Princess, 124, 176.
Elphinstone, Adm. George Keith, Viscount Keith, 57.
Enfans trouvés, Hôpital des, 109, 184.
Englefield, Sir H., 162.
—, Ethelinda C., 162.
—, Teresa A., 162.
Etherege, Sir George, 206.
Eton, 9.
European Magazine, 64, 234, 246 f., 255, 257.
Exeter Change, 109.

F

Face, 80.
Fazio, 40.
Félibien, M., 150.
Felix, Father, 71 f., 154, 164, 192.
Fellowes, Sir James, 37 f.
Fénelon, Archbishop, 154.
Fermor, Mrs., 120, 144, 173, 204.
Fife, Lord, 37.
Fitzgerald, Mr., 54.
Fitzherbert, Miss, 144.
Flanders, houses in, 74, 153, 155.
Fleury, abbé, 30.
Flint, Lucy, 240.
—, Mr., 240.
Florence, 2, 35.
Florence Miscellany, 41.
Foire St. Ovide, 92.
Fontainebleau, 74 f., 102 f., 120, 124 f., 133, 175, 218, 230, 233.
—, palace at, 127 ff.
—, play at, 128 f., 139.
Food, French, 74 f., 102 f., 125, 212 f.
Foote, Samuel, 72, 96, 131, 184.
—, works of, 72, 131.
Forbes, Dr., 55.
Forster, G., 51.
Fossée, see Austin Nuns, English.
Francis, St., 83.
—, Miss M., 36, 38.
Francis I, of France, 97.
Francken, Frans, 113.
François, abbé, 110, 120, 130, 133, 139, 141, 170.
Frazer, Capt. Andrew, 161 ff.
—, Mrs., 161 ff.
French, habits of, 75, 89, 91, 95, 100 ff., 107, 109 f., 125, 137 f., 148, 195, 199 f., 203 f., 210, 220 ff., 230.

French, indelicacy of, 100, 133, 138, 140.
— journal, Mrs. Thrale's, 67 ff.
— —, Johnson's, 167 ff.
— —, Mrs. Piozzi's, 189 ff.
— journey, cost of, 57.
— language, 208, 218.
— master, 96.
Fréron, M., 173.
Friars, manners of, 121 f.
Fry, Mr. 28.
Fust, printer, 185.

G

Gabriel, J. A., 166.
Gagnier, see Gagny.
Gagny, M. de, 112, 119, 171.
Gallia Christiana, 181.
Gamester, The, 98.
Gardening, French, 87, 108, 115, 142, 150 f., 212 f.
Garrick, D., 39.
Gartside, J., 136.
Gay, J., 206.
Geeraerts, M. J., 154.
Geneste, 79, 80.
Gentilly, 183.
Ghent, 136, 162.
Gibbes, Sir G. S., 56.
Gibraltar, 171.
Gifford, W., 51.
Gillon, J., 37.
Glasse, Rev. G. H., 37.
Gobelins tapestry, 110 f., 115, 170, 205, 211.
Goldoni, 207.
Goldsmith, O., 39, 112.
Gough, Sir H., 143, 182 f.
Gratiano, 212.
Gravelines, see Poor Clares.
Gray, Dr., 187.
—, Dr. Robert, 34, 38.

Gray, Thomas, 93.
—, Mrs., see Grey, Miss.
Greatheed, B., 39 ff.
Great Yarmouth, 148.
Green, jockeys in, 101, 230, 232.
Greenwich, chapel at, 131.
Grenville, H., 102.
Gretna Green, 37.
Grêve, the, 179.
Grey, Miss, 71 f., 165, 192 f.
—, Sir H., 72.
Guemené, Mme. de, 124, 176.
Gutenberg, J., 185.

H

Halifax, Lord, 14 f.
Hamilton, Duke of, 46.
Hamlet, 199.
Hampstead, 142.
Hanover, 190.
Hanover Square, 170.
Harris, James, 15, 207.
Haslewood, 163.
Hatzfeld, 143.
Hawkins, Sir J., 44.
Hayward, Autobiography, etc., 11, passim.
Hebrides, 2.
Hector, Mr., 221.
Heinel, Mlle., 114.
Henley, Robert, Earl of Northington, 108.
—, —, daughters of, 108.
Henry IV, of France, 132.
Henry the Fifth, 131.
Henry VII, of England, 14.
Herrick, Robert, 135.
Highgate, 142.
Hill, G. Birkbeck, 1, 18, 20, 22, 23, 31, 41, 50, 194.
—, —, Johnsonian Miscellanies, 217 ff.

Hill, G. Birkbeck, *Letters of Samuel Johnson*, 10, 18, 20 ff., 47 ff., 64 f., 217 ff., 227 ff., 237 ff., 253.

—, —, See Boswell's *Life of Johnson*, 1, *passim*.

Hilton, Elizabeth, 106.

—, J., 106.

Hinchcliffe, Dr., 38.

Hoare, Mrs. Merrik, see Thrale, Sophia.

Holker, J., 106, 111.

—, Mrs., 106.

Holland, 1.

Holman, J. G., 39.

—, Mrs., 39.

Hooke, Dr. L. J., 139, 181, 226 f.

Hooker, see Holker.

Horse-race, 98 ff., 230.

Horton, Mrs., 213.

Hôtel d'Angleterre, 70.

Hôtel de la Croix de Malthe, 211.

Houses, French, 74, 76, 113, 116 f., 119 f., 127 f., 138, 142, 149, 169, 172 f., 176 f., 187, 195 ff., 220.

Howard, Catherine, 136.

—, —, Lady, 136.

—, Henry, Duke of Norfolk, 136.

—, Mrs., 106, 134.

—, Philip, 136.

—, Lady Philippa, 60 f.

Hughes, Charles, 160, 203.

Hulton, see Hilton.

Huntingdon, Lord, 37.

Hutton, James, 37.

I

Iceland, 1.

Inns, French, 76, 79, 90, 197, 208, 211 ff.

Invalides, chapel of the, 145 f., 149, 205.

Ireland, 65.

Irnham, Lord, 213.

Irwin, Capt., 110, 171.

—, Mrs., 110.

Isham, Lt.-Col. Ralph Heyward, 236.

Islington, 93, 110.

Italy, 1 ff., 35 ff., 231, 250 ff.

J

Jackson's Oxford Journal, 22.

James II, of England, 97.

James, George, 37, 198.

—, Dr. R., 194.

Jebb, Sir Richard, 19, 246, 252, 254.

Jesuits, 72, 104, 186.

Jockeys, 101.

Johannes Bonifacius, 185.

John Rylands Library, 14 ff., 22, 202.

—, letters in,

—, —, Burney-Thrale, 36.

—, —, Byron-Thrale, 37, 60 f.

—, —, Cecilia Thrale (Mostyn), 32 f., 62 f.

—, —, Chappelow-Piozzi, 38.

—, —, Conway-Piozzi, 39.

—, —, Delap-Thrale, 39.

—, —, Francis-Piozzi, 36.

—, —, Gillon-Piozzi, 37.

—, —, Gray-Piozzi, 38.

—, —, Greatheed-Piozzi, 39.

—, —, Kirkwall-Piozzi, 37.

—, —, Ladies of Llangollen-Piozzi, 37.

—, —, Lort-Thrale, 37.

—, —, Lysons-Piozzi, 37.

—, —, Mrs. Piozzi to her daughters, 28.

John Rylands Library, letters in, Murphy-Thrale, 38.
—, —, Pennant-Piozzi, 37.
—, —, Pennington-Piozzi, 34.
—, —, Piozzi, 37.
—, —, Piozzi-Chappelow, 38.
—, —, Piozzi-Salusbury, 21, 34.
—, —, Salusbury-Piozzi, 55.
—, —, Seward-Piozzi, 38.
—, —, Siddons-Piozzi, 39.
—, —, Thrale-Johnson, 11, 23 ff., 26, 112, 139, 223, 225, 234 ff., 247, 250 f., 256.
—, —, Whalley-Piozzi, 38.
—, —, Williams-Piozzi, 38.
—, MSS. in,
—, —, Adventurer, 40.
—, —, British Synonymy, 51.
—, —, Cervantes de Saavedra, trans., 16.
—, —, continental journey, 190.
—, —, Don Quixote (fragment), trans., 16.
—, —, Endovellicus, 41.
—, —, French journal, 68.
—, —, Humourist, 40.
—, —, Retrospection, 52 ff.
—, —, Sketch of Europe, trans., 54.
—, —, Streatham portraits, 41.
—, —, Three Dialogues, 41.
—, —, Three Warnings to John Bull, 52.
—, —, Two Fountains, 40.
—, —, Una and Duessa, 54.
Johnson, Dr. Samuel, 76, 90, 106, 128, 142 f., 153, 155, 164, 166, 203 f., 207.
— and art, 206.
— and Baretti, 219, 255.
— as traveller, 1 ff.
— at play, 233.

Johnson at Streatham, 3, 9, 20.
—, birthday of, 71, 203.
—, character of, 42 ff., 47, 88.
—, dislikes French, 184, 230 f.
—, journal of, 5 ff., 167 ff.
—, letters of, see Hill, G. Birkbeck.
—, Miss Reynolds and, 229 ff.
—, note-books of, 168.
—, observations by, 69, 71, 85 ff., 92, 131, 156, 159 ff.
—, portrait of, 39.
—, Prayers and Meditations, 175, 184, 217.
—, purchases by, 174.
—, Rambler, 6.
—, Rasselas, 78, 82, 144.
—, wager of, 124.
—, wig of, 164.
—, with Benedictine monks, 8, 140, 186, 222 ff.
Johnson, Mrs., 175.
Jonson, B., 80.
Julius Cæsar's well, 70.
Justice, Courts of, 172, 177.

K

Keene, Mr., 143, 182 f.
Keith, Lady, see Thrale, H. M.
—, Lord, see Elphinstone.
Kempelen, Wolfgang von, 207.
Kendal, 61 f.
Kensington, 77, 244, 253.
Killpatrick, Capt., 114, 141, 183.
King's Library, Paris, 138, 180, 227.
Kingston, Duchess of, 71.
Kinnaird, Lord, 148.
Kipping, apothecary, 239 f.
Kirkham, Lancs., 105.
Kirkwall, Lady, 37.

Knapp, O. G., 39, 64.
Knight, Ellis C., 38.

L

Lancashire, 212.
Langdale, W., 163.
—, Jane, 163.
Langton, B., 48.
Lansdowne, Marquis of, 22, 31, 33, 57, 257.
Laon, 213.
Lathomi, P., 185.
Laud, Archbishop, 173.
Lauzun, duc de, 98.
La Vallière, Louise de, 97.
Leasowes, the, 209.
Lee, Harriet, 37, 202.
Leicester Square, 92.
Le Liever, M., 139, 158.
Le Roy, J. D., 99 f., 110, 116 f., 120, 138, 148 f., 170.
—, P., 117 f., 149, 172.
Le Sueur, E., 183.
Lethe, 140.
Lever, Sir Ashton, 111.
Leverian Museum, 111 f.
Levet, R., 178, 217 ff., 225.
Leviez, M., 91.
Lewis, see Louis.
Lewis, Mrs., 38, 42, 44 ff.
—, —, letter from, 44 ff.
Lichfield, 69, 221, 237.
Lille, 158 ff.
Lillers, 73 f.
Lisbon, 202.
Little Newport St., 93.
Little Trianon, 178.
Liverpool, 60.
Llangollen, ladies of, 37.
Llanrhaiadhr, 156.
Loirelle, B. de, 98.
London, 119, 137.

Longitude, 117 f.
Lorenzo, 213.
Lort, Dr. M., 37.
Louis XIV, of France, 93, 170, 178.
— XV, of France, 92, 97, 119, 141, 166.
— XVI, of France, 124 f., 131, 175 f., 179, 183, 206, 218.
— XVIII, of France, 133.
Louise Marie, Princess, 150.
Lower Ditchford, 153.
Lungs, 80.
Luther, M., 166.
Luton, 15.
Luxembourg, gallery, 110.
— gardens, 114, 116, 123, 147, 183.
Luynes, Duchess of, 127.
Lyford, E., 53.
Lyford Redivivus, 53.
Lyons, 185, 210 ff.
Lysons, D., 37.
—, S., 37.
Lyttelton, W., 9.

M

MacArdell, J., 91.
Maffei, J. P., 186.
Maittaire, M., 185.
Malahide Castle, 236.
Malone, Edmond, 168.
Malvezzi de' Medici, Marquis, 202.
Mammon, Sir Epicure, 80.
Manchester, 106.
Mandeville, B., 210.
Mangin, Rev. E., 41, 53, 56.
Mann, Sir H., 41, 107.
Manucci, Count, 59, 64 ff., 102 f., 106, 108, 110, 114, 118, 120, 137 f., 170, 175, 222, 253.

Margate, 66.
Mariage de Figaro, Le, 206.
Marie-Antionette, Queen of France, 98 f., 125, 131, 141, 218, 220.
—, —, apartments of, 132 f.
—, —, at theatre, 128 f.
—, —, goes riding, 126 f., 175, 177.
Marie-Louise-Josephine, Princess, 133.
Marie-Thérèse, Princess, 91.
Marlborough, 71.
Martène, E., 180.
Masterman, Mrs., 164 f.
Mayans y Siscar, G., 16.
Mazarin, 182.
— Library, 227.
Mead, Dominick, 103, 120.
Mediterranean, 2.
Meerman, G., 185.
Menagerie, 130 f., 187 f.
Merchant of Venice, The, 213.
Merritt, P., 39, 54.
Merry, Robert, 41.
Meudon, 142, 182.
Meursius, J., 185.
Mignard, Pierre, 132.
Milan, 35, 66, 201 f.
Milman, H. H., 40.
Milman St., 205.
Milton, 85 f., 102.
Minucci see Manucci, Count.
Mirrors, manufacture of, 178 f.
Molly, servant, 70, 148, 165.
Montagu, Mrs. Elizabeth, 18, 42. ff.
—, —, letter of, 43 f.
Montesquieu, president, 226.
Montmartre, 142.
Montpellier, 224.
Montreuil, girl at, 196.
Mont Valérien, 142.

Monville, M., 113, 169 f.
Moore, Mr., 111.
—, E., 98.
—, J. B., 104.
—, Miss, 104.
—, Thomas, 54.
—, Sir Thomas, 182.
More, Hannah, 37, 42, 48.
Morgue, 137 f.
Morley, Lacy Collison-, 16, 57, 235, 252, 257.
Morres, Henry Redmond, Viscount Mountmorres, 114.
Morris, Miss, 256.
—, Mrs., 256.
Mostyn, J. M., 32 f.
—, Mrs., see Thrale, Cecilia.
Motteux, Mr., 137, 184.
Mount Calvary, see Mont Valérien.
— Cassell, 160.
Mulgrave, Lord, 224.
Munich, 190.
Murphy, A., 9, 38 f.
Murray, David, Earl of Mansfield, 128.

N

Napier, A., 172.
Naples, 2.
National Gallery, 148.
Naudæus, 182.
Neer, A. van der, 211.
Neilson, J., 111.
Netherlands, 1.
Neufchâtel, 76 f., 79.
Newcastle, Duke of, 202.
Nice, 224.
Nicholson, Miss, 28 f.
Niggey, see Thrale, H. M.
Nîmes, 171.

Norfolk, Duke of, 61.
Normandy, 178.
Norwood, 142.
Notre Dame, Paris, 95.
Notre Dame de Syon, 120.
Nova Scotia, 15.
Noyon, 152, 166, 188.
Nuncio, papal, 128.
Nuns, lives of, 193 f. ; see Calais,
    Paris, Rouen.

O

Offley Place, 15.
Opera, French, 115, 148, 175.
Oppian, works of, 227 f.
Oratory, Fathers of the, 169.
Orleans, 171.
—, Philip, Duke of, 150.
—, —, palace of, 103 f.
—, —, —, pictures in, 103 f.,
        115, 119, 132, 147,
        201.
Ossory, Dean of, 38.
Owen, Rev. H., 227.
Oxford, 1, 9, 18, 47, 73, 86, 132,
    186, 222 ff., 227 f.
—, All Souls College, 73, 132.
—, Jesus College, 227.
—, Pembroke College, 1, 222 f.

P

Padua, 1.
Palais Bourbon, 174 f.
— Marchand, 139, 147, 172, 174.
— Royal, 147, 149, 173, 198,
    205 f.
Palmer, Rev. J., 229.
Panchaud, M., 107.
Panthéon, 95.
Panting, Dr. M., 1.
Paris, passim.

Paris, cleanliness of, 119.
—, Parliament of, 174.
—, Playhouse at, 96.
—, streets of, 94, 148 f.
Parker, Alexander, 105.
—, Dr., 15.
—, Dorothy, 105.
—, Capt. T., 105.
Parr, Dr. Samuel, 37.
Parson, W., 41.
Paulmy, see D'Argenson.
Payne, Mrs., 58.
Pembroke, Lord, 35, 37.
Pennant, T., 37 187.
Pennington, Mrs., 34, 38 f., 56,
    64, 202.
Pennyman, Sir J., 72.
—, Lady, 72.
Penrice, I., 148.
Penthièvre, Duke of, 76.
—, —, villa of, 107.
Penzance, 53.
Pepys, Sir Lucas, 19, 37, 239 f.
—, W. W., 28.
Perkins, Mr., 11.
Pernon, M., 211.
Perron, Mme. du, 78, 83, 86.
—, M. du, 78.
Peterborough, Bishop of, see
    Hinchcliffe, Dr.
Petit Dunkerque, 143.
Petite Vienne, 131.
Petrarch, 181.
Phèdre, 78 f.
Philippe Egalité, 198.
Piccioni, L., 57.
Piozzi, G., 3, 7, 21 ff., 33, 36, 66,
    190 f., 208, 213, 256 f.
—, H. L., see also Thrale,
    Hester Lynch.
—, —, Anecdotes, 4 f., 10, 26 f.,
    41 ff., 47, 69, 85 f., 88,
    131, 244.

Piozzi, H. L., *Letters to and from the late Samuel Johnson*, 3, 4, 234.
—, —, *British Synonymy*, 51.
—, —, *Intimate letters of H. Piozzi and P. Pennington*, 39, 64.
—, —, *Observations*, etc., 50 ff.
—, —, *Retrospection*, 52 ff.
—, —, *Three Warnings to John Bull*, 52.
—, John Salusbury, see Salusbury, Sir J. S. P.
Piozziana, 41, 53, 56.
Pitt, Thomas, 150.
—, William, 52.
Place de la Concorde, 92.
— Louis Quinze, 173.
— Vendôme, 170.
— de Victoire, 93, 183.
Planta, Mr., 185.
Plato, 182.
Plays, 78 f., 96, 98, 128 f., 137, 140, 143, 148, 176, 206, 212, 233.
Poelenburgh, C. van, 113.
Poetry, French, 133.
Pompadour, Mme. du, 141 f.
Pompignan, J. J. le Franc de, 137.
Ponsonby, Miss Sarah, 37.
Poor Clares, Dunkirk, 162.
—, Gravelines, 164.
—, Rouen, 79 f., 83 f., 146, 163 f.
Pope, A., 15, 102, 120, 166, 174, 204.
Porcelain, French, 132, 141, 182.
Porter, Miss Lucy, 174, 221 f.
Port Royale, abbey of, 136.
Preston, 62, 105.
Primaticcio, 127.
Printing, 180 f.

Provence, Mme. de, 133.
Psalmorum Codex, Mainz, 185.

Q

Quarterly Review, 51.
Queeney, see Thrale, H. M.

R

Racine, Jean, 15.
—, Louis, 78 f.
Ramsay, Sir J., 15.
Raphael, 6, 148, 173.
Rapin, Paul de, 192.
Rationale divinorum officiorum, 180, 185.
Raucourt, Mlle., 140.
Ray, Robert, 28, 33.
Recueil des historiens des Gaules, etc., 181.
Red Lyon Square, see Bath.
Rembrandt, 142.
Revett, N., 116.
Revolution, French, 73, 173, 206.
Reynolds, Frances, 36, 42, 245.
—, —, MS. notes of, 229 f.
—, Sir Joshua, 36, 39, 45 f., 229, 245.
—, Mary, 229.
Rhone, river, 209 ff.
Ribbleton, 105.
Richelieu, Cardinal, 98.
Roads, French, 74, 76, 87, 137, 164, 171, 174, 197.
Robert, brothers, 203.
Roberts, S. C., 4, 53.
—, W. W., 36.
Rochester, 69.
Rodney, Sir G., 184.
Roehampton, 76.
Roffette, abbé, 47, 82 ff.

Rogers, S., 32, 37, 168.
Romano, G., 142.
Rome, 2.
Rosier, P. de, 203.
Rouen, 77 ff., 86, 144 ff., 163 f., 218.
Rousseau, 135.
Royal Academy, 228.
Roydon, Diss, 38.
Rubens, 113, 132, 147, 173.
Rue d'Enfer, 183.
Rue des Fossés St. Victor, 120.
Rue de Varenne, 171.
Rue Jacob, 137.
Rue St. Antoine, 104.
Rue St. Jacques, 97.
Rue St. Victoire, 120.
Russia, Empress of, 211.
—, ambassador of, see Bariatinski.

S

Sacchini, 66.
Sadlers Wells, 110.
St. Asaph, Bishop of, 38.
St. Cloud, 181 f., 227.
St. Denys, 89, 149 f., 186, 228.
St. Edmond, monks of, 139.
Sainte-Marthe, brothers, 181.
St. Eustache, church of, 184 f.
St. Germain des Prés, library at, 185.
St. Germaine-en-Laye, 88 f., 185 f.
—, forest of, 89.
St. Hilaire, mitre of, 150.
St. Hyacinthe, Cordonnier de, 172.
St. James Chronicle, 15, 40.
St. Julien, M., 117, 119, 149, 172.
St. Louis, King of France, 183.
St. Maur, Benedictines of, 181.
St. Olave, church of, 227.

St. Omer, 72 ff., 217.
—, college at, 72, 74, 79, 95.
St. Quentin, 188.
St. Roque, church of, 96, 144 f., 197 f.
—, —, procession at, 144 f.
St. Vaast, church of, 73.
Salford Hall, 153.
Salusbury, Hester Lynch, see Thrale, Hester Lynch.
—, John, 14 f., 17, 21.
—, Sir John Salusbury Piozzi, 21, 34 f., 40, 55, 68.
—, Thomas, 14.
—, Sir Thomas, 15, 17.
Sam, servant, 70, 88, 145, 156 161, 165.
Sandys, G., 182.
Santerre, A. J., 178.
Sausmarez, Admiral Sir J., 55.
Savoy, 213.
Sceaux, 107, 119.
Schoeffer, printer, 185.
Scotland, 60.
Scott, William, Lord Stowell, 168.
Scrase, Mr., 237.
Seeley, L. B., 40.
Segre, C., 57.
Seine, 87 f., 118, 142.
Serpentine, 200.
Sèvres china, 132, 141, 182.
Seward, Anna, 38, 42, 50.
—, William, 65.
Shakespeare, 102, 108, 131, 199, 213.
Sharpe, William, 168.
—, —, daughter of, 168.
Sheldon, Catharine, 153.
—, Elizabeth F., 153.
—, Mary, 153.
—, Mrs., 163.
—, William, 153.
Shenstone, W., 209.

Sheppard, Charles, 37.
Sheward, Mr., 45.
Ship, model of, 71, 193.
Shops, 92, 101, 175.
Siddons, Mrs., 33, 39.
—, —, daughters of, 33.
Signs, street, 115, 130, 160, 201.
Simpson, Elizabeth, 105 f., 136.
—, Mary, 105.
—, Richard, 105.
Simson, see Simpson.
Singleton, jockey, 99.
Sisterna, Prince of, 35.
Sizergh Castle, 60 ff.
Solander, Dr., 2.
Soldiers, 70, 92, 137, 156, 171, 177.
Sophie de Brabant, 212.
Sorbonne, 180 f., 186.
Sotheby, Sale Catalogues, 53, 148.
Spain, 171, 194.
—, Ambassador from, 22.
—, language of, 257.
Speculum humanae Salvationis, 180.
Speed, Henrietta J., 102.
Spencer, John, Earl, 108.
Sport, 75, 77, 195.
Stafford, Lady Anastatia, 105.
—, Lady Anne, 105.
Stafford-Howard, William, Earl of Stafford, 105.
Stanbrook, 153.
Standish, Ralph, 59.
Stephenson, Mrs., 64.
Stevenson, Mr., 31.
Stewart, see Stuart.
Stockdale, J., 52.
Stokes, F. G., 70.
Streatfield, Sophia, 13 f.
Streatham, 3, 9, 20, 64, 66, 108, 202 f., 218, 234, 238 ff., 244.
Streets, lighting of, 149.

Stretford, Manchester, 106.
Strickland, Mrs., 59 ff., 78, 80 ff., 89 ff., 97, 105, 121, 136, 138, 144 ff., 154, 163, 183, 222, 231 f.
—, —, letter from, 63.
—, Charles, 60.
—, George, 60.
—, Gerard, 60.
—, Gerard Edward, 61.
—, Mary, see Stephenson, Mrs.
—, Thomas, 60.
Stuart, James (Athenian), 116, 132.
Sunday, in France, 210.
Swaine, Mr., 110, 139.
Swale, Count, 148.
—, Mr., 148.
Swales of Swaledale, the, 148.
Sweden, 2.

T

Taaf, 184.
Taaffe, D., 184.
Talbot, George, Earl of Shrewsbury, 105.
—, Lady Lucy, 105, 136.
Tapestry, 110; see Gobelins.
Tavistock St., 109.
Taylor, Dr., 220, 251.
Teignmouth, abbey of St. Scolastica at, 163.
Teniers, D., 113.
Thames, river, 118.
Thiebault, M., 208.
Thomas, Mrs., 244.
Thrale, Cecilia Margaretta, 20 f., 28, 62 ff.
—, —, letters from, 32 f., 62.
—, Frances Anna, 236.
—, Henrietta Sophia (Harriet), 256.

INDEX

Thrale, Henry, 2, 5, 9 ff., 39, 58, 70, 85, 88 ff., 143, 152, 158 f., 205, 217 ff., 224, 244, 250 ff.
—, —, accident to, 88 ff.
—, —, character of, 12 f., 16 ff.
—, —, death of, 14.
—, —, scholarship of, 17 ff.
—, Henry Salusbury, 4, 19, 64, 77, 90, 160, 236, 241, 244, 246 f.
—, Hester Lynch, see also Piozzi, Hester Lynch.
—, —, accident to, 55, 195.
—, —, as mother, 20, 29, 234 ff., 252 ff.
—, —, bathes, 54 f.
—, —, behaviour of, 26 ff.
—, —, children of, 19 ff.
—, —, criticism of, 42 ff.
—, —, death of, 54 f.
—, —, French journal (1775) of, of, 5, 7 ff., 47, 67 ff.
—, —, French journey (1784) of, 8 f., 189 ff.
—, —, friends of, 35 ff.
—, —, German journey of, 190.
—, —, handwriting of, 55.
—, —, illness of, 198 f.
—, —, inaccuracy of, 46 ff.
—, —, Italian journey of, 190.
—, —, letters of, see John Rylands Library, letters in.
—, —, marriage certificate of, 22.
—, —, MSS. of, see John Rylands Library.
—, —, religious opinions of, 38, 145, 156 ff.
—, —, superstitions of, 158 f.
—, —, theatrical interests of, 38 f.

Thrale, Hester Lynch, writings of, see John Rylands Library.
—, Hester Maria, 2, 20, 22, 28 ff., 56 f., passim.
—, —, appearance of, 56, 192.
—, —, dances in priory, 139 f.
—, —, marriage of, 57.
—, —, portrait of, 29, 198.
—, —, shyness of, 90.
—, Lucy, 239.
—, Popey, see Thrale, Sophia.
—, Ralph, 236 ff.
—, Sophia, 20, 28, 198, 244.
—, Susanna Arabella, 20, 28 ff., 198, 244.
Thraliana, 21, 57, 159 f., 202 f.
Thurlow, Lord, 3, 37.
Times Literary Supplement, 49.
Tinker, C. B., 3.
Titi, Prince, 172.
Titian, 103, 148.
Tooke, Horne, 51.
Townley, Cecilia, see Strickland, Mrs.
—, Charles, 60.
—, William, 59.
Townley-Standish, Edward, 60.
Toynbee, Mrs. Paget, 41.
Trent, 190.
Trianon, 131, 178.
Trotti, Marquis, 201 f.
Tuileries, 93, 173.
Tumblers, 116.
Turconi, Conte, 201.
Turin, 35.
Twelfth cake, 134.
Tyson, M., 14.

U

Udson, Mr., 184.

V

Varese, 35.
Vavasor, Mme., 80.
—, Mrs., 163.
—, Sir Walter, 163.
—, Sister Margaret Teresa, 80.
Venice, 2.
—, Republic of, 97, 178.
Verdure, 209.
Vernon, 87, 89.
Verona, 190.
Versailles, 96, 131 ff., 177 ff.
Vestris, G. A. B., 118.
Victor Amadeus III, of Savoy, 133.
Vienna, 190.
Villa vetera, J. de, 185.
Vineyards, 87 f., 119, 208.
Virgil, 224.
Virgin, statues of, 74, 158 f.
Viry, Comte de, 102.
—, Comtesse de, 102.
Voltaire, 108.

W

Waagen, G. F., 103, 148.
Wales, 1, 10, 60, 69, 202.
Walpole, Horace, 41, 50 f., 98, 102, 107, 114, 183.
Wanstead House, 107.
Welch, Father, 153 f., 188.
Westcote, Lord, see Lyttelton, W.
West Indies, 2.
Weston, Jacob, 37.
—, Sophia, see Pennington, Mrs.
Whalley, Dr. Thomas Sedgwick, 38, 207.
Wheatley, H. B., 93.

White Knights, Berks, 162.
Wilkes, Father, 222, 224 f.
Williams, Anna, 40, 219.
—, Helen Maria, 37 f.
—, Mrs., nun, 80, 83.
Willitoft, Yorks, 61.
Willoughby, Miss, 55.
Willughby, F., 112.
Wilsick, Count, 35.
Wilson, Dr., 15.
—, Father, 82, 170.
—, Dr. Thomas, 95
Wilton, Mr., 254.
—, Mrs., 253.
Wimbledon, 108.
Windsor, 89.
Wine, 74, 208.
Winefred, St., 83.
Withington, Richard, 105.
—, Mary, see Simpson, Mary.
Woffington, Margaret, 107.
—, Mary, see Cholmondeley, Hon. Mrs.
Woolton, 153.
Worcester, 69.
Worthington, Dr., 156.
Wovermanns, 113.

X

Xenophon, 227.

Y

Yonne, river, 208.
York, Archbishop of, 228.

Z

Zamick, M., 41.